HOW TO QUEER THE WORLD

How to Queer the World

Radical Worldbuilding through Video Games

Bo Ruberg

NEW YORK UNIVERSITY PRESS
New York

NEW YORK UNIVERSITY PRESS
New York
www.nyupress.org

© 2025 by New York University

All rights reserved

Please contact the Library of Congress for Cataloging-in-Publication data.

ISBN: 9781479831999 (hardback)
ISBN: 9781479832002 (paperback)
ISBN: 9781479832057 (library ebook)
ISBN: 9781479832033 (consumer ebook)

This book is printed on acid-free paper, and its binding materials are chosen for strength and durability. We strive to use environmentally responsible suppliers and materials to the greatest extent possible in publishing our books.

Manufactured in the United States of America

10 9 8 7 6 5 4 3 2 1

Also available as an ebook

For Eli and Jonah, who are my world

CONTENTS

Introduction: Rethinking (Queer) Worldbuilding through Video Games   1

1. Nine Thousand Little Worlds: Worldbuilding and Queer Worldmaking in *What the Golf*   35

2. Inverting the Laws of the Universe: Trans Time Mechanics and Queer Astrophysics in *If Found...*   69

3. Queer Bodies in Motion: Game Physics as Worldbuilder in *Goat Simulator* and *Wobbledogs*   106

4. Building Worlds through Graphical Depth: The Queer Dimensionality of 2.5D in *OlliOlli World*   141

5. Straight Paths through Queer Video Games: Overbuilding the World in *Gone Home*   170

6. Unplayable Worlds: Queer Posthumanism and the End of Agency in *San Andreas Deer Cam*   194

Conclusion: How to Queer the World   221

Acknowledgments   239

Notes   245

Works Cited   263

Index   283

About the Author   293

Introduction

Rethinking (Queer) Worldbuilding through Video Games

We stand now in a historical moment when we desperately need the ability to build new worlds. This is a moment of immense concern for the future of the world as we know it today—threatened by climate crisis, the ongoing effects of a pandemic, and a turn toward right-wing extremism across the globe—but it is also therefore a moment of immense worldbuilding potential. For marginalized people, the pressure of this moment feels all the more palpable. In the United States, with legal protections for LGBTQIA+ (lesbian, gay, bisexual, transgender, queer, intersex, asexual, etc., shortened here as "queer") people in jeopardy and violent incidents of racism, xenophobia, transphobia, and homophobia on the rise, it has become clear that the world we currently inhabit is broken and deeply unjust. Judith Butler explains in *What World Is This?*, her reflection on life during COVID-19, "The pandemic makes us reconsider the world as an object of scrutiny, register the world as a cause for alarm, mark the fact that this present version of the world was not anticipated." In its way, says Butler, the pandemic has laid bare "the revelation of the world as a different world than we thought it was," thrusting upon us "a newer sense of the world, if not a newer world."[1] We now see the world before us more clearly. And this new clarity brings with it an urgent longing to deconstruct and reconstruct the world, to try again, to experiment with radically alternate ways of being, to build the world otherwise.[2]

Before we can build the world in alternate ways, however, we need to be able to envision alternate worlds. Works of science fiction and other forms of speculative art have long been at the forefront of efforts to build new worlds through imagination. Worldbuilding of this sort is never a neutral endeavor; designing the world anew always entails resisting or reinforcing (sometimes simultaneously) existing structures of power. As Kara Keeling explains in *Queer Times, Black Futures*, in which she contrasts speculative futures imagined by creators fighting for Black liberation with those proposed by large corporations, "the politics of imaginative knowledge production are by no means guaranteed."[3] The cultural stakes inherent in worldbuilding have been made particularly clear through creative and scholarly work around Afrofuturism and Black speculative worldbuilding.[4] As performance studies scholar Jayna Brown argues in her writing about Black mystics and musicians, structures of white supremacy have placed Black communities into a "bleak and bloody dimension we are taught to call reality." In response, Brown calls for "build[ing] alternative worlds, in this dimension and in others," as a way to "practice alternative ways of being alive."[5] Drawing from the authors' respective works as both creative writers and public scholars, Alexis De Veaux, Alexis Pauline Gumbs, and Walidah Imarisha have proposed reframing discussions about Black speculative worldbuilding through the concept of "visionary fiction." Visionary fiction, Imarisha explains, is rooted in "the experience of oppressed peoples creating decolonized dreams of the future."[6] Gumbs describes how the spirit of visionary fiction shapes her own approach to worldbuilding. "It has made me a more generous participant in the present," she says, "because I understand that I have a creative role in not just the future that we can have, but importantly, the future that we can imagine."[7] Imagining alternate worlds, then, is a critical step toward bringing more socially just worlds into being.

In addition to turning to fiction, art, and music to find the speculative worlds that inspire us, it is a central contention of this book that there is another media form we should be taking closely into consideration when we look for "alternative ways of being live": video games. Video games have often been derided or dismissed precisely because they seem disconnected from the "real world." Yet, in truth, the relationship between video games and the world around us is much more complex than these critiques would suggest. As many game studies scholars have argued, video games are intimately bound up with the real world; they shape and are shaped by the conditions of their production and reception.[8] At the same time, video games offer opportunities to inhabit worlds that differ from our own. Indeed, we can understand video games themselves as alternate worlds. In their own ways, they are each models for other ways that the world might operate. They offer us opportunities to "question the order of things," as the disability studies scholar Robert McRuer writes in *Crip Theory*, to ask how this order has been "constructed and naturalized . . . and how it might be changed."[9]

Certainly, not all video game worlds offer visions of empowerment for those who are pushed to the margins. Video games are a vast and varied medium, and games culture is still marred by discriminatory attitudes toward race, sexuality, and gender.[10] Kishonna Gray, writing in *Intersectional Tech*, explains that "video games provide chilling examples of . . . gendered and racialized practices of diminishing, devaluing, and excluding women of color in particular."[11] At the same time, games themselves offer powerful opportunities to experiment with strategies for rebuilding the world we currently live in, one where many forms of oppression currently reign. The researcher-practitioners Kaelan Doyle-Myerscough, Patrick Jagoda, Sarah Edmands Martin, and Allison Yang Jing expressed a similar view when they asserted, in their 2023 panel on worldbuilding at the Digital Games Research Association Conference, "We view games not only as commercial objects or media texts but as vehicles for testing out alternative systems, infrastructures, and relations."[12] Players, as well as game designers and developers, perform a critical role in video game worldbuilding. In games, Cody Mejeur notes, players become "active agents" who help determine "what form and meaning the possible world will take."[13]

This book puts forth two main arguments about the relationship between video games and worldbuilding. First, it argues that we should fundamentally rethink and dramatically expand worldbuilding as a concept. Traditionally, in video games as well as other forms of media and art, worldbuilding has been used to refer to the creation of fictional narrative worlds. Queer media studies scholar Alexis Lothian explains that science fiction writers largely understand worldbuilding as being "about creating a plausible imaginary universe, one that will generally be contemplated from the outside by readers, rather than lived within."[14] Worldbuilding is therefore imagined to be enacted through the development of characters, cultural backdrops, and other representational elements that contribute to a rich story world.

By contrast, video games show us that worldbuilding means so much more than storytelling. Video games offer precisely what Lothian says more traditional forms of science fiction do not: built worlds that players "live within." Every video game is a world, including video games that have no storytelling elements. Throughout this book, I demonstrate how worldbuilding in video games operates on the level of systems and structures. The game worlds that I analyze take shape through nonrepresentational elements like game mechanics, software, computational physics, graphic dimensionality, and level design. For game makers and game scholars, I argue, this shift toward seeing all video games as worlds has the potential to open new avenues for critiquing games' ideological implications. Just as crucially, expanding how we understand worldbuilding in video games challenges us to expand how we think about worldbuilding in general. Through games, we can see that building (or unbuilding and rebuilding) the world necessitates a revolutionary redesign of the foundational logics and underlying operations of the world we inhabit. Changing the story that we drape over those systems will not change the fundamental inequities of our world.

The second main argument of this book is that video games build worlds in ways that resonate powerfully with LGBTQIA+ lives, even when these games do not include on-screen representations of queer characters. Through video games, I theorize a practice that I term *queer worldbuilding*. Queer worldbuilding is not the same thing as building worlds that feature queer stories or communities, though such worlds themselves have immense value. Instead, queer worldbuilding describes the practice of constructing new worlds through methods, frameworks, and tools that can themselves be understood as queer. Drawing from the work of queer theorists like José Esteban Muñoz, Lauren Berlant, Michael Warner, and Sara Ahmed, queer studies has long explored the concept of queer world*making*.[15] Queer worldmaking posits that queer people make worlds through their practices of community building, art making, and moving through their everyday lives. Drawing connections between queer worldmaking and video game worldbuilding, as I do here, prompts us to reflect on worldbuilding as a process rather than a product. In this spirit, I offer the video games analyzed across the chapters that follow as examples of building worlds through a process that itself challenges or rewrites norms around sexuality, gender, identity, and desire.[16] In them, we find tools for both building queer worlds and queering the world around us.

Every Video Game Is a World

The alternate vision of worldbuilding that I am proposing is premised on understanding video games themselves as worlds. When we think of video games and worldbuilding together, it is common to think of large-scale, expansive, story-focused games with extensively developed narratives. These games, certainly, are worlds. But so are all video games, regardless of their content. Small games are worlds. Abstract games are worlds. Puzzle games, mobile games, experimental games, absurdist games, games with no characters: all of these video games are worlds, in their own right. Each video game is a bounded space that players enter into, a terrain with its own geographies of possibility that players temporarily inhabit (more on the problematic colonialist implications of this inhabitation in chapter 4). Riccardo Fassone, in his book *Every Video Game Is an Island*, describes video games as being characterized by their pervasive use of endings.[17] These endings manifest themselves in many forms, says Fassone, from the dramatic conclusions of narratives to the invisible walls that mark the edges of levels to the constraints placed on players by specific mechanics. For Fassone, playing a video game means constantly running up against these limitations, making each game feel like "an island surrounded by cliffs and rocks," a "contained simulation" that has been encircled by "jagged borders."[18] While I find this to be a compelling image—it is no coincidence that many of the games discussed in this book are set on islands—I am myself interested less in the limits of games than in what lies within those limits. Inside the boundaries of each video game lies a playable world.

This argument—that all video games are worlds—is simultaneously novel and self-evident. In many ways, ideas about video games and worlds already go hand in hand. A great number of video games are set in what we commonly refer to as alternate worlds: science fictional or otherwise fantastical universes that notably differ from our own. As mentioned, across the history of their cultural reception, video games have been positioned in opposition to the so-called real world. By contrast, game studies scholars have argued for decades that video games are inextricably tied to the realities of their social and political contexts and the real lives of their players. Sociologist T. L. Taylor captures this spirit in referring to the experiences of early 2000s massively multiplayer online roleplaying game (MMORPG) participants as a "play between worlds."[19] More recently, Alenda Chang, writing about the role of ecology and the natural world in games, has explained that all "games straddle multiple real and imagined worlds."[20] It is also standard to use the language of worlds to conceptualize video games themselves. Since at least the release of *Super Mario Bros.* (Nintendo) in 1985, groupings of levels contained within a single game have been described as "worlds."[21] The term is now often used more broadly to describe any large area within a game that is, in some sense, distinct from the rest of the playable space. Simultaneously, "world" can also refer to a video game as a whole; often, in the discourse of game creators, players, and scholars, the term "game world" describes the full diegetic contents of a video game. Already, in these rhetorical interplays between video games and worlds, we can see how games surface some of the multifaceted and even contradictory elements that go into conceptualizing worlds. Sometimes the world is a separate space, a world apart; sometimes a world nestles inside other worlds; sometimes a world is everything around us, a terrain stretching out as far as the eye can see.

Many video games and game genres embrace their role as worlds. MMORPGS and their precursors, such as multiuser dungeons (MUDs), are referred to as virtual worlds: what Mia Consalvo defines as shared, synchronous, and persistent spaces that involve some form of embodiment for players and "allow a number of people to come together from different locations to interact."[22] As online ethnographers like Celia Pearce and Tom Boellstorff have shown, these environments operate as complex cultural ecosystems: digital civilizations that rise and fall, like worlds unto themselves.[23] Approaching game worlds from a historical perspective, Carly Kocurek and Matt Payne describe how the early *Ultima* games—released at the start of the 1980s—established norms for worldbuilding in computer role-playing games that have persisted for decades; some of these norms include "character creation, buying and selling items, completing minor and major quests, dungeon crawling, and open-world exploration."[24] Fittingly, a number of the most prominent AAA video games (large-scale games developed by the mainstream industry) from the past decade have been "open-world" games, like *The Legend of Zelda: Breath of the Wild* (Nintendo, 2017) (figure I.1) and

Figure 1.1. The vast open world of *The Legend of Zelda: Breath of the Wild* (Nintendo, 2017) stretches out in front of the protagonist, Link. (Screenshot by author)

Genshin Impact (miHoYo, 2020). Open-world games present players with expansive environments that they can explore (more or less) along paths of their choosing.[25] Worlds also feature prominently in the design of video game spaces. Many games and game levels are depicted as self-contained worlds, such as the islands mentioned earlier, or planets floating in outer space. Consider an early computer game like *Myst* (Cyan, 1993) (figure 1.2), set on its remote, fog-shrouded island, and the many subsequent games that have borrowed the visual trope of the mysterious island locale in the intervening years, from *Dear Esther* (The Chinese Room, 2012) to *The Witness* (Jonathan Blow, 2016). It is as if, when we set out to imagine where a video game should take place, we know instinctively that it should exist in its own world.

Video games are also surrounded by social and commercial worlds. Amanda Phillips has explained that gamers are commonly thought of "as immersed in their own worlds, virtual or otherwise."[26] These worlds are both the worlds of video games themselves and the insular spheres of toxic gamer culture: echo chambers that produce discriminatory, self-affirming worlds of thought.[27] At the same time, while gamer culture may look like a singular world from the outside, it in fact contains multiple subcultural worlds, full of affinity groups that play different kinds

Figure I.2. Exploring the mysterious island of *Myst*. Original game developed by Cyan, released 1993. Screenshot is from 2021 remastered release: *Myst* (Cyan Worlds Inc., 2021). (Screenshot by author)

of games and for different reasons.[28] The video game industry too is a world: a strange, looking-glass land where the logic of labor has gone topsy-turvy and developers are expected to work overtime in the name of "love."[29] It is often in these worlds around games that problems of exclusion, racism, and toxic boundary policing make themselves most visible. As the new media scholar and artist micha cárdenas has suggested, the worlds of video game culture as they exist today may be too rotten at their core for marginalized people to inhabit them.[30] One of the values of recognizing how video games form worlds is realizing that we have the power to walk away from those worlds—to live and work and play in other realms.

However, when I argue that we should see video games as worlds, I do not simply mean that we should address the rhetorical constructs of worldness that surrounds games. I mean something more blunt and more brazen: I mean that we should think of video games themselves, first and foremost, as worlds rather than as games. Yes, a sizable percentage of video games include what players would typically consider gamey elements—rules, challenges, competition, goals.[31] But there are innumerable exceptions. Genres like interactive visual novels and so-called walking simulators clearly push the boundaries of what counts as a game.[32] On distribution platforms like Itch.io, independent developers have posted thousands of experimental video games that have no rules, no points, or no win states; some require no skill, and others even play themselves. Even many of those big-budget games that win the hearts of mainstream gamers are, let us be honest, really barely games at all. Wildly popular titles like *Baldur's Gate 3* (Larian Studios, 2023), *Elden Ring* (FromSoftware, Inc., 2022), and *God of War Ragnarök* (Sony Interactive Entertainment, 2022), to name a few blockbusters from recent years, may technically include some formal elements that transform the freeform act of play into a structured game. However, these elements are all secondary to the basic point of these games: for the player to explore and experience the game world that unfurls around them.

Stephanie Boluk and Patrick Lemieux make a related point when they contend that video games are not really games but instead the raw material for making metagames.[33] For my part, I would say that video games do sometimes *contain* games, but what they *are*, above all, is worlds: universes in miniature. At the risk of putting too fine a point on it, I want to emphasize that I am not referring here to the narrative heuristics that have been skinned over the structural elements of video games (e.g., its story, characters, and setting). I am referring to video games as holistic media objects made up of an assemblage of parts: software, interface, interaction design, on-screen representation, aesthetics, atmosphere. Each of these elements contributes in critical ways to the formation of the game world. They form the ground on which the player stands and the air that they breathe. No matter how the video game industry tries to hype video games as machines for performing hypermasculine mastery, they are something very different from that at their core. They are ecosystems and habitats. They are spaces to be.

As I have suggested, reframing video games as worlds opens up new opportunities for making sense of the cultural meaning that games contain. Every game world enacts its own ideological position. In many prominent video game genres, these ideologies are inherently extractive and even violent, as Soraya Murray explains in her work on the imperialist implications of landscapes in first-person shooter games.[34] However, video game landscapes also have the potential to manifest counterhegemonic ideologies, subverting white and Western conceptualizations of the world. For example, the 2020 virtual reality installation

Along the River of Spacetime, developed by Indigenous studies scholar and game designer Elizabeth LaPensée, communicates teachings from the Anishinaabe people by using 360-degree video to bring players to various natural sites dotting a river system near what is now commonly known as Lansing, Michigan. Jumping across seasons and locations, the game prompts players to construct constellations through two-dimensional drawings overlaid on the game space (figure 1.3). LaPensée has described the construction of the game world as intentionally disjointed. "You travel this way, between landscapes, which change in a non-linear manner," she explains, to experience space through Indigenous "ways of knowing."[35] *Along the River of Spacetime*, then, is an example of a video game that encodes a postcolonial and indeed anticolonial ideology into the physical design of its world.

Simultaneously, as game designer Tracy Fullerton suggests in her writing on the Thoreau-inspired *Walden, a Game* (USC Game Innovation Lab, 2017), understanding video games as worlds also allows us to reflect on different *worldviews*—ways that games see the world and who matters within it.[36] Conversely, approaching video games through the concept of worlds shifts our own perspective on what matters in games. If games are worlds, then the importance of competition, achievements,

Figure 1.3. A two-dimensional drawing of a crane constellation overlays three-dimensional video footage in *Along the River of Spacetime* (Elizabeth LaPensée, 2020). (Image printed with the permission of Elizabeth LaPensée)

and technological prowess fades into the background. In its place, what comes to hold meaning in a video game is its qualities as a space for existing. In this game world, who has power? Who is afforded freedom, and who is placed under constraint? How do beings connect with one another? Even as we reformulate video games as worlds, it is crucial to remember that these worlds are never truly separate from our own world. Far from being cordoned off in a "magic circle" (a concept for describing game worlds that has long been both deployed and refuted within game studies), video game worlds have boundaries that are permeable, shifting, and incomplete.[37] They are constantly changing, leaking, collapsing, and being rebuilt.

Worldbuilding beyond Storytelling

Video games are worlds, but they are also more than that. They are works of world*building*. As stated, worldbuilding is commonly understood as the practice of imagining a fictional, constructed world and implementing it in a work (or works) of media.[38] Transmedia studies scholar Marta Boni writes that elaborate narrative worldbuilding is an increasingly "common practice in the current media landscape"—a practice that is embarked on by media creators and media fans alike.[39] Within this vision of worldbuilding, the task of establishing worlds plays out in a number of ways. Some elements of a built world may be communicated through dialogue; others may be presented through environmental storytelling elements (a topic that we will return to in chapter 5).[40] Worldbuilding is often described as being most overt in works of literature and film from genres like science fiction and fantasy.[41] However, in truth, all works of media (even those that present themselves as *non*fictional) engage in worldbuilding, creating a backdrop for their contents and providing a sense that the specific material they present emerges from within a broader world. Video games are no exception. As many authors offering guidance for aspiring game makers have argued, worldbuilding is an especially key—and especially complex—element of video game design, since players do not merely read about or view game worlds but instead interact within them directly.[42]

To anyone who studies or contributes to the design of video games, the idea that developing a video game entails worldbuilding may seem, on its surface, wholly unsurprising. Scholars and game industry professionals have been publishing on and speaking about the role of worldbuilding in video games for years, with work in this area picking up steam.[43] Within these spheres, it is widely understood that worldbuilding represents a useful implement for game developers and that many video games—especially those that are positioned within intricately constructed imaginary worlds—can be productively read as examples of worldbuilding.[44]

However, I am arguing that these current conceptualizations of worldbuilding in video games remain notably limited, preventing us from recognizing the full range of ways that video games build their worlds. This limitation stems from the fact that the preponderance of existing work on worldbuilding in video games understands worldbuilding as synonymous with—or, at least, fundamentally an expression of—narrative and storytelling. Mark J. P. Wolf, who has written extensively on worldbuilding in video games, illustrates this with his description of "world design." He states,

> All stories occur within some kind of setting, which becomes the world of the story and its characters. Storyworlds can be developed to varying degrees, with the minimum development including only the world data necessary to tell the story for which the world exists. Even in such a case, the information we receive about a world will suggest a certain type of world, along with an attitude or feeling toward the world being depicted, one which is particularly crafted to suit the needs of the story. Many imaginary worlds go well beyond the world data needed for the story or stories set in the world, providing a great degree of detail about the world and its locations, inhabitants, cultures, technologies, flora, fauna, and so forth. . . . Typically, a world is designed as the backdrop for a story, so the design of the world develops out of the needs of the story and its audience.[45]

What I find striking in this passage, and the approach to worldbuilding that it epitomizes, is the fundamental assumption that imaginary worlds are built in the service of *stories*. Wolf refers to such worlds as "settings" where stories take place and explains that, technically, an imaginary world need only be built out to the extent that it supports the story its creators intend to tell. This world, no matter how detailed, takes shape in service of the narrative. First and foremost, in this formulation, worldbuilding is the building of a "backdrop" that facilitates and enriches storytelling by putting it into context.

A similar set of presumptions about the relationship between worldbuilding and storytelling can be seen in talks at industry events like the annual Game Developers Conference. Such talks are often presented by individuals who have worked on large-scale video games with wide-reaching narratives constructed by teams of writers. They address topics like the challenges of designing worlds that cater to different player interests in *Dragon Age: Inquisition* (Bioware, 2014) or the process of envisioning settlements and their inhabitants in *Horizon: Forbidden West* (Guerrilla Games, 2022).[46] While these presentations do typically recognize the importance of nontextual elements of how video games tell stories, such as the visual representation of in-game locales and non-player characters, their presenters too describe game worlds as backdrops to narratives. *Horizon: Forbidden West,* for instance, is an action-adventure game set partly in a post-apocalyptic San Francisco "where nature has reclaimed the land" and human beings attempt to relearn the ways of their lost society while fighting off giant, dinosaur-esque machines (figure 1.4).[47] In a talk about worldbuilding in the *Horizon: Forbidden West*, lead concept artist Roland Ijzermans explained how the game's narrative premise—that its human settlers must deal with the constant threat of "extremely dangerous wildlife"—formed the foundation for the various local cultures that the developers created within the game.[48] A case such as this illustrates how, often, a video game's story does not really take place within the context of its world; instead, the game world itself takes shape around the story. Story comes first. World trails behind.

However, as we will see time and again, this is far from a complete picture of how and why worlds operate in video games. Storytelling represents only one component of video game worldbuilding because stories represent only one component of video games. To be sure, many video games tell powerful stories; many video game players care deeply about these stories; and, as Phillips has explained, efforts from within the field of game studies to sideline the importance of stories have often constituted thinly veiled attempts to push women, people of color, and queer people out of the study of video games.[49] Thus,

Figure I.4. Alon, the protagonist of *Horizon: Forbidden West* (Guerrilla Games, 2022), rides past a post-apocalyptic vista of San Francisco's Golden Gate Bridge. (Screenshot by author)

it is important not to dismiss the value of games' narrative content. However, across their many forms, video games are a medium characterized by their interactivity. Video games may *tell* stories, but what they *are* are opportunities for action, exploration, and play. Worlds themselves are not stories; they are places, spheres, and conditions of possibility. If all video games are worlds, then all decisions about the design of a video game are acts of worldbuilding. And all elements of a video game, from the construction of its mechanics to the layout of its levels to the aesthetic quality of its graphics and sound, contribute to building its world.

Consider one example of a game that looks almost nothing like *Horizon: Forbidden West*—an indie game about spending time in nature called *A Short Hike* (2019), designed by Adam Robinson-Yu. In a 2020 presentation titled "Crafting a Tiny Open World," Robinson-Yu describes *A Short Hike* as a small-scale game that he initially began while taking a break from a more elaborate project.[50] The game does have a loose narrative: it is about Claire, an anthropomorphic bird, who goes for a scenic hike around the wooded, mountainous island of Hawk Peak Provincial Park (figure I.5). Along the way, as she heads to the top of the mountain, Claire occasionally stops to go swimming, chat with other animal characters, or spread her wings and soar from area to area. However, the narrative component of the game is minimal, a light-touch pretense for the admiration of nature. What matters in *A Short Hike* is, instead, the world of the game itself—a place for strolling amid an autumn-inspired color palette and semipixelated graphics, set against a whimsical soundtrack that communicates the pleasures of getting lost in the wilderness. This game world does not support a story. This game *is* its world.

Robinson-Yu's talk about how he "crafted" this tiny world reflects a vision of video game worldbuilding that is not bound to—and, in fact, is largely uninterested in—traditional forms of storytelling. In describing the elements that make up his game's world, Robinson-Yu discusses its art style, its cameras, its use of postprocessing effects, and how its blue-tinted shadows help the world "feel more alive." He explains that his design process began not with building a narrative but with building topography: playing around with the terrain tools in the development engine Unity to sculpt areas "that felt fun to climb and fly on." In turn, those experimentations, he says, inspired the full design of the island and the paths that Claire can take to the summit. Robinson-Yu also describes some of the emergent behaviors that he observed in players when conducting play tests; for instance, players tried to avoid taking

Figure 1.5. Claire from *A Short Hike* (Adam Robinson-Yu, 2019) receives a compass and heads off to explore the mountain park. (Screenshot by author)

demarcated routes by swimming around the island (figure 1.6). "Players like to test the bounds of a game when they first start," Robinson-Yu states in his talk. "They want to see, will the game just let you swim into the ocean? And I wanted to say yes, you can."[51] The world of *A Short Hike*, then, was shaped through feeling (the feeling of "aliveness," the feeling of fun) and pleasure (the pleasure of goofing around with new software, the pleasure of pushing the boundaries of a game) rather than through story.

Notably, what Robinson-Yu barely mentions in describing his worldbuilding process is narrative: Who is Claire? What is her background? What motivates her on her hike? At the end of his talk, Robinson-Yu does briefly discuss his experience writing the short moments of dialogue between characters that pop up throughout the game, but he does so mostly to state the minimal importance of writing in his worldbuilding process. "Writing is hard," he says. "I didn't put much pressure on myself when I was working on *A Short Hike*. I approached the writing in a silly, improvisational kind of way. I didn't really expect it to carry the game and be a main part of the gameplay."[52] In this way, Robinson-Yu drives home the marginal role that storytelling elements like text played

Figure 1.6. Adam Robinson-Yu, designer of *A Short Hike*, illustrates players' attempts to swim off the island in a presentation about worldbuilding. (Image printed with the permission of Adam Robinson-Yu)

in building the world of *A Short Hike*. To be clear, Robinson-Yu's game is not exceptional in building its world primarily through technical, aesthetic, and affective considerations. What is useful is how Robinson-Yu's frank description of developing his game underscores the centrality of nonnarrative elements in the process of worldbuilding.

The story behind *A Short Hike* also highlights how players participate in the work of worldbuilding. Sometimes they do this by serving as playtesters; in response to playtests, developers may change the design of their games. At other times, such as in virtual worlds, players may literally construct the digital locales and items that populate the online world.⁵³ In a broader sense, though, players serve as worldbuilders through the simple act of transforming game worlds from preprogrammed sets of conditions into lived realities. They may follow directions and pursue established win conditions. Or they may ignore preset paths, jump into the ocean, and swim as far as the game will allow. In such moments, players animate a game's geography and map its borders.

To an extent, the kinds of worldbuilding that players enact within video games mirror worldbuilding done by players—and other media fans—outside of games. Fan studies scholars have described practices like fan fiction writing as acts of worldbuilding, for instance.⁵⁴ Surely, video game fans participate in worldbuilding through these fannish practices as well. However, conceptualizing video game play as worldbuilding helpfully reframes the very act of engaging with media (watching a film or a television show, listening to music, navigating content on the internet) as a mode of building the world. Understanding players as co-worldbuilders also reminds us to reflect on the role of liveness in animating video game worlds. Describing the continued allure of theater, the performance studies scholar Jill Dolan writes that audiences are drawn to live performance because of their desire to "participate in its world-making" and thereby to experience "how a different world could feel."⁵⁵ Video games similarly invite players to participate in alternate worlds of feeling, brought to life through play.

Queer Video Game Worlds

The spirit of video game worldbuilding has much in common with the spirit of queerness. Both describe a mode of imagining alternate ways of being in the world. The meaning of the word "queer" is notoriously slippery. In the US context from which I write, the word "queer" is used as an umbrella term for anyone who falls within the LGBTQIA+ spectrum or whose gender or sexual identity otherwise does not fit with dominant social norms. In academic contexts, as gender studies and African American studies scholar Siobhan B. Somerville articulates, queer is also used "as a term that calls into question the stability of any such categories of identity." Somerville explains, "To 'queer' becomes a way to denaturalize categories, . . . revealing them as socially and historically constructed identities that have often worked to establish and police the line between the 'normal' and the 'abnormal.'"[56] Approaching queerness through considerations of race, Chandan Reddy describes the political valence of the term "queer," which is used "by those who seek to disturb, shatter, or undermine the heteronormative cultural order." At the same time, Reddy emphasizes, "queer—especially when used in conjunctions such as *queer of color*, *queer Latinx*, *Black queer*, and so on—signifies a broad, if at times contradictory, set of political critiques and alternative ideologies *within* LGBTQIA+ politics and *among* intersectional feminist movements."[57] Queerness has long been conceptualized alongside media. Karen Tongson explains that the term "queer media" encompasses media objects that offer overt LGBTQIA+ representation (that is, representation of discrete, nonnormative gender and sexual identities) as well as media objects that "make themselves available to queer interpretation, queer worlds, and queer people."[58]

When I say "queer," I am referring precisely to this nexus: the place where intersectional identities overlap with the meaning contained in media. As a bisexual, nonbinary (white, neurodivergent, Jewish, anti-Zionist) person who is deeply invested in queer community, I hold queerness as an identity marker close to my heart. Simultaneously, I value the more conceptual dimensions of queerness: queerness as nonnormativity and counternormativity, as radical resistance, as a mode of desiring against the grain, as a way of building intimacy through unexpected connections, as a politics of visibility and opacity, as the name for feeling or loving or fucking the wrong way, as a strategy for imagining the unimaginable. At the same time, I remain cognizant that not all the forms of identity-based expression that we might place under the umbrella of queerness are synonymous with progressive or intersectional politics.

Critical theorist Jasbir Puar has theorized the concept of "homonationalism" to describe a US "national homosexuality" that seeks to normativize gayness while also contributing to the "global dominant ascendancy of whiteness that is implicated in the propagation of the United States as empire."[59] These concerns also extend beyond the United States. Writing about anti-Muslim rhetoric among white gay and lesbian groups in Britain, Jin Haritaworn, Tamsila Tauqir, and Esra Erdem have described how "gay assimilationism" makes certain forms of LGBTQIA+ identity complicit with imperialism.[60] In order to resist this assimilationist complicity with the oppression of people of color, queer activism and queer scholarship must remain critical of hegemonic power structures and self-aware about their own place within racialized systems of privilege.

As I and my fellow queer game studies scholars have argued elsewhere, video games are rich sites for locating and expressing queerness.[61] While some video games (whether mainstream or independent, shorthanded as "indie") contain the presentation of LGBTQIA+ identities, a great many more contain queer meaning—offering themselves as opportunities for exploring queer play, engaging with queer design, or undertaking queer analysis. Insisting on the queerness of video games, in its many forms, is a way to reclaim a medium that has long been exclusionary to queer people. To say that video games can model queer worlds is to expand on this reclamation, to move beyond making a place for queer people in the world of video games by insisting that video games can aid us in making the world itself more queer.

There are many ways in which queer worlds manifest themselves in video games. Multiple AAA games of the sort that engage in elaborate narrative worldbuilding now prominently feature queer characters. One high-profile example is *The Last of Us Part II* (Naughty Dog, 2020), which includes a lesbian protagonist and a transgender side character and was the recipient of a 2021 GLAAD Award for Outstanding Video Game.[62] Beyond the sphere of mainstream video games, the rise of queer avant-garde game makers has brought with it an explosion of indie video games whose worlds are directly structured around queer experience.[63] Mattie Brice has noted that white designers were centered in the early days of the queer games avant-garde, which began to take form at the start of the 2010s.[64] Today, a growing number of these games are being made by, about, and for queer people of color, ranging from *The Black*

Trans Archive (Danielle Brathwaite-Shirley, 2021), which wrestles with the erasure of Black trans people from documented histories, to the upbeat roller derby "rhythm ga(y)me" *Skate & Date* (Geneva Hayward, 2020). In *Skate & Date*, players skate to a musical beat in the role of Maggie, a Black femme roller derby team captain with a crush on a woman from a rival team. A game like *Skate & Date* creates its own vision of a queer world: a world where femmes are, as a matter of course, powerful physical competitors who romance other femmes.

The realm of non-digital games is an increasingly important space for envisioning queer worlds. Numerous table-top role-playing games have been developed over the past decade that are set in worlds filled with queer characters, queer romance, and opportunities for building queer societies. Citing examples of analog games like *The Quiet Year* (Avery Alder, 2013), *Microscope Explorer* (Ben Robbins, 2011), and *The Ground Itself* (Everest Pipkin, 2019), Kaelan Doyle-Myerscough terms these "worldbuilding games." Such games, writes Doyle-Myerscough, are ones "in which players imagine other societies, places, worlds or cultures through play." They often use explicitly prescribed rules to prompt players to see the world in new ways, inviting them to become collaborators in imagining "alternate futures and radical possibilities." These futures bring wide-reaching "problems of capitalism, colonialism and restrictive gender norms" into question, often creating spaces for queer love to thrive.[65]

Queer video game worlds also manifest themselves as queer communities. Many queer and transgender people have shared stories about using online role-playing games to explore their identities and connect with others who share similar experiences: a way of forming queer games worlds while using game worlds to understand oneself as queer.[66] Approaching video games through the lens of queer anthropology, Spencer Ruelos has explained, "Playing games allows queer players to flourish in between physical and digital worlds," which in turn allows them "to create new senses of queer belonging."[67] Beginning in 2012 and 2013, events like GaymerX and the Queerness and Games Conference built temporary worlds where queer people who made, studied, or simply loved video games could come together to play.[68] Today, queer gaming continues to represent an important thread in spaces like the Game Developers of Color Expo, IndieCade, and art gallery shows about video games both within the United States and internationally.⁶⁹ Each of these arenas is, in its own way, a world: a location, a group, a culture, a way of seeing, a set of possibilities.

At the same time, many video game worlds that do not appear queer can be understood queerly. As we will see throughout this book, these worlds are places where the norms that we often mistake for universal truths—our unquestioned beliefs about *how the world works*, both socially and physically—are sidestepped, rewritten, or overturned. Indeed, the relationship between video games and queer worldbuilding goes deeper than the queerness of any individual game world. I am not alone in making this connection. Others from game studies and queer studies alike have gestured toward worldbuilding as a meaningful element of video games' queer potential. Some of these scholars include Jack Halberstam, Edmond Chang, Adrienne Shaw, Jennessa Hester, and Jeffrey Sens.⁷⁰ I myself have made initial inroads into mapping the myriad interplays between video games and queer worldbuilding, looking at how queer worlds can be made or unmade through "no fun" feelings and structures of life and death.⁷¹ Much of this existing work points to echoes between video games and José Esteban Muñoz's writing on utopia as a queer world that sits forever on the horizon.⁷² For example, game designer Colleen Macklin writes in her contribution to the 2017 volume *Queer Game Studies*, "Games are more about world building than about linear storytelling. If it's worlds that we are exploring with games, then isn't it possible for these algorithmic worlds to evolve to allow for more flexibility and diversity in player desire? . . . I would propose that games are queer because they provide us with a notably different way of looking at and living in the world. The queer utopia may already be here, in our games."⁷³

Video games are also tied to queer worlds through play. I stated earlier that players can be seen as worldbuilders, since they collaborate in the work of bringing game worlds to life. As I discuss at length in chapter 1, this vision of game worlds as animated by play closely parallels the queer theory concept of worldmaking, especially as articulated by Muñoz in texts like "Ephemera as Evidence" and *Disidentifications*. For Muñoz, worldmaking is bound up with performance: both artistic performance and the everyday performance of living a queer life. Worldmaking embodies "the spirit of *doing* queerness," writes Muñoz, as a way to "establish alternate views of the world" that "function as critiques of oppressive regimes of 'truth.'"[74] Video games are built worlds, in that they are explicitly constructed by their developers, but they are also made worlds, in the sense of queer worldmaking. They too operate through a spirit of doing; they make worlds through the praxis of play. Video games also speak back to the theorization of queer worldmaking itself. Queer worldmaking, as a subject in queer studies, often remains elusive, intangible, and abstract. Video games serve as opportunities to transform queer worldmaking into something concrete. They offer us playgrounds where we can reach out and touch, as trans studies scholar Susan Stryker writes in describing the process of transing, "the material truth of a potential for worlding otherwise."[75] They show us worldmaking in action.

Certainly, the queer worlds we find in video games offer us (as queer people, as others from marginalized groups, and as critically engaged game makers and players) a critical entry point into imagining how we might queer the world around us. Arguing for the activist implications of transmedia worldbuilding, fan studies scholar Henry Jenkins writes, "Before we can build a better world, we need to imagine what a better world looks like. Popular culture often provides the most vivid images of alternative worlds or alternative futures."[76] Video games fit this description. However, queer video game worlds are not tidy, unambivalent, or easily instrumentalized. Like all queer works of art and ways of living, they are messy.[77] Queer video game worlds are often silly, improbable, or impossible, ecstatic and joyful but also broken or mournful, posthuman and nonhuman, post-apocalyptic, counterhegemonic in some ways and complicit with dominant structures of power in others. They engage simultaneously in the creation and destruction of worlds, interweaving Donna Haraway's vision of "worlding" with what Jack Halberstam terms "unworlding."[78] Queer video game worlds balance the longing to fix worlds and the hunger to destroy them. In this way, they embody the contradictory yet resilient spirit that Marquis Bey voices in describing Black trans feminism: "Taking hold of the world . . . in effect ends the world in order to claim the world, a world emerging in the rubble of this world, anew, in order for something that used to be us to live."[79]

The messiness of video game worlds is part of what makes them queer. It is also why they serve as such generative objects for thinking through the work of queer worldbuilding more broadly. These worlds are many things at once. They are an invitation to remake the world through play. They are whole universes, shrunk down to the scale of tiny dioramas, galaxies under glass. Video game worlds challenge us to question how the universe—our universe, any universe—functions. Simultaneously, often, these games operate as cautionary tales and imperfect guides: raising specters of the ongoing toxicity of video game culture or falling short of their revolutionary potential. Even the most explicitly counter-hegemonic video games remain complicated cultural objects, emerging from the contexts of an exploitative games industry or the precarious labor of indie game making. The messiness of these video games reminds us that the work of making and remaking the world is always ongoing and that making the world more queer is not necessarily one and the same with making it better.

Games will not fix a broken world.[80] They will not save a world on the brink of collapse. But they will inspire us to explore new ways of rebuilding our world. And, when necessary, they will remind us that some worlds cannot be saved. "The queer utopia may already be here, in our games," proposes Macklin.[81] Claudia Costa Pederson too, writing in her book *Gaming Utopia*, describes "video games and video game culture as an available, open space for utopia."[82] Yet, as will become clear, queer worlds in video games are, in fact, rarely utopias. Nor are they dystopias. Instead, they are mirrors, reflecting back to us the shortcomings and possibilities contained within our own reality, showing us how queer our world already is and how queer it could become.

A Structural Approach to (Queer) Worldbuilding

To truly queer the world requires looking past the surface of the world that we see—whether on a screen or all around us—and confronting the underlying structures on which a world is built. Just like the more immediately visible aspects of the world, these structural aspects too must be questioned, destabilized, reenvisioned, and remade in order for the world to meaningfully take on new form. In one sense, I am talking about the kinds of structures on a grand, global scale that operate far beyond video games: structures of governance, structures of capitalism, structures of access, interlocking structures of oppression, structures of power. Such structures fundamentally give shape to our world, dictating both how it functions and whom it functions for. In another sense, I am talking about the structures on which media worlds are built: structures of genre, structures of media-making technology, structures of distribution, material infrastructures. Though such structures and their attendant structuring logics play a formative role in the creation of all media worlds, it is a core premise of this book that these structures make themselves especially apparent (and therefore especially open to critique and reimagining) in video games. For video games, these are structures of design norms, structures of software, structures of simulation, structures of human-computer interfaces, structures of agency. These structures are themselves shaped by structures of cultural thought: the often unquestioned "regimes of truth," to call back to Muñoz's phrase, that dictate how we conceptualize personhood, pleasure, time, embodiment, realism, and, by extension, the very nature of our material reality.

Long before narratives or cultural backdrops or even visual landscapes enter the picture—those things that seem most obviously to make a media world a world—these structures themselves act as worldbuilders. They are the forces that simultaneously make worldbuilding possible and constrain the possibilities of any given world. Structures build worlds in the ways that wood framing builds houses, in the way that load-bearing beams hold up walls. They set the fundamental conditions of the world as well as the conditions under which it can persist. Queering the world, or changing it in any deeply impactful way, must mean changing these structures. Understanding worldbuilding in media must mean accounting for these structures. There is no world without them. In this sense, such structures are the world itself. Though not all media worlds are queer, queer thinking is valuable for the analysis of all media worlds. Queer studies methods teach us to always look beneath the surface, questioning the norms of what is "real" and challenging us to unearth and confront the ways of thinking that shape our world.

I have said that my approach to understanding worldbuilding is unique in that it looks beyond narrative. It is perhaps more accurate to say that my approach is unique because it opens the door to so many alternate ways of analyzing media worlds, which I have found myself free to consider only after leaving storytelling (largely) behind. Here, investigating video game worldbuilding means investigating interactive rule sets, software functions, the physics of computational simulation, divergent approaches to human-computer interaction design, and constructions of graphical depth—to name only a few approaches to this work. In the pages to come, this will become a refrain: video games make visible the fundamental systems that underlie their worlds and reveal the mutability of those systems; in this way, they prompt us to question the fundamental systems of *our own world* and to ask whether those facts about our universe that we consider profoundly immutable might not also be open to change. Often, in the history of studying video games and other forms of digital media, this kind of call to attend to the technical and formalist elements of the medium has been issued by scholars promoting a not-so-implicit agenda to shift the field away from considerations of culture, identity, and power.[83] By contrast, my goal is precisely to understand and illuminate how the machinery of video game worlds—the cogs and gears under their hoods—are themselves at the very root of their cultural meaning. By extension, this approach serves to illustrate how many of those more technically inclined video game industry workers who have been left out of the present-day fanfare around worldbuilding (such as engineers and user interface designers) are in fact equally responsible for, and therefore also equally accountable for, the meaning that video games express through worldbuilding. The technical is always political.

Each of the chapters in this book offers a humanistic close reading of a video game (or, in the case of chapter 3, two video games) that models a different approach to the practice that I am calling queer worldbuilding. These are worlds that, in one way or another, embody queerness through the functions of their underlying systems. I have chosen to focus explicitly on video games that do not fit the mold of the large-scale, narrative-based games typically presented as exemplars of worldbuilding. Most of these are what we would consider indie.[84] They have largely been released between 2013 and 2023, a period of considerable growth and diversification for indie game creation.[85] All are video games rather than analog games, since I study digital media, but there is also a growing body of work on worldbuilding in tabletop games.[86] I am particularly drawn to games that are experimental, absurdist, vibrantly colorful, or otherwise unabashedly strange; I find that such games are joyfully provocative as objects to think with and helpfully flagrant in their reimagining of systems. I read these video games as queer objects. However, my purpose in identifying them as such is not to perpetuate some endless push toward reading every piece of media queerly, a critique one might offer in the spirit of Kadji Amin's argument against queer objects.[87] Establishing these games as queer is only the beginning. For game studies scholars, game makers, and game students, my hope is that these analyses offer jumping-off points for further exploring the transformative potential of using video games to reimagine the structures of our world. For queer studies scholars and other queer readers, I hope they will demonstrate how video games serve as prisms. By shining our analytical light on them, we make visible the multiple aspects of queer worldbuilding and worldmaking (and unmaking and remaking) that might otherwise remain unseen.

My analyses of these games draw from an array of interpretive frameworks. Most directly, this work is in dialogue with game studies, queer studies, and trans studies. In chapters with specific relevance to transgender identities and experiences, I have endeavored to walk a line between respecting trans studies as distinct from queer studies while also recognizing the centrality that trans people have always played in queer scholarship, queer activism, and queer worldbuilding.[88] In this way, I hope that this work might serve as a bridge for a rising cohort of game studies scholars who are pivoting toward analyzing video games through trans lenses, including Whit Pow, P. S. Berge, Madison Schmalzer, Ari Gass, Cody Mejeur, Hibby Thatch, and more.[89] Simultaneously, however, many of this book's most vital interlocutors are from neither game studies nor queer studies. The analyses offered here are deeply indebted to critical race theory, African American studies, posthumanism, performance studies, and geography studies. In particular, scientific thought—in the form of astronomy, physics, and computer science as well as new materialism, feminist technoscience, and Afrofuturism—is a constant guide in this book. We might think of this text, then, as an entry into science and technology studies or perhaps as a model for a new materialist approach to studying video games. Alternatively, we might think of it as presenting a mode of analysis that has come delightfully unmoored from the typical boundaries of disciplinarity. The very notion of worldbuilding scrambles the imagined divide between the humanities and the sciences. How can we draw a line between the study of the worlds we imagine and the study of the world we inhabit? How can we question how worlds have been built within media objects without questioning how our own world has been built?

My interpretations of these games are often simultaneously celebratory and skeptical. I aim to make sense of them through a set of intersectional lenses that account for race, ethnicity, white supremacy, imperialism, and colonialism as well as gender and sexuality. This approach commonly raises points of tension or even concerns within game worlds. I see this as a critical component of the new theorizing about worldbuilding that I am putting forth. These worlds are full of potential in some ways, but they are far from perfect; a world that is liberatory to some may be oppressive to others. As Mark Jerng writes in his book *Racial Worldmaking*, attending to how race is built into speculative worlds in ways that go beyond overt representations of racial oppression or liberation—that is, how race is manifest "at the level of context, atmosphere, sequence, and narrative explanation"—gives us valuable strategies for noticing how racism is built into the world around us and questioning "our ongoing participation in the structures of our racial worlds."[90] Worldmaking, as Dorinne Kondo similarly reminds us in her work on theater, always goes hand in hand with "race-making."[91] Learning to see worldbuilding in more structural ways also gives us the language for seeing and ultimately challenging the racialized structures of power that characterize the world around us.

Taken together, these chapters offer a toolkit for both doing and analyzing video game worldbuilding. They call on game makers to account for the impact that their technical and design decisions have on their playable worlds. They also call on scholars to unpack the underlying systems of games in analyzing their meanings as worlds and as media objects in the world. This toolkit is simultaneously aimed toward LGBTQIA+ creators and those (including artists, activists, and community leaders) invested in building worlds that are not only queer in their content but also queer in their structures and form. The work of building new worlds through video games is a project that resonates deeply with the work of living queer lives: constantly making and remaking the world around us, exploring alternatives, and creating different ways to live, love, desire, resist, and be. In providing this toolkit, I am inspired by race and technology scholar Ruha Benjamin's words at the end of her introduction to *Captivating Technology*: "Ultimately, my hope is for you, the reader, to imagine and craft the worlds you cannot live without, just as you dismantle the ones we cannot live within."[92]

A Toolkit for Queering the World

This book is broken into six chapters. Chapter 1 uses the absurdist golf video game *What the Golf* (Triband, 2019) to demonstrate how designers build and rebuild worlds each time they change the rules of a game. *What the Golf* continuously scrambles the conditions of play, presenting players with thousands of golf-course iterations, each positioned on its own floating mountaintop. By constantly creating and re-creating new mini game worlds, all equipped with their own challenges and win states, *What the Golf* models how video games create alternate worlds when they shift actions, desires, and even ontologies: reimagining what players can do, what players want, and who players are. *What the Golf* also serves as a useful illustration of how video game worldbuilding parallels theories of queer worldmaking. Each new mini world is brought to life through play much in the way that Muñoz describes queer worldmaking as an active, performative practice. Additionally, through both the game's sheer proliferation of worlds and its continuous efforts to overturn expectations, *What the Golf* suggests that the very act of worldbuilding in video games might be understood as queer: a way of creating what Muñoz refers to in *The Sense of Brown* as "other worlds," whether "contestatory, oppositional, or merely alternative."[93]

In chapter 2, I turn to the visual novel *If Found . . .* (Dreamfeel, 2022) to explain how video games build worlds through their interactive mechanics and interfaces. *If Found . . .* is a game that challenges normative structures of time. Its story, which is about a young trans woman who returns to her family home in remote western Ireland, moves forward in time. Meanwhile, the game's mechanics, which center around erasing drawings and writing from the protagonist's diary, move backward. In this way, the game models an alternate trans temporality, one that resists what I describe, drawing from trans studies scholars like Jian Neo Chen and Hil Malatino, as transnormative narratives about linear progress and transition. *If Found . . .* is also fascinated with astrophysics, black holes, and the fabric of space-time, which the game's protagonist refers to as "the building blocks of the universe." Yet the backward-moving mechanics of *If Found . . .* scramble the dictates of contemporary astrophysics—the very laws of our material world. In this way, the game models an approach to queer worldbuilding that stops short of nothing less than rewriting scientific truths at the grandest possible scale, remaking time and space in the spirit of feminist theorist and physicist Karen Barad's assertion that "there is something inherently queer about the nature of matter."[94]

Chapter 3 shifts from a discussion of game design to an analysis of game development—the ways that game worlds are built as technical, computational systems. Specifically, this chapter focuses on physics software, which dictates how simulated physical objects move and interact within a video game world. After explaining the long-standing ties between game physics and sexualized bodies, I present two games that build their worlds around differing queer reconfigurations of physics. The first, *Goat Simulator* (Coffee Stain, 2014), changes the operations of gravity, building a world that feels intentionally "floaty" and rewriting the logics of attraction between bodies. The second, *Wobbledogs* (Tom Astle, 2021), is a game about raising and breeding geometric doglike creatures with rubbery, gelatinous bodies: the very embodiment of life that exists between the animate and the inanimate, as described by scholars who have theorized the nature of animacy, like Jane Bennett and Mel Chen. Here, I draw from developer logs posted online by the game's creator, Tom Astle, to demonstrate how these wobble physics actively shaped the worldbuilding of *Wobbledogs*, steering Astle's decisions about design and story. These examples underscore how the rendering of the tangible world in video games gives form to the messages that such worlds communicate. They also remind us that software tools (and other tools for media making) can serve as valuable nonhuman collaborators in the work of envisioning alternate worlds.

Next, in chapter 4, I return to Jayna Brown's call to imagine alternate dimensions as a springboard for addressing the worldbuilding potential of visual dimensions in video games. As a medium, video games operate across different modes of dimensionality, from the two-dimensionality of side-scrolling platformers to the supposedly immersive three-dimensionality of elaborate graphical worlds. Each dimensional perspective creates a different version of a game world. To demonstrate this, I look at the strange case of what is known as 2.5D games, which combine two- and three-dimensional elements. Through a reading of the 2.5D skateboarding game *OlliOlli World* (Roll7, 2022), I argue for 2.5D as a tool that adds depth and materiality to a video game world. 2.5D, I explain, also represents a queer orientation toward space; it exists in the impossible liminal zone between rational dimensions, literalizing concepts from queer geography studies scholars like Jen Jack Gieseking about the in-betweenness of queer geographies. *OlliOlli World* uses its 2.5D perspective to fill its foreground and background with layers of worlds, including communities of implicitly queer characters and intriguingly strange creatures. Yet *OlliOlli World* ultimately resists players' entry into many of these layers, showing us how 2.5D simultaneously builds worlds and restricts access to them. This, in turn, offers us a much-needed reminder to avoid the colonial and imperialist logics that would have us assume that every world we come across (in a video game or elsewhere) is built for us to enter.

Sara Ahmed, writing in *Queer Phenomenology*, describes how the way we move through space changes the worlds that come into view around us.[95] Indeed, movement and space are two components of worldbuilding that recur throughout the book. Chapter 5 takes Ahmed's insights as an entry point for addressing how video games build worlds through their design of navigable space: the paths along which player-characters can move.[96] In contrast to previous chapters, which foreground the speculative potential of worldbuilding tools, this chapter argues that video game worlds can be *overbuilt*—structured so tightly that they lose their potential for expressing queer meaning. I demonstrate this through the case of *Gone Home* (The Fullbright Company, 2013). Well-known as an influential video game featuring lesbian central characters, *Gone Home* seems to invite players to meander through the protagonist's family home in the spirit of queer, nonlinear wandering. Yet, upon closer analysis, *Gone Home* operates more like a game on rails, straightening the experience of play by requiring players to move through the world in a highly linear fashion. In this chapter, I also return to the concept of queer worldmaking through play. Here, I explain the practice of speedrunning *Gone Home*, in which players find the straightest possible paths through the game world. Through speedrunning, I reflect on how emergent play practices can simultaneously undermine and enrich the work of queer worldbuilding.

Chapter 6 asks: What happens when the worlds of video games, a medium so often defined through opportunities for player interaction and agency, are no longer built for us?[97] To answer that question, I look at Brent Watanabe's online installation art piece *San Andreas Deer Cam* (2013), which live streamed real-time footage of a digital deer controlled by preprogrammed algorithms roaming the streets of *Grand Theft Auto V* (Rockstar Games, 2013). *San Andreas Deer Cam*, I argue, shows us that the construction of player agency is part of video games' worldbuilding toolkit—a point that Watanabe's piece makes precisely by taking away any ability for players to control the deer or the game world that it inhabits. Drawing from critical theorists like Zakiyyah Iman Jackson whose work interrogates racialized divides between the human and nonhuman, I argue that *San Andreas Deer Cam* models an approach to worldbuilding characterized by the spirit of queer posthumanism. Ultimately, Watanabe's piece suggests that the truly radical potential of building alternate video game worlds may lie in building worlds that cannot be played, worlds that destabilize our belief in our own human centrality in the world and serve as implicit arguments for recentering other forms of living.

The conclusion of this book distills the analyses presented in the previous chapters into a concrete set of actionable guidelines and provocations for worldbuilders. At a number of points in this introduction, I have insisted that video game worlds are of striking importance because they have the power to model alternate worlds in action, transforming our speculative imaginings (whether from the realms of science fiction or queer worldmaking) into functional spaces and systems that we can step inside. Here, I return to make good on this claim, translating my conceptual readings of the video game case studies into lessons oriented toward game makers, community leaders, and political activists. Interspersed with these lessons, I also offer supplemental examples of video games that embody these approaches to queer worldbuilding. I provide these additional examples to demonstrate that the video games I have focused on are not monolithic; they do not represent the only possible paths for building (queer) worlds through their respective tools. These games offer us one set of strategies—among many possible strategies—that we can take with us into the world beyond games.

As we move into the chapters ahead, let me offer a personal note: Much like every video game is a world, every academic monograph is a world, for its author if not for its reader. The process of writing such a book requires constructing a zone in one's mind, carving out time and physical space in one's day-to-day life, and living inside that space (literally or figuratively), sometimes for years on end. For me, the world of this particular book first took shape during a time when my own queer world was in the process of falling apart. In addition to living alongside a series of overwhelming political, ecological, and global health-related crises, as we all have done during this period, I was processing the loss of the intimate, interpersonal world I had built for myself and the world I had envisioned for my future. In one fell swoop, I lost a sixteen-year relationship, my chosen queer family, my surrogate biological family, and the beautiful (if deeply flawed) queer city of San Francisco that I called my home. I was left in the emotional rubble, starting a new job in a new town where I felt entirely out of place, trying to stay afloat among unending waves of gender dysphoria and a futile search for a new queer community. What was this strange world, and what place did I have within it? To try to answer that question, I turned, as I have throughout my life at times of uncertainty, to video games. And in video games, I have found, over the course of time, a language for talking about how we might build new queer worlds, broadly conceived, but also how I might rebuild my own.

A lot has changed in my life since this book's earliest days. I have formed a new family; I call a different city my home; I am learning how to exist within my own nonbinary body. I cannot say that I have fully succeeded in the work of building my own new queer world, but I am taking steps each day. As is the case for so many of us whose identities and histories are situated at the margins, living my life is itself an act of worldbuilding. I mention this context to explain that rethinking worldbuilding and envisioning queer worlds are not abstract concepts to me. The tools that I describe in this book are tools that my communities need, but they are also tools that I need myself. When I say that we can build radical new worlds by destabilizing norms, rethinking underlying logics, and moving our bodies queerly, I am thinking about how I too need to move differently through the world. There is no going back to the way the world was before, for me or for any of us, but there are ways of reimagining the path forward: a path that is winding and uncertain and full of contradictions, a path that carves out the contours of a queer world.

1

Nine Thousand Little Worlds

Worldbuilding and Queer Worldmaking in What the Golf

What the Golf (2019), as its irreverent title might suggest, is a video game that has very little to do with golf—at least, not as we typically imagine it. In the face of a long-standing and ever-expanding lineup of sports simulator video games that are promoted through their increasingly "realistic" graphics and gameplay, *What the Golf*, developed by the Danish independent development studio Triband, operates as an absurdist parody of the very idea of a golf video game. The game opens with the scene of a tiny, one-hole golf course perched on top of a mountain, which sticks up into the clouds (figure 1.1). At one end of the course, a golf ball sits waiting in the grass. A short distance away stands a putting green with a hole marked by a flag. Players quickly learn the game's incredibly simple controls: pull back on the cursor (using a touch screen, mouse, or controller stick, depending on which platform one is playing on) to power up an arrow, which, when released, will knock the ball in a chosen direction. Successfully directing the ball into the hole constitutes a win. After each win, a burst of confetti shoots forth from the hole, an unseen crowd bursts into cheers, the game pops up a short congratulatory message, and the player moves on to the next level. Sending the ball off the steep cliffs that border the course constitutes a loss. In the event of a loss, the invisible spectators groan in disappointment, and the game quickly reloads the level so that the player can try again.

If this sounds like a relatively normal way to translate the game of golf into a video game, *What the Golf* rapidly overturns that sense of normalcy. Each successive course, positioned on its own craggy mountain top, makes golf incrementally weirder. In the second level, players must shoot their ball around a triad of cats sitting in front of the hole. In the third level, a human figure holding a golf club appears next to the ball, as if about to strike. When players pull back and release the directional

Figure 1.1. The opening level of *What the Golf* (Triband, 2019). (Screenshot by author)

arrow, however, the resulting force hits the human golfer, not the ball; the player must now fling the golfer, whose floppy body tumbles awkwardly across the grass, toward the flag. In level four, the terms of play are swapped again, and the player must now hit a golf club, hurling it over increasingly disjointed terrain and navigating around a set of pink toasters that, when touched, eagerly launch slices of toast (figure 1.2). Level seven seems straightforward enough until the player takes their shot and the hole itself moves, scooting several feet to the left with a mischievous giggle. And all of this takes place before the game's title screen has even rolled. Thus, from its opening moments, *What the Golf* clearly establishes its gameplay premise: to unravel the basic concept of golf piece by piece and to put those pieces back together again in the most ridiculous iterations possible.

Each level of *What the Golf*—and by "level," I mean both the game's separate mountaintop courses and the varying setups that appear on those courses—operates like a hypothetical. Those hypotheticals only get more and more gleefully unhinged as the game goes on. What if, instead of hitting one ball, you hit lots of them simultaneously? What if, every time you hit the ball, holes popped up from the ground to swallow it up? What if you transformed a golf course into a track and field arena, and instead of hitting a ball you flung a single, flat-soled sneaker? What if you took that track, flipped it straight up and down, swapped the ball for a horse, and had the horse fall through the air for an alarmingly long distance before crashing into the hole? The list of hypotheticals goes on. *What the Golf* has hundreds of levels and literally thousands of "holes," that is, specific arrangements of scenarios, obstacles, and goals. The original version of the game, which was released in 2019, shipped with a main campaign that takes about six hours to play.[1] In 2021, Triband began releasing additional "episodes," new clusters of levels with themes like "Sporty Sports," "Slime Time," and "It's Snowtime!"[2] For a sense of scale, each of these takes only about an hour to play, yet the third such episode alone (a donut-themed collection of levels conveniently titled "A Hole New World") alone includes fifty new courses and *one thousand*

Figure 1.2. In an early level of *What the Golf*, players fling a golf club past toasters that launch toast. (Screenshot by author)

new holes.³ Given the overall play time of the game, this suggests that *What the Golf* currently includes, in total, roughly nine thousand holes.

This sheer magnitude of the game's iterations is staggering. It is so large, in fact, that at times it seems big enough to swallow up the world. In a 2020 interview, Rune K. Drewson, one of the game's designers, explained that some potential players steer away from the game because it has "golf" in the title. In reality, said Drewson, "it's a golf game that doesn't have anything to do with golf, except to show you that everything in the world is actually golf. . . . Even life itself is golf. We get born, and we all end up in a hole."⁴ Drewson delivers this claim—that everything in the world, even life itself, is actually golf—with an air of deadpan humor but also a sense of earnestness. What is golf, he seems to be saying, but the word we use to name our repeated attempts to move an object toward a goal? In that sense, what are any of us ever doing in life but playing our own endless iterations of golf? For Drewson, the expansive implications of *What the Golf* seem to extend most concretely to other video games. He continues his claims: "*Super Mario* is a golf game. *Assassin's Creed* is a golf game. *Counter-Strike* is a golf game. *What the Golf* is not a golf game. It's a game that shows you that all the games you've been playing all along are just golf games."⁵ It seems that, for someone who has helped design thousands of increasingly abstracted golf holes, both the world of video games and the world itself have come to look like one giant golf course.

For my part, I want to take this idea that *What the Golf* reveals the underlying golfiness of the world and flip it on its head. Rather than arguing that the world is golf (though I am open to that possibility), I am interested in how *What the Golf* itself contains a multitude of worlds—thousands and thousands of hypothetical ways of imagining a gameplay universe. When we think of building new worlds, whether in video games or other media forms, we often conjure up grand visions: far-off galaxies, complex ecological environments, multilayered alternate cultures, or post-apocalyptic wastelands in which society must rise from the ashes. *What the Golf* is about none of these things. It is, from a storytelling perspective, largely about nothing at all. Nonetheless, *What the Golf* is precisely a video game about building and rebuilding worlds. This is because, as we will see, each of its levels constitutes a game world premised on a new combination of interactive rules. Given that it takes only five to ten seconds to play each of its levels, we might say that *What the Golf* makes and remakes the world every few moments. In this way, it echoes and yet also differs from a game like Anna Anthropy's *Queers in Love at the End of the World* (2013), a text-based Twine game in which, as Claudia Lo has explained, the world ends and begins again in a repeating, ten-second queer time loop.[6] The micro worlds that appear in *What the Golf* are played just as briefly, but they do not repeat.[7] Instead, they model an approach to worldbuilding in which gameplay proliferates outward into a seemingly infinite array of possible worlds.

In this chapter, I present *What the Golf* as a particularly legible and therefore instructive example of a video game that models many of the foundational premises of this book outlined in the introduction. First, through *What the Golf*, we can see how video games of all sorts contain (and, indeed, *are*) worlds. Second, because *What the Golf* is a nonnarrative game that emphasizes shifting mechanics, it models how video game worldbuilding is enacted through the design of interactive systems rather than through storytelling. Third, the game's campy, tongue-in-cheek references to queer culture draw attention to the queer implications of its worldbuilding. Indeed, by constantly reimagining the playable world, the game destabilizes norms of identity, agency, and desire; it unmoors notions of what a game world should be and who *we* should be when we play it. By extension, *What the Golf* helpfully demonstrates how worldbuilding in video games might itself constitute a queer practice, even when the worlds represented in video games do not contain explicit LGBTQIA+ representation. At the same time, the relative lack of markers of racial diversity in the game serves as a reminder that even game worlds that can be interpreted as queer may remain exclusionary along other vectors of identity and privilege.

Finally, because each of the game's level-worlds (as we might call them) is set into motion through acts of play, *What the Golf* illustrates with more specificity how worldbuilding in video games resonates with theories of queer worldmaking, a connection also gestured at in the introduction. Queer worldmaking, as I have briefly explained, is a queer theory concept that describes the ways that people with LGBTQIA+ identities set new queer worlds into motion through both their art and their everyday lives. By nature, queer worldmaking, like queerness itself, is a nebulous concept. My own conceptualization of queer worldmaking draws heavily on writing by José Esteban Muñoz, who, across his career, described queer worldmaking as an active, performative practice. Though worldbuilding has typically been envisioned as distinct from worldmaking, *What the Golf* sheds light on the connections between them. Much as Muñoz describes queer of color subjects as making alternative visions of reality, *What the Golf* demonstrates how video game worlds are not only *built* (by their designers) but also *made* through play.

What Makes a World?

What the Golf is full to the brim with playable worlds. However, worldbuilding in *What the Golf* does not look like the kind of worldbuilding we—as scholars, developers, or players—have come to expect from video games. As mentioned, most existing work on video game worldbuilding largely equates worldbuilding with the development of narratives, in-game text, character backstories, and the creation of diegetic cultural milieus that serve as backdrops to gameplay.[8] *What the Golf*, by contrast, has no story; it has no true characters; it has what we might loosely call a setting, but that setting is fractured and nonsensical. The game's levels are connected through (what are commonly termed in video game parlance) hub worlds, but these are little more than interconnected rooms that feature their own pleasingly illogical tableaux. In one such room, a dog DJs a disco dance party. In the next, a man riding a cannon shoots hot dogs onto a soccer field while an anthropomorphic tomato sobs in the corner (figure 1.3).

These scenes are not part of a larger story. They are absurdist in the spirit of dadaist or surrealist collage: cut and paste, out of place, intentionally incongruous and nonsensical.[9] A different game might offer a framing narrative to explain why the player should work their way through level after level of bizarre pseudo-golf. Indeed, many of the video games to which *What the Golf* pays homage, such as the *Katamari Damacy* series (Bandei Namco Studios, 2004–2018), *Donut County* (Ben Esposito, 2018), and *Octodad: Dadliest Catch* (Young Horses, 2014), include story elements that contextualize their characters' otherwise ridiculous behavior.[10] By contrast, *What the Golf* presents itself as a work of pure aesthetics and gameplay. And yet, despite the fact that it lacks

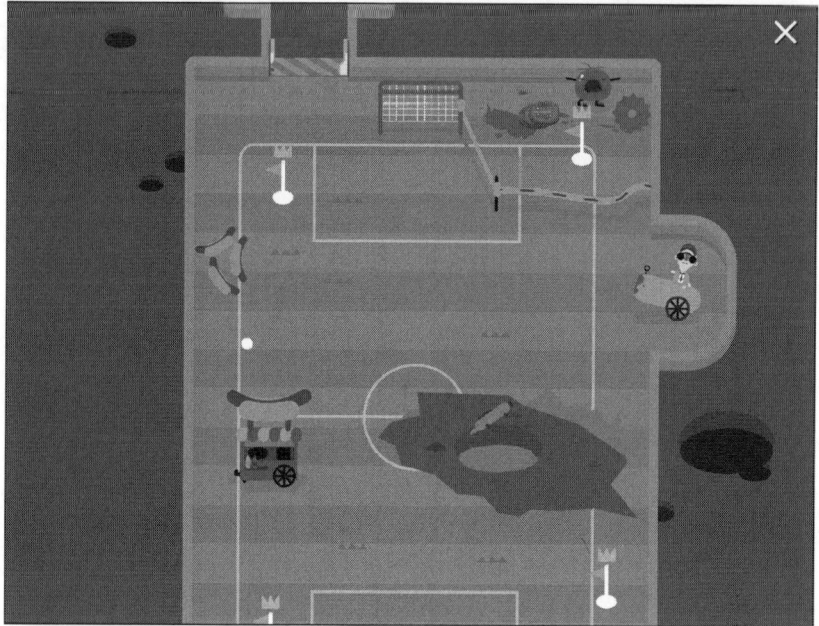

Figure 1.3. A room in the hub world through which players access the levels of *What the Golf*. (Screenshot by author)

almost all of the elements traditionally associated with worldbuilding, *What the Golf* has built—and continues to build, through the ongoing release of additional content—an immense multiplicity of worlds.

Understanding how each of the game's levels constitutes its own world requires first stepping back and articulating the factors that transform a place, whether inside a video game or out, into a world. What makes a world? If we are setting aside notions of worldbuilding that conceptualize worlds as constructed narrative settings, then what *do* we mean when we call something a world? If a media object itself, rather than the locations and cultures it portrays, can be a world, then what qualities give a piece of media its worldliness? The definition of "world" may seem self-evident. Yet, upon closer consideration, it too reveals itself to be capacious, mercurial, and surprisingly hard to pin down. "World" has a deceivingly commonsensical quality, as if we all know one when we see it.[11] Much to the contrary, thinking about worlds through a video game *What the Golf* is productive, in part, because such games strip away this commonsensicalness. By building and rebuilding the world again and again, video games challenge us to test the terms by which we understand the world itself.

Within *What the Golf*, multiple possible definitions of a world manifest themselves simultaneously. Perhaps the most straightforward way to conceptualize a world is as a bounded physical space: a self-contained terrain that is, in some way, separated off from the expanse around it. The levels of *What the Golf* each literalize this particular vision of a world. Most are perched high in the sky, like a series of floating islands. Around them, we see only an endless, undifferentiated sea of blue. In certain levels, players actually catch sight of the bottom of these courses. Because no land has been graphically rendered beneath them, they appear to hover in the ether, truly separated from what we might call, colloquially, the rest of the world. To an extent, the levels of *What the Golf* are similar to the floating courses found in other video games, such as the *Super Monkey Ball* series (various developers, 2000–2021).[12] In the *Super Monkey Ball* games, players roll giant balls down tilting tracks that levitate high above a variety of terrains, including tropical oceans and jutting rocky outcroppings. When the balls fall off the sides of these tracks, they (and the flailing monkeys contained within them) plummet toward the Earth below, and the level begins again. In contrast to the depictions of the surrounding world presented in *Super Monkey Ball*, however, *What the Golf* removes all visual information about the ground beneath its mountaintop courses, heightening the sense that its levels are truly tiny worlds unto themselves. Each of these thousands of levels is, paradoxically, the only thing in the universe.

At the same time, *What the Golf* prompts us to see the ambiguity inherent in defining worlds as bounded terrains. The boundaries of the game's many levels, as players discover through various flirtations with failure, are more elastic than they first appear. If players knock their ball (or whichever object they control in a given level) past the edge of a course's cliff, they sometimes have the opportunity to recover, most commonly by using the directional arrow to knock their ball back onto the green in midair. At other times, the boundaries of a course are not merely external; they are also internal. Many levels incorporate obstacles within the seemingly bounded space of the mountaintop course, such as large holes that objects can fall into. Falling into these holes produces the same results as falling off the side of the mountain—that is, the player loses and must try again—despite the fact that the ball has not technically left the space of the floating course. Presumably, it has instead rolled inside the mountain, sucked up into the bowels of the world. For this reason, if we understand the physical terrains of *What the Golf* as models for the larger concept of a world, we come to anticipate that the boundaries of a given world (whether physical, social, or media based) are likely to be blurry, contradictory, and even misleading—perhaps especially when those boundaries seem particularly clear.

What the Golf simultaneously prompts us to expand this vision of a world as a specific, defined space by thinking about *atmosphere*. Considered from a different angle, we could say that a world is a sphere that contains within itself a certain set of atmospheric conditions. Atmosphere is spatial yet diffuse; one can stand inside it, yet it is hard to say with accuracy where it starts and ends. In discussing atmosphere, I am thinking literally about the atmosphere that surrounds our planet—a swirl of nitrogen, oxygen, and water vapor inside which life (as we know it) is possible and beyond which life (under most circumstances) cannot survive.[13] When we talk in common parlance about the Earth as a world, we do not mean simply the ground under our feet but also the miles of atmosphere that extend up into space. In this sense, atmosphere describes the physical thing that both encircles the world and demarcates its conditions of possibility.

At the same time, I am thinking of atmosphere as a concept that describes a specific world-like quality within visual media: that thing that lends a piece of media its particular ambiance, its feeling. Writing about the use of Mexican American extras to create racialized atmosphere in silent films, Laura Isabel Serna explains atmosphere as an "aesthetic category" used "to produce realistic filmic worlds."[14] Says Serna, filmic atmosphere should be understood as an "emotional or affective force that can shape social life," playing off dominant cultural feelings about what makes a world real, who should feature prominently within it, and who should be positioned as set dressing.[15] We need atmosphere to survive (again, I am thinking of the atmosphere that surrounds the Earth), but atmosphere can also be toxic. Serna, for instance, describes how "the creation of cinematic worlds . . . naturalized racial hierarchies to the extent that they became, for many viewers of Hollywood films, as unremarkable as the air we breathe."[16] In this way, atmosphere participates in the creation of new worlds while simultaneously perpetuating beliefs from existing worlds, reinstating cultural ideas about whom a world should place front and center and who should remain in the background.

Each video game too creates its own atmospheric conditions: the swirling, nebulous bubble that enfolds the game, establishing the aesthetic and affective—and, by extension, cultural and political—qualities of its world. Broadly speaking, the atmosphere of *What the Golf* can be described as bright, colorful, and upbeat: qualities that manifest themselves through the game's vibrant palette, blocky graphic style, cartoonish character design, and quirky soundtrack. These atmospheric conditions, while endearing, admittedly seem somewhat unremarkable in comparison to the importance of the Earth's atmosphere or atmospheres of racial oppression. Yet, once again, *What the Golf* offers a useful illustration; it shows us the techniques that video game worlds more generally use to establish atmosphere by presenting us with a proliferation of level-worlds, each of which constructs its own atmosphere differently. What we find across these levels is that atmosphere takes shape largely through the use of non-interactive elements. In *What the Golf*, these elements include the placement of structures (like buildings) or natural elements (like trees) around the terrain of the level. Most prominently, though, *What the Golf* establishes its shifting atmospheres by dotting its levels with a rotating roster of non-player characters (NPCs), who themselves function like extras on a film set. These NPCs contribute to both the fictional world (such as it is) of a given level and also the individual atmospheric mood that differentiates that level from other worlds in the game.

Consider, for instance, a level in the "A Hole New World" episode in which the player uses the directional arrow to navigate a wobbly bicycle through a long, narrow course. (After all, everything is golf, so why not riding a bike?) Along the way, the bicycle passes a motley cast of characters, mostly anthropomorphic animals who mull about or lounge in the sunshine. The most striking of these is a horse who reclines on a pool chair propped up on a rocky outcropping in the middle of the course (figure 1.4). Seemingly taking no notice of the passing bicycle, the horse shields his eyes with a cowboy hat and holds, with one outstretched

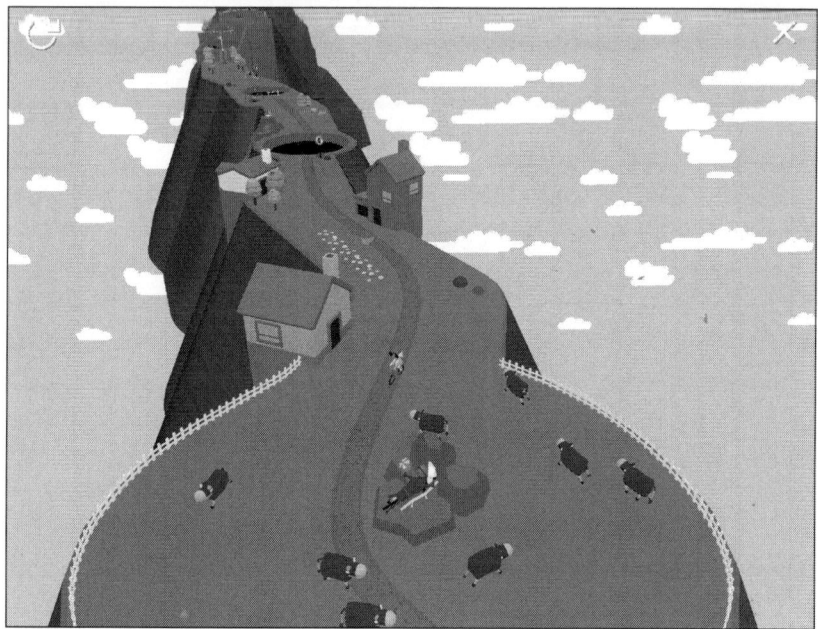

Figure 1.4. In a bicycle-riding level of *What the Golf*, players leap over a sunbathing horse. (Screenshot by author)

hoof, what appears to be a tropical cocktail, complete with a festive paper umbrella. Because the horse's chair is surrounded by cows who will push the bicycle off-course, the player is likely to proceed through this area by launching the bicycle straight up and over the horse. Still, the horse remains entirely unperturbed; no matter how many times the player rides near or simply over him, the horse does not deign to stop sunbathing. In his character design and placement, then, the horse embodies the atmospheric tone of the level. His presence imbues this world with a sense of languidness and leisure, while communicating to the player the stinging feeling that the inhabitants of the world they are riding through could not care less about their presence. Wafting on the air that the player breathes are the intermingled scents of barnyard animals, tanning oil, dark rum, unapologetic idleness, and the sour sweat of a cold-shouldered social slight.

What the Golf's depiction of NPCs also establishes the game's own racialized atmosphere. In addition to its cast of animal characters, the game does feature some human NPCs, the majority of whom are white. The golfer character, who on occasion functions as a player-character, is depicted as white as well. Admittedly, *What the Golf* includes some Black and brown human NPCs. These NPCs are few and far between, however, and they typically appear only among large crowds in levels where the non-interactive scenery includes a cheering audience. In this way, though the game does not depict the kinds of active racial stereotyping and anti-Blackness that are troublingly common in many video game genres, it does operate under a "color-blind ideology" that, as André Brock explains, allows whiteness to operate as the "default, 'normal' identity in video games."[17] This, in turn, perpetuates what anthropologist and Black game studies scholar Akil Fletcher describes as "the magic circle of whiteness," in which play spaces are envisioned as places that privilege and uphold white identities while sidelining the identities of people of color.[18] The atmosphere of *What the Golf* is thus one in which racial diversity is deployed occasionally to acknowledge—while still sidelining—experiences of difference: a quick nod to the world of racialized identities that is positioned as largely external to the game's own many worlds.

Serna describes the use of racialized extras to establish atmosphere in silent films as part of an effort to produce (what were being presented to white audiences by film creators as) "realistic filmic worlds."[19] Yet the atmospheres that each level-world conjures in *What the Golf* are also instructive for encouraging us to think beyond cultural notions of realism—or, perhaps more accurately, to complicate realism—when we look for the worlds contained within video games. In a game like *What the Golf*, techniques for establishing atmosphere often foster a distinctly disjointed unreality that characterizes many of the game's worlds. That is, far from establishing a sense of realism, atmosphere in *What the Golf* is often used to heighten the sense that each of the game's worlds is, in its own way, absurd. Indeed, there are many video games—all of which constitute worlds in their own rights—that are so abstracted that they begin to make the very concept of realism seem ridiculous. What is a realistic match-three mobile game? What is a realistic online word puzzle? By distancing themselves from realism, the atmospheric conditions we find operating in *What the Golf* serve to emphasize the affective rather than the ontological qualities that contribute to defining worlds.

The boundaries that border any given world are always, in one way or another, boundaries of feeling. Whether or not we know a world when we see it, we know it when we *feel* it.

Building Worlds through Interactive Design

Thus far, I have talked about how *What the Golf* builds its multiplicity of worlds through visual and non-interactive elements, like its level design and NPCs. However, even more crucial for understanding how worldbuilding operates in *What the Golf*—and in video games more generally—is how the game uses *interactive* elements. At its most foundational level, *What the Golf* makes and remakes its worlds not by shifting golf courses or swapping out NPCs but by changing the fundamental terms of gameplay. These are the terms that form the very premise on which each micro world within the game is built. When these premises shift, the game world shifts with them. *What the Golf* illustrates how game design, then, rather than narrative design, establishes or changes the conditions around which video game worlds emerge. Changing these conditions sets a new world into motion.

What makes *What the Golf* such an instructive example of worldbuilding through design is, once again, its multiplicity, which offers us ready-made points of comparison between individual game worlds. Unlike in most video games, which tend to use a relatively consistent set of core mechanics over the course of a game, every level in *What the Golf* is built around a different combination of interactive elements that give shape to its unique playable world. Speaking in a 2019 interview with *Game Developer* magazine, Tim Garbos, the creative director of Triband, explained that *What the Golf* was designed to maximize the experience of surprise.[20] Each time that the player begins a new level, they find that the game has shifted. Consider, side by side, a few of the levels already described. In one, the player hits a ball; in another, the player steers a bicycle; in a third, the player pushes a horse from a platform. These scenarios are not mini-games: short playable diversions from a central gameplay experience. Instead, each of these scenarios represents its own alternate reality imagining of golf—a set of multiplying parallel universes in which golf, translated into a video game, is played in distinct ways. This proliferation of different approaches to play is itself what gives structure and meaning to each of the thousands of worlds that populate *What the Golf*. Put otherwise, what solidifies these different levels into distinct worlds is how they play and are played.

This constant shifting of the terms of play in *What the Golf* takes three main forms. I map them here to articulate how *What the Golf* performs its worldbuilding but also to offer them up as a more general framework that we might apply (and expand on) while analyzing how other video games build their worlds. First, across its array of levels, *What the Golf* is constantly reimagining what players can *do*. Until they shove their avatar-object with the directional arrow, the player has no way of knowing how that object will behave or what kinds of movement it is capable of in this particular level-world. They also do not know what obstacles will stand in their path (many of which do not become visible until the player makes their first hit) or how those obstacles will operate. Therefore, as they begin each new level, players know almost none of the terms of play. In this regard, the game intentionally plays with expectations. Often, it produces a sense of surprise, as Garbos says, by creating precedent for certain forms of action and then enacting a bait-and-switch.

A pair of levels in the "Sporty Sports" expansion pack illustrates these rapid, intentionally vertiginous shifts with typical *What the Golf* humor. Here, initially, the player finds themself playing as a giraffe. Seated at one end of a mountaintop golf course, the giraffe holds a can of spray paint aimed at a large canvas. The player quickly learns that the directional arrow, rather than launching the giraffe as they might expect, moves the spray paint, which allows the player to paint. To progress, players must successfully trace the image of a hot dog on the canvas. The next level again opens with a giraffe seated in front of a canvas; this time, poised in a very similar position, the giraffe holds a paintbrush (figure 1.5). Yet, when the player attempts to paint, the in-game camera moves rapidly away from the giraffe and to a nearby cow. The directional arrow, once released, now flings the cow down the course toward a waiting flag. Meanwhile, the giraffe is left in the dust at the starting line. This level, it turns out, was never a giraffe painting level at all; it was always a level about flinging cows. Thus, as quickly as the game has acclimated players to a world defined by one type of action (a world in which all you can do is paint), it swaps out this premise and places players into a totally different world (one in which all you can do is prod a flopping cow toward a finish line).

Figure 1.5. *What the Golf* regularly surprises its players, such as in a level where players expect to paint and instead fling a cow. (Screenshot by author)

Game studies scholar Cameron Kunzelman, in his book *The World Is Born from Zero*, describes what he terms "mechanics of speculation." Discussing how narrative-forward science fiction video games perform worldbuilding through their interactive mechanics, Kunzelman explains that such games prompt players to engage in speculative thinking by "putting us in a position to think about the outcomes of our in-game actions."[21] To paraphrase Kunzelman, we might say that, each time a video game (of any sort) invites us to interact, it simultaneously invites us to speculate about the potential effects of our in-game actions: what the game will do with our chosen inputs and what those consequences will suggest about how the game understands the meaning of our choices. Of course, *What the Golf* is not a science fiction video game of the sort that Kunzelman has in mind. Nevertheless, it leans hard into its own version of the mechanics of speculation. The one thing that players of *What the Golf* can rely on is the knowledge that the game is constantly changing. Every time they pull back the directional arrow in a new level, players are prompted to engage in their own act of speculation, one that is simultaneously pragmatic and affectively charged. What will happen when I release this arrow? Will it cause me to advance toward the flag or to fall off the mountainside? What kind of action is possible in this world? Will it surprise me? Will I feel amused, or will I feel tricked?

This pair of giraffe painting levels also illustrates the second main way that *What the Golf* changes the terms of play that define its worlds: by constantly shifting what the player *wants*. Across its levels, the game regularly shifts the goals it sets for its players, as well as the challenges that the player must overcome to reach those goals. Just as players do not know what actions they will take until they release the directional arrow at the start of each level, they do not know what the conditions for winning or losing a given level will be until they reach its end. Often, learning this lesson requires dying once or twice—trial runs of the course that function as momentarily fatal fact-finding missions. Will success, this time, mean hitting an object into a flag? Steering a bicycle into a mountainside cave? Spray painting a convincing representation of a hot dog? Will achieving this goal require dodging holes? Navigating around pushy cows? Tiptoeing (to the extent that a golf ball can tiptoe) past hair-trigger toasters?

Win and loss conditions are key characteristics that give shape to many forms of video game worlds. These conditions simultaneously describe the boundaries of a game world—that is, under what circumstances it will come to an end, whether for better or for worse—and the longings that shape that world. One of the fundamental characteristics of any game world is what kinds of actions it rewards or punishes, what it does or does not seem to *desire* players to do, and by extension what it prompts players themselves to desire. Given that each of *What the Golf*'s levels brings with it different goals, each can also be understood as a unique world powered by a distinct set of desires. I use "desire" here intentionally for the way it conjures up associations with sexuality, attraction, and the erotic. As Audre Lorde writes, "Recognizing the power of the erotic within our lives can give us the energy to pursue genuine change within our world."[22] Fueled by alternative desires, we create alternative worlds.

Third, *What the Golf* constantly remakes its interactive worlds by changing the terms of what players *are*. Just as the game regularly switches out the action that occurs when players release the directional arrow, it swaps what object is moved by the force of the arrow. In this way, with each new level, the game changes what object the player *plays with* and thereby *plays as*. Technically, players take on the role of the arrow itself—the abstracted, disembodied force that moves other objects through the world. However, in effect, the object that the player moves comes to feel like their avatar on screen: rolling, running, flopping, or falling in fits and starts across the golf green.[23] As players progress in quick succession through various levels, that avatar switches again and again. In one sequence of levels, for example, players first find themselves playing as a small snowball rolling through a wintery course. In the next moment, they are a man running on top of a moving snowball. And then, another moment later, they are a moose encased in a giant ball of snow, its head trapped deep inside and its limbs pointed straight out in all directions.

Indeed, another one of the foundational premises that defines a video game world, whether or not it contains a specific protagonist with a discernible identity, is its answer to the question, "Who am I when I play this game?" Each level of *What the Golf* answers that question differently. In turn, each of these levels offers a new worldview: an alternate perspective that originates from a new creature, a new mode of being. Simultaneously, *What the Golf*, as an overall collection of worlds, offers its own answer to the question, "Who I am when I play?" You are everything and nothing, the game seems to say, or perhaps you are the spirit of golf itself—ready to inhabit an array of movable objects toward some unknown goal. It seems that, just like all the world, you too are nothing more and nothing less than golf.

Thus, *What the Golf* demonstrates how the interactive qualities of play, those building blocks of video games, establish the fundamental conditions of a game's world. This is true whether that world takes just one form within a given video game or, as in the case of *What the Golf*, thousands of them. However, before moving on from my discussion of how *What the Golf* models video game worldbuilding, I want to return to a point that I presented in the introduction that complicates this focus on design. While game creators doubtless play a formative role in establishing the rules that set the conditions for each video game world, the act of play itself is what sets the wheels of that world in motion. In this sense, we can think of video game design as the construction of a world-building *machine* rather than the actual building of a world. Only when players begin to act within the game space do the cogs of that machine start turning, spinning up a world that takes shape around (and in direct response to) them. To an extent then, we might equate video games to early cinematic technologies that required embodied input from viewers to bring imagery to life. A video game world is, in at least one way, not unlike a flip book or a hand-cranked Mutoscope, which presents viewers with a series of photographs they can flip through in quick succession to create the impression that they are watching a world in motion.

Let me illustrate the way that play animates video game worlds by returning to a level of *What the Golf*. Consider, again, the level in which the player rides a bicycle past a sunbathing horse. This level is, in fact, part of a longer, culminating sequence of levels strung together in the equivalent of a boss battle. Even within this one extended sequence, the world of the game is multiply made and remade as the player enters each new sublevel. Initially, the player is greeted with the scene of a typical, one-hole mountaintop golf course. It appears they will be playing as a human wearing sunglasses and holding a hot dog. The hole they need to reach, marked by a now-familiar orange flag, seems to be immediately in front of their character. Yet, as soon as they release the arrow, the game world transforms. With the flag's characteristic impish giggle, it runs off into a cave, calling on the player to follow and changing the win conditions for the level. After the player launches their character a few hops forward, additional holes begin appearing in the ground, transforming the terrain into treacherous Swiss cheese. The game world as it appears at first glance, it turns out, was an illusion. Only when the player begins to play does that world take on its true form.

Next in this sequence, after the player flings their character into the gaping mountainside cave, they find that they have landed in a new world: the long, winding bicycle course with its unflappable, day-drinking horse. Now playing as the same human character on a bike, players learn that using the arrow conjures a whole new set of actions and movements. Holding down the arrow allows the human to ride the bicycle forward; releasing the arrow hurls him spinning up into the air, in the style of an ill-advised BMX trick. The unexpected physics of this action contribute to the pleasure of its surprise. Players soon realize that, with very little momentum, the bicyclist can catapult himself over large obstacles, somersaulting five or six times before landing on both wheels and rolling onward.

Having completed this area, the player moves into the next world in the sequence: a long stretch of seaside road, bordered by glowing golden sand and dotted with palm trees. Once again, the characteristics that define the interactive world are made anew. Now the player's character drives a car—which, it turns out, must be steered carefully lest it be catapulted off the level by spring-loaded platforms or barrels of explosives. Finally, the player lands back on one last mountaintop course. Now, suddenly, they play as a hovering rain cloud (figure 1.6). Floating the cloud toward the waiting flag reveals a final surprise: as it passes by, the cloud sheds raindrops into a series of holes, out of which sprout eager clusters of flags that spring up haphazardly, like weeds. In the span of less than two minutes, the player has moved through multiple ways of doing, wanting, and being. Having begun as a person, they end as a force of nature.

In this way, *What the Golf* serves as a reminder, as we move forward in our investigation of how video games build their worlds, to attend to the ways that play interfaces with design. This emphasis on play makes players equal participants in the work of building worlds. Thinking about play as an integral part of worldbuilding will also allow us to see, in this book's final chapters, how placing limitations on play likewise limits the radical potential of certain video game worlds. Additionally, as I discuss more later in this chapter, highlighting the role of play in video game worldbuilding serves as a valuable bridge between worldbuilding and queer worldmaking, bringing to the surface rich yet underexplored connections between the ways that video game worlds and worlds of queer experience take shape.

At the same time, it is important to remain vigilant of the complexities of play itself, rather than idealizing play or presuming that play holds the same meaning for all people. Play has been variously theorized in game studies, where it has been envisioned in turns as transformative, transgressive, emancipatory, discriminatory, and oppressive. Tara Fickle has demonstrated how texts commonly seen as foundational for theorizing play are themselves rooted in colonialist thought, often

Figure 1.6. In one level of *What the Golf*, players float a rain cloud over holes that respond by sprouting flags. (Screenshot by author)

depicting ludic cultures of Asia, Africa, and the Middle East as Orientalist curiosities.[24] Writing in *Repairing Play: A Black Phenomenology*, Aaron Trammell similarly contests established theorizations of play as a universal act of leisure and pleasure.[25] Far from being simply liberatory, Trammell argues, dominant cultural and intellectual histories of play are equally bound up with pain, torture, and the trauma of slavery.[26] A more "inclusive and reparative definition of the term," writes Trammell, "must rethink the very definition of play to make space for those it has oppressed, as well as those it has elevated."[27]

We must bring this same critical spirit to our analysis of play within video game worlds. Work like Fickle's and Trammell's challenges us to embark on an ongoing process of interrogating—rather than merely describing or uniformly celebrating—video game worlds. Of each world (whether found in a video game or elsewhere), we can and should ask: By and for whom is this world built? In this world, who gets to act and who is acted on? What forms of pleasure does this world offer to the player and at whose expense? Whose eyes do we encounter this world through, and how might this world look different if played from another perspective? In what territories and on whose backs are these worlds constructed? Which existing hierarchies does this world abolish, and which does it replicate? Who has the privilege of rebuilding the world, and who is themself forcibly rebuilt, part of the collateral damage of breaking and reshaping reality?

The Queer Worlds of *What the Golf*

I have said that *What the Golf* models how video games build worlds through design. Yet, I want to pivot here to add a second layer to this claim about the game. *What the Golf* is doubly useful as a model because its approach to worldbuilding resonates with queerness, enacting a particular mode of queer worldbuilding while suggesting that we might see the act of building (and rebuilding) the world in video games itself as queer. Though each of the subsequent chapters in this book will discuss another video game that enacts its own version of queer worldbuilding, reflecting the diversity of ways in which worlds might be built queerly, I find *What the Golf* to be a particularly compelling example to use as a springboard for identifying queer worldbuilding in action. Despite its shortcomings, the game helps us move past limited, supposedly commonsensical notions of what constitutes a queer world. Just as the game looks little like the kind of narrative-heavy video games typically celebrated for their worldbuilding, it bears little resemblance to video games (I am thinking here of titles like *Gone Home*, the subject of chapter 5, or Game Grump's 2017 *Dream Daddy*) that most overtly place people with LGBTQIA+ identities at the center of their worlds. Nonetheless, *What the Golf*, which has its own queer-coded representational overtones, embodies an approach to building the world that echoes queer experiences.

On its face, *What the Golf* seems like a strange candidate for queer interpretation. Given that the game has no narrative elements, it also has no overtly queer characters, romances, or direct engagement with queer politics. Indeed, both its premise and the execution of that premise are deeply farcical and therefore may seem an ill fit to a topic like queerness, at least from the vantage point of those who expect issues of sexual and gender identity to be confined to so-called serious games.[28] *What the Golf* also offers none of the opportunities for empathy with marginalized people that, as Teddy Pozo has explained, are commonly expected by straight players who encounter queer games.[29] Indeed, the game overtly sidesteps identification or immersion, refusing to allow players to rest comfortably within any one identity (person, golf ball, golf club, snowball, horse) for longer than the span of a level. In its energetic absurdity, *What the Golf* similarly resists any attempts to instrumentalize the game as an instructive social object. It gives straight and cisgender players no queer lesson to be learned.

Yet, if we scratch the game's surface, we find that the worlds of *What the Golf* are queer in a number of ways. As has perhaps already become apparent, these worlds are populated by a decidedly queer and campy cast of NPCs: human figures of indeterminate genders; animals enjoying the everyday hedonistic pleasures of human life; typically inanimate objects that suddenly fling themselves across golf courses with reckless abandon; holes that move at will with a cheeky, mischievous glee. The very concept of *What the Golf* comes with queer implications. Across its vast collection of levels, the game notably sidesteps humor related to sexual innuendo. However, a shadow of crass sexuality hangs over the game. Its title (*What the Golf*) is funny precisely because it plays off the phrase we expect to hear ("what the fuck"). Each time the player reopens the game, a chorus of upbeat voices sing the game's title; when they do, we cannot help but feel the shadow of "fuck" behind the word "golf." To call a game *What the Golf* is to insist that we consider, each time we hear or speak or write its name, that fucking and golfing may not be so different—an implicit argument for a line of thinking that Caroline Bem and Susanna Paasonen describe, in their introduction to a special issue of *Sexualities* titled "Play!," as "thinking sex in and as play."[30] After all, it is easy enough to extend Drewson's claim that "everything in the world is actually golf" to include an array of sexual acts, queer and otherwise. What is more queerly erotic or polymorphously perverse than trying, thousands of times, to repeatedly propel an unlikely variety of objects into a vast array of eager, waiting holes?[31]

On occasion, *What the Golf* makes it connections to queer culture more explicit through visual references and inside jokes. Another set of levels in the "A Hole New World" expansion (right in its name we have an entire world defined by hungry holes!) appears to be themed around gay pride. In one level, players, in the role of a stretchy-legged dachshund dog, shimmy past a cardboard box full of rainbow flags. The dachshund then scoots up the side of a building and joins a rooftop

Figure 1.7. A rooftop dance party with rainbow pennants and wiener dogs in *What the Golf*. (Screenshot by author)

dance party, decorated with rainbow pennants and attended exclusively by fellow wiener dogs (figure 1.7). To complete the level, players must cook hot dogs, then dress up like a hot dog and dance for their friends. Finally, they must clean up the bottles that litter the ground at the party's end. The scene has obvious Pride-month-party-and-its-aftermath vibes. It clearly revels in translating the concept of a "sausage fest," normally a crude term used to describe a group of straight men, into a goofy gay party where wieners wear wiener costumes and eat other wieners.

What the Golf also tips its hat to queerness by mocking the norms and rituals of heterosexuality. This is clearest in the "Valentine's Day" pack—a set of six levels released in February 2023 as part of ongoing, incremental updates to the game. In the first of these levels, players steer a delicate vase attached to a bundle of heart-shaped balloons, which must be flown past obstacles to reach the flag. Positioned along the course are two couples who seem to be celebrating the holiday. These include a pair of cats who are staring intently into each other's eyes and a pair of

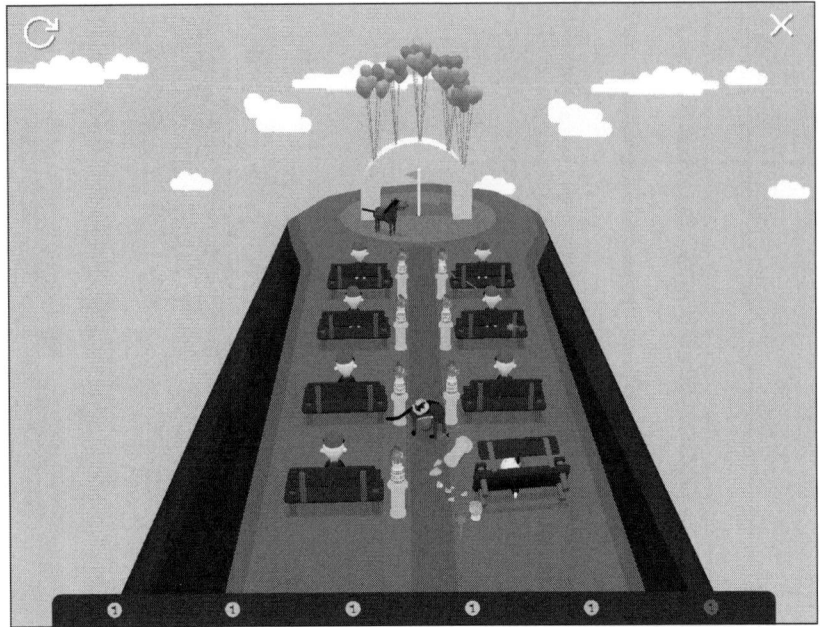

Figure 1.8. The *What the Golf* "Valentine's Day" pack includes a level in which players fling a horse bride down the aisle to her groom. (Screenshot by author)

dogs, one of whom gives the other a bone for a present. In the second level, players play as a car with the simple task of driving down a path; however, seated across this path are four couples enjoying their own Valentine's Day meals, complete with candlelight and flowers. All eight members of these couples are identical horses. In the fourth level, players throw a giant, diamond-studded engagement ring at the flag in the manner of a horseshoe toss; in the fifth, they fling a horse dressed as a human bride (complete with a white veil) down a makeshift church aisle to her horse groom (figure 1.8).[32] Each of these levels offers its own parody of straight courtship, queering Valentine's Day by leveraging the game's preposterous spirit to highlight the inherent ridiculousness of coupling up for romantic dinners or lassoing a partner into marriage with the largest possible engagement ring. The whole world is an absurdist game of golf, apparently, but heterosexual love is the most absurd golf game of all.

Yet, importantly, the worlds of *What the Golf* are not only queer when they reference queer culture or poke fun at the bizarre rituals of straight people. These worlds—as interactive spaces and systems—can themselves be understood as queer. This queerness manifests itself in multiple ways, but, first, I am thinking of queer theory that describes the nature of queer social worlds. Lauren Berlant and Michael Warner write in their 1998 essay "Sex in Public" that certain forms of queer publics, especially those that are tied to sexuality but where sex itself does not take place, can be seen as "queer zones and other worlds estranged from heterosexual culture."[33] *What the Golf* embodies the physical geography of such worlds. In a queer reading of the game, these "estranged" zones take on concrete form, becoming the floating grassy courses that hover disconnected from the ground below. In turn, each level assumes the qualities of a queer public space, a zone where sex may not take place but the relevance of sexuality is nonetheless palpably present.

The design of *What the Golf*'s levels, with their proliferating experiments in navigability, similarly literalize Berlant and Warner's vision of queer worlds. "The queer world," state Berlant and Warner, "is a space of entrances, exits, unsystematized lines of acquaintance, projected horizons, typifying examples, alternate routes, blockages, incommensurate geographies."[34] This description brings to mind many spatial elements of *What the Golf*. The game's holes, for instance, serve simultaneously as sites of entrance, exit, and blockage. A player directs their ball-avatar into a hole in the hub world to begin a level; they complete many levels by reaching the hole at the end of the course; along the way, players must navigate past all the "wrong" holes (the obstacles that periodically appear to swallow them up midlevel) on their way to the right one. And "incommensurate geographies" is practically *What the Golf*'s middle name. How else would we describe the spatial logics of a video game in which—as is the final sequence of "A Hole New World"—a mountaintop connects seamlessly to a floating bike path, which connects to an island, which connects to another mountain? In a similar spirit, sexuality studies scholars Gust A. Yep, Miranda Olzman, and Allen Conkle write that "a queer world is not necessarily coherent and neatly delineated because it embraces all the intersections and complexities of human relations. In many ways, it is plural—queer worlds—and includes liminal spaces for transformative, symbolic, collective, and material possibilities."[35]

Bringing together these descriptions, we might say that a queer world is a messy one that does not fit dominant notions of space and refuses to cohere into a singular whole. The worlds we find in *What the Golf* epitomize this ethos.

The very fact that *What the Golf* makes and remakes its worlds time and again also lends these worlds an inherently queer quality. Muñoz, in his posthumously published book *The Sense of Brown*, describes how queer of color artistic performance can operate as an "opening to other worlds, a passage to alternative realities, as a way to build worlds that are contestatory, oppositional, or merely alternative."[36] This work of creating alternative worlds is itself inherently linked to queerness. Writing earlier, in *Cruising Utopia*, Muñoz famously argued that queerness itself "is essentially about a rejection of a here and now and an insistence on potentiality or concrete possibility for another world."[37] By connecting these ideas, we can understand the work of creating alternative realities as a queer practice in its own right, one that insists on envisioning other worlds. Because alternative worlds stand in contrast to the world around us—the "here and now"—they are, by their nature, imbued with a queer spirit that longs to find other ways of being. (We will return to this idea of the radical speculative potential of envisioning alternative dimensions, building from Jayna Brown's related theorizations in *Black Utopias*, in chapter 2.)[38]

To the extent that all video games build new worlds, we could argue that all video games engage in this kind of queer alternative worldbuilding—though, as numerous scholars remind us, many of the video game worlds that may seem alternative in fact replicate structures of racism, misogyny, imperialism, and ableism that are very much drawn from our own world. The mere idea of video games as worlds likely conjures up, for certain gamers, visions of open world games, which game studies scholar Christopher Patterson describes as "a metagenre of AAA (blockbuster) video games . . . that reiterates the desire to conquer and dominate foreign spaces."[39] Yet *What the Golf*, itself far from an open world game, magnifies the basic practice of building new worlds, offering not just one such "other world" but thousands. Thus far, I have been discussing the game mostly as a collection of individual level-worlds. However, if we consider *What the Golf* as a whole, we can also understand it as an insistent, ecstatic performance of worldbuilding rendered nearly ad infinitum. It is "contestatory" and "oppositional," to use Muñoz's words, precisely in its frantic, impassioned refusal to allow any one world to solidify and become normative before moving on to the next (and the next and the next).

This refusal lies at the core of *What the Golf*'s practice of queer worldbuilding. One way of building worlds queerly, as modeled through *What the Golf*, is to make them again and again without the expectation of permanence or finality. Drawing inspiration from the lived experiences of queer people—who commonly face increased material precarity, whose own personal and cultural worlds may crumble at any time due to the systematic forces of racialized homophobia and transphobia, and whose own lives are often quite literally cut short—this mode of queer worldbuilding embraces the power of imagining a new world briefly, fleetingly, and then letting it go. In this way, queer worldbuilding does not so much result in the creation of a single queer world as it results in a fundamental reframing of the world as a place that is molten, uncertain. Queer worldbuilding at this rapid pace calls on us to constantly question the world as it is now (if only for a few seconds) and to prepare to build it once again anew.

Indeed, precisely through the design elements that I outlined earlier, *What the Golf* illustrates how building new worlds means destabilizing the norms of the world as we know it—norms that are themselves intimately and inextricably tied to sexuality and gender. I have explained how *What the Golf* rebuilds the interactive structures that define its worlds by constantly shifting three elements of gameplay: what the player can do, what the player is prompted to want, and who the player is. In this way, the game regularly overturns any sense of stable categories, desires, and identities. As we have discussed, in the academic context, queerness itself is widely understood to describe not only LGBTQIA+ identities or even nonnormative forms of gender and sexual expression but also, more broadly, a push to undermine the very assumption that identity and pleasure can be rendered into tidy, immutable categories. As feminist studies scholar Jane Ward writes, in addressing the tensions between queer thought and structured disciplinary research methods, queerness is "defined by its celebrated failure to adhere to stable classificatory systems."[40] *What the Golf*, through its insistence on constant reiteration, demonstrates how worldbuilding in video games too can undermine classificatory systems and, along with them, the very possibility of a hegemonic normativity. No form of action, no form of longing, no form of being is natural or "normal" in *What the Golf*. All of these factors, which together make up our sense of who we are as gendered and sexual subjects in the world, are perpetually in flux. Thus, through its worldbuilding (and rebuilding), *What the Golf* queers the world itself.

In a sense, we can see *What the Golf* and its proliferation of worlds as a small-scale replica of the medium of video games more generally. Video games too represent a collection of thousands of alternate worlds. When we, as players, engage with different video games, we also hop between their worlds. As we traverse this far-reaching landscape of games, the identities, longings, and forms of agency that we take on regularly change. This is one way, among many, that video game worldbuilding as a general practice might itself be imagined to queer the world around us. It invites us to actively participate in the unmooring of presumptions about who we are, what we do, and our place in the world. By extension, video game worldbuilding offers us the chance to play our own role in revealing the truth about the worlds we inhabit: that they are never built on solid ground, that they are always predicated on social constructs, that there is no such thing as a natural order of the universe (let alone a natural order of identity), and that the way we understand the world and our place within it always remains available for reimagining.

Queer Worldmaking through Play

The worlds of *What the Golf* shift how we think about video game worlds, video game worldbuilding, and the queerness of worldbuilding. At the same time, they offer us new perspectives on the work of queer *worldmaking*. I dedicate considerable space here, in this last section of the chapter, to the interplays between worldbuilding and worldmaking because they demonstrate how the practice of building video game worlds already has deep ties to the creation of queer worlds as understood through queer theory. Drawing out the connections (as well as some key differences) between worldbuilding and worldmaking shows us that video game worlds and queer worlds are linked not only in how they are *built* but also in how they are *made*. I have said that video game worlds are brought to life through acts of play. So too are queer worlds made, according to queer theorists, through acts of queer living.

As I mention in this book's introduction, queer worldmaking is a widely used concept in queer theory and related areas of scholarship, such as performance studies and queer geography. Originated by Muñoz in 1996 and taken up shortly thereafter by Berlant and Warner, queer worldmaking has been defined and deployed by scholars in differing ways over the intervening decades.[41] In the broadest terms, queer worldmaking refers to the ways that the lived practices of LGBTQIA+ people create worlds that stand in contrast or opposition to the mainstream world of heteronormativity. Thomas K. Nakayama and Charles E. Morris III, editors of *QED: A Journal in GLBTQ Worldmaking*, write in the journal's inaugural issue, "Queer worldmaking takes place in all kinds of places, at all different times, involving all kinds of people, who work toward creating a different world. It is not a strategic plan, organized by anyone, but a bottom-up engagement with the everyday."[42] Explains Karen Zaino, writing in the context of education, "Queer worldmaking, as a framework, encourages the scholarly conversation . . . to move from narratives of resistance to narratives of creation."[43] While the concept of queer worldmaking can be applied widely, it is valuable to remember that it emerges from and remains closely intertwined with queer of color theory. As Muñoz writes in *Disidentifications*, "Queers of color and other minoritarians have been denied a world." Thus, for racialized subjects, the "project of worldmaking . . . is to continue disidentifying with this world until we achieve a new one."[44]

Muñoz's writing in particular proves fruitful for thinking about the connections between queer worldmaking and video game worldbuilding. For Muñoz, queer worldmaking represents a mode of performance. While Muñoz looks to forms of artistic performance (for instance, those found in theater, film, music, and dance) to illustrate how queer creators envision new worlds, he also explains that the concept of performance extends to the everyday practice or *praxis* of queer living. Whether performed by artists or LGBTQIA+ communities, making new queer worlds is an active task, a kind of work, and a form of *doing*—one that queer people undertake each day. In "Ephemera as Evidence," Muñoz describes how attending to performance allows scholars to focus on "what acts and objects do" rather than simply what they might mean. Attending to action, in turn, reveals how "the spirit of *doing* queerness" operates as the engine that drives the work of "*making* queer worlds."[45]

In *Disidentifications*, Muñoz expands on this description of queer worldmaking as doing, specifying that worldmaking operates by presenting alternate points of view. He writes (to expand on a quote given briefly in the introduction of this book), "The concept of worldmaking delineates the ways in which performances—both theatrical and everyday rituals—have the ability to establish alternate views of the world. These alternative vistas are more than simply views or perspectives; they are oppositional ideologies that function as critiques of oppressive regimes of 'truth' that subjugate minoritarian people. . . . It is my contention that the doing that matters most and the performance that seems most crucial are nothing short of the actual making of worlds."[46] Thus, in Muñoz's formulation, the worlds that queer people envision through their performances are meaningful because they challenge oppression. Yet, what is equally meaningful is the act of performance itself: the way that queer action animates these visions, breathing life into the new worlds.

Video games, as an interactive medium, align compellingly with Muñoz's descriptions of queer worldmaking. They too are worlds that come to life through a form of active performance—namely, the performance of play. When I refer to video game play as a performance, I am not thinking primarily of a performance put on for an audience. Granted, a growing number of forms of video game play being broadcast for a public viewership (such as professional esports, speedrunning fundraisers, and video game live streaming) can be seen as performances in a near-theatrical sense.[47] I also do not mean for the term "performance" to connote a falseness: the idea that players, when they step into a video game, are posturing or dissimulating rather than acting as their true selves. I am not even referring, really, to the ways that video game players step into performative identities when they take on the roles of variously gendered or racialized playable characters—whether through what Lisa Nakamura has termed "identity tourism" or through a more meaningful, if vicarious, "personal performance of the self," to borrow a turn of phrase from social media researcher Zizi Papacharissi.[48]

Instead, I am offering the framing of play as performance in the spirit of performance studies, which understands performance—as game designer Clara Fernández-Vara writes in describing her own framework for studying video games as performance—to refer to "the study of actions, of how things are done," as well as the processes by which these actions make meaning.[49] While it may seem that a player serves merely as an audience for a video game's content, Fernández-Vara explains that "the player is an active performer because she is also an interactor."[50] Players literally take action as they move through a game world, performing the act of play. Without players to play them—to explore their terrains, to engage with their rules, to test out their boundaries—there are no video game worlds. Thus far, I have argued that all video games are worlds, that all video game development is worldbuilding, and that play itself is integral to the building of video game worlds. Here, inspired by Muñoz's formulation of queer worldmaking as performance, I am taking this line of argumentation a step farther and saying that all video game play is itself world*making*. Every time we play a video game, we engage in the performative work of "establish[ing] alternate views of the world," as Muñoz writes, participating in "nothing short of the actual making of worlds."

Thus, guided by concepts of queer worldmaking, we can understand video games as worlds that are simultaneously built (by developers) and made (by players). In this way, they stand in the often otherwise murky overlap between worldbuilding and queer worldmaking. As mentioned previously, though these two terms seem nearly identical at first glance, they are typically used to refer to very different kinds of creation. In her book *Old Futures*, Alexis Lothian describes the traditional distinction between worldbuilding and worldmaking. She explains that speculative worlds like those found in science fiction are often referred to as being "built" rather than "made" because they have been intentionally planned by their creators. This mode of worldbuilding "focuses more on structures and institutions than on experiential and interpersonal realities."[51] Queer worldmaking, by contrast, has largely been theorized as far less deliberate and, indeed, often resistant to the very notion of structure. "Queer world-making is the opening and creation of spaces without a map," writes Yep, "the invention and proliferation of ideas without an unchanging and predetermined goal, and the expansion of individual freedom and collective possibilities."⁵² In a similar vein, Berlant and Warner describe queer culture as "a world-making project, where world . . . differs from community or group because it necessarily includes more people than can be identified [and] more spaces than can be mapped beyond a few reference points."⁵³

Video games stand, then, at the place where worldbuilding and worldmaking meet. They scramble these very differentiations. They are rooted in computational structures and often use game mechanics to reflect on the operations of institutions. Yet they are also deeply experiential in nature and frequently invested in interpersonal dynamics. Video games are made worlds that, rather than being unmappable and goalless, often quite literally come with a map and clearly delineated goals. I have said that video games show us how worldbuilding means more than the storytelling. In a similar vein, video games offer us a critical new way of conceptualizing queer worldmaking: not just as an intangible gesturing toward a set of possibilities but as the actual making of a new world (or an array of new worlds) that queer people can step inside. At the same time, video games prompt us to think productively about how worldbuilding and worldmaking might clash, even within the same media object. How might we, as players, choose to *make* new worlds within video games that differ from the worlds that developers have *built* for us? When does queer worldmaking go hand in hand with queer worldbuilding, and when does worldmaking represent a kind of rebellion—a refusal to accept the world as built?

What the Golf also helps illuminate what queer worldmaking, as a conceptual framework, offers the field of game studies. Queer worldmaking energizes the cultural and political implications of video game worldbuilding. It emboldens us to understand play, which we might otherwise think of as a way of "playing along" (in the sense of complying with a system), as a mode of work. By this, I do not mean the kind of work, repackaged as play—operating under the sign of what Braxton Soderman terms "playful capitalism"—that uses "playfulness to increase worker productivity and mask exploitative working conditions."⁵⁴ Instead, I am using work as a way of describing an action that makes change. Play does the work of transformation—enacting what Muñoz calls "transformative politics and possibilities"—that is inherent to remaking the world. Relatedly, the framework of queer worldmaking underscores that the building and playing of alternate worlds in video games can constitute an activist project: one that may position players within fantastical, improbable, or even impossible worlds but that might do so for the express purpose of changing the lived realities of queer and other minoritarian people.

At the same time, queer worldmaking raises productive complications around video game worldbuilding, challenging us to identify and confront points of tension in arguing for the radical potential of video game worlds. Queer worldmaking, as Muñoz clearly articulates, is what he describes as a "disidentificatory" practice—a way for marginalized subjects (and especially queer people of color) to simultaneously reject and reclaim the products of a dominant popular culture, often using media as the "raw material" for "acts of conjuring that deform and re-form the world."[55] By contrast, when players animate a video game world through the worldmaking power of their play, they may well be deforming and re-forming the larger hegemonic world beyond the game, but they may not be disidentifying with the game itself. In a similar vein, trans studies scholar Benny LeMaster, writing about the formation of queer and transgender communities, states that queer worlds are made when individuals respond to the "imposition" of "institutional constraints and affordances."[56] Like Muñoz, LeMaster is underscoring queer worldmaking as a way to push back against systems of power. Yet video games too represent systems of power. Can we truly call video game play an act of worldmaking if the worlds that players make are one and the same with the predetermined worlds that video game developers have built? Perhaps the queerest worlds that players make within video games are those that they construct through what Edmond Chang has termed "queergaming," a concept that encompasses many forms of queer play, including play that operates "against the intent of the game's design," a way to "repurpose or resist the rules."[57] Making video game worlds through play is always an ambivalent practice, then. It positions itself at the place where the counterhegemony *of* video game worlds runs up against the counterhegemony that players enact *within* video game worlds.

Video game worldbuilding also adds new dimensions to theorizations of queer worldmaking by provocatively entangling queer worldmaking with ideas about play. As a model for making new worlds, play prompts us to consider how queer worldmaking may be not just a productive or even a performative act but a playful one. The lens of play, which calls to mind both lightheartedness and erotic play, casts the task of making new queer worlds as simultaneously joyful and sexual. At the same time, as demonstrated by the game studies scholars who critique play through considerations of race and power mentioned earlier, play brings to the fore a set of potential problems with queer worldmaking that queer studies itself must likewise address.

As we proceed into the chapters that follow, we take with us a set of foundational insights from *What the Golf* and the reflections on queer worldmaking it sparks. *What the Golf* makes manifest the claim that video games are worlds, that they contain worlds, and that they engage in worldbuilding through the design of their interactive elements. It also offers us a chance to practice the task of looking for how video games build queer worlds, how they do so queerly, and how attending to the worldmaking power of play may point us toward important contradictions in the worlds of video games. Each of the games considered in the coming chapters builds a queer world and sets its own conditions for structuring that world and its meaning. In this regard, *What the Golf* is instructive but far from exceptional. Let me close, then, by circling back one last time to Drewson's statement that *What the Golf* is "not a golf game" but instead "a game that shows you that all the games you've been playing all along are just golf games." We could, in fact, say the same thing about *What the Golf* and its relationship to video game worldbuilding more broadly. Perhaps *What the Golf* is not so much a worldbuilding video game as it is a game that challenges you to ask yourself whether all the video games you have been playing all along were really just games about building worlds.

2.

Inverting the Laws of the Universe

Trans Time Mechanics and Queer Astrophysics in If Found . . .

Let me begin with an admission: over the course of researching and writing this chapter, which is about mechanics of time, I have become obsessed with black holes. As you read, you'll see why. This chapter presents an analysis of the 2020 video game *If Found . . .* (hereafter simply *If Found*), which was developed by a small creative team operating under the name Dreamfeel and headed by the game's lead designer, Llaura McGee.[1] *If Found* is an interactive visual novel—a story presented, over the course of the game, through subsequent screens of two-dimensional imagery—with an unusual core mechanic. Instead of providing players with buttons or arrows to advance through its narrative, as would be standard in the interactive novel genre, the game operates through erasing.

Specifically, the story of *If Found* is told through text and drawings scrawled in the diary of its protagonist, Kasio, as well as other artwork rendered in a similarly sketch-like style. Kasio is a twenty-three-year-old trans woman who is returning to her family home in rural western Ireland. Kasio's diary, with marks and notes scratched across its yellow lined pages, serves as her inner voice, the place where she tells her own story (figure 2.1). However, rather than simply reading this story, the player's task is to wipe each subsequent scene of it away. In place of a cursor, players control a rectangular, white rubber eraser, which they use to remove Kasio's writing, drawings, and other scribbling from each page. Once a page has been rendered blank, a new page of the diary appears, describing another step in Kasio's story, only to be erased like the page before. In this way, the game proceeds both forward (in its relatively linear storyline, which covers a period of roughly a month following Kasio's return) and backward, unwriting what she has written, undoing what she has done, winding back the clock on who she has been.

Figure 2.1. Players advance through the storyline in *If Found . . .* by erasing writing and drawing from the protagonist's diary. (Screenshot by author)

In what follows, I argue that *If Found* models a form of worldbuilding that operates through the design of gameplay mechanics, a concept that I introduced in chapter 1 but extend here. In particular, *If Found* shows us what a world might look like if it were built around mechanics of time that resonate with transgender lives. In *If Found*, we find a roadmap for deepening our thinking about the role of game design in worldbuilding as well as a provocation to radically reimagining the fabric of space-time itself. By using what I am terming *trans mechanics* to reflect on and distort the operations of astrophysics (more on astrophysics in a moment), *If Found* proposes an approach to worldbuilding that offers nothing less than a reconfiguration of the foundational scientific logics of our universe. At the same time, the game suggests that our universe may already be deeply queer. Writing about the slippery temporal ontologies of quantum physics—that is, physics that describes the working of our world on the *smallest* possible scale—new materialist Karen Barad proclaims in her essay "Nature's Queer Performativity" that "there is something inherently queer about the nature of matter."[2] *If Found* and by extension my analysis of the game make a parallel argument, expanded out to astrophysics, the physics that describe the workings of our world on the *largest* possible scale. When considered through a reading of the game's trans mechanics, *If Found* itself seems to proclaim that there is something inherently queer about the nature of time.

Why I have become obsessed with black holes is this. *If Found* is actually composed of two intertwining narratives, one seemingly real and one science-fictional. The primary narrative is indeed the story of Kasio, which takes place in December 1993. Kasio has been away in Dublin, where she has earned both her undergraduate and master's degrees in astrophysics. She plans to return to Dublin in January, after the winter break, to begin pursuing her doctorate. Her family home is on the island of Achill, which hangs just off the western coast of Ireland: a remote area with windswept vistas that stretch out over the chilly Atlantic Ocean. Kasio's homecoming is a fraught and painful one, since her mother, Brid (Kasio's father has passed away), neither understands nor accepts that Kasio is trans. Over the course of the game, Kasio tries multiple times to connect with her mother, but these attempts end in emotionally crushing fights. Ultimately, Kasio spends most of the month crashing with friends in an abandoned, decaying house. It is not until Kasio nearly dies of exposure that her mother comes to her rescue and finally embraces her as her daughter.

Simultaneously, interwoven with Kasio's story, *If Found* presents a second narrative: a tale about Doctor Cassiopeia (named for the constellation), an astronaut exploring a dangerous anomaly in the depths of outer space. The anomaly, it turns out, is in fact a rapidly growing black hole. Cassiopeia, Kasio's fantastical doppelganger, must jump between wormholes to find the source of the black hole's power and stop it from swallowing up the entire world. Along the way, she makes radio contact with a mysterious person calling himself "Control," who directs her to the source of the anomaly—which is located, it turns out, on the island of Achill. In the game's concluding stretch, Cassiopeia and Control fail to stop the black hole. Cassiopeia's story ends as she roams a post-apocalyptic Ireland and finds new community among the rubble. As with Kasio's storyline, this second narrative is told through the erasing mechanic. Though it remains unclear whether the images that tell Cassiopeia's story also appear in Kasio's diary (or perhaps in Kasio's dreams, since these science-fictional sequences are often interspersed into moments when Kasio is sleeping), the player proceeds through these images in the same fashion, rubbing away the sketchy drawings on the screen to reveal each subsequent step in Cassiopeia's saga (figure 2.2).

Figure 2.2. The secondary narrative in *If Found...*, a story about an astronaut attempting to stop the growth of a massive black hole, similarly uses the erasing mechanic. (Screenshot by author)

This second narrative thread of *If Found* differs considerably, then, from better-known examples in what science and technology historian Alexander Mirowski terms the "space games" genre. Across video game history, writes Mirowski, "space-themed games [have] often embodied the genre conventions of space opera—science fiction tales featuring high adventure, outsized foes, and damsels in distress. In practice, this involved game mechanics revolving around the piloting of interstellar crafts to defeat extraterrestrial foes and save (defend, liberate) terrestrial allies from their predations."[3] In *If Found*, by contrast, the only "damsels" are fearless astronauts with doctoral degrees, there are no interstellar crafts to pilot, and the extraterrestrial foe—the black hole itself—can never be defeated. To the extent that *If Found* is a "space game," it is a game not so much about outer space as it is about what outer space represents: a place of mystery and wonder where one can float away from the restrictions and oppressions of life on Earth, a place for confronting one's fears about the nature of the universe, a place for accepting that the power of human agency pales in comparison to the force of a world far beyond our grasp.

Yet, as we will see, the black hole is more than a metaphorical villain in *If Found*, where we might well expect it to stand in for the gaping maw of social bias that Kasio regularly faces on the earthly plane. Instead, the black hole functions as a constant familiar backdrop, an ambivalent omnipresence that serves a variety of roles, some of them seemingly contradictory. The black hole gives (admittedly well-trod, even cliché) apocalyptic stakes to Cassiopeia's celestial adventures. But for Kasio, who is herself passionate about astrophysics and fascinated by the world of the stars, the black hole is a more complicated figure. Scribbles of the black hole appear in her notebook again and again—half visual motif, half recurring thought that she cannot shake. There, the black hole operates as a looming reminder that Kasio, who struggles with homelessness and deteriorating mental health, teeters on the brink of her own personal pit of despair. At the same time, visually, the black hole becomes the aperture through which Kasio's story unfolds. Often, when transitioning between scenes or sequences, the in-game camera will zoom in on the darkness of the black-hole-like images in Kasio's diary, as if traveling through the hole (like a window onto a new world) to reach the next section of the game on the other side. As I discuss later in this chapter, black holes are also presented explicitly as worldbuilding tools. Kasio and Cassiopeia both muse dreamily about how, even as black holes threaten destruction, they may sprout whole new worlds: places where new universes grow in the cracks that form when our own universe has been ripped asunder.

I linger here with black holes before delving into my analysis of *If Found* because they offer us a valuable model for thinking about how we might build new worlds—whether through video games or otherwise—by shifting our perspective on the world as we already know it. Like *If Found*'s twin protagonists, I am drawn to the contradictions that black holes embody. They are simultaneously theoretical concepts and real astrophysical phenomena.[4] They are pinpricks in the fabric of space-time where matter becomes so dense that it gobbles up everything (more matter, light, information itself) that dares come near it.[5] They are frightening but are also immensely attractive, both in the sense that the idea of them captivates us and in the sense that they exercise overwhelming gravitational pulls. What lies inside them is death, almost certainly, but also new possibilities. The physics of a black hole push our current scientific understanding of how the universe functions to its limits.[6] A black hole is an absurdity that teaches us about how our world is built precisely by breaking it.

Black holes are also immensely queer.[7] There is a surprisingly long history in astrophysics of straight, white, cisgender male scientists refusing to believe in the existence of black holes precisely because the very idea of them has been seen as too "absurd" or "unnatural," a perversion of logic—rhetoric that clearly echoes the condemnation of homosexuality and other non-heteronormative sexualities.[8] Black holes are the astrophysics equivalent of queer identity, queer intimacy, or queer sex. Though they are now almost universally recognized by their relevant scientific communities, they spent years shuffled out of sight under a kind of "don't ask, don't tell" policy (one colored by a notable streak of anti–South Asian racism).[9] Don't ask about how the laws of physics suggest that there should be points of infinite gravity. Don't tell about the holes in our universe. In the winding intellectual history of black holes, we find a reminder that the world around us is constantly being built and rebuilt, imagined and reimagined, even as it simultaneously remains the same. Science too is a way of building the world. Though the science of the present day—whatever that present day might be—typically presents itself as objectively true, science itself is always changing.

Thus, in black holes, we also find inspiration for turning our gaze toward alternate worlds that already exist within the dominant world, worlds that may go overlooked or may deliberately render themselves unseen. Black feminist studies scholar Michele Wallace, in her 1990 book *Invisibility Blues*, uses the image of the black hole to describe the social invisibility of Black women's creativity.[10] Wallace explains that the black hole may look empty to a theoretical observer, but it is in fact, as Evelyn Hammonds points out in her reading of Wallace's essay, "a dense and full place in space."[11] In this sense, by calling to mind the double meaning of "blackness/Blackness," the black hole conjures questions raised by scholars of race like Simone Brown, Édouard Glissant, and Marquis Bey, who interrogate the logics of visibility for marginalized and especially racialized people.[12] When does increased visibility, commonly envisioned as a positive step toward promoting social equity, bring with it increased surveillance? What "diverse" ways of being can only thrive when they remain obfuscated? The world contained within the black hole may flourish precisely because it cannot be perceived from the outside.[13]

You hear the obsession, right? While I write these words, I am sitting in my bedroom, next to a shelf lined with dog-eared books with titles like *Black Holes: The Key to Understanding the Universe*.[14] I pour over diagrams detailing how time distorts around black holes; I read and re-read passages about how, at the center of a black hole, space and time functionally become one. This is all new to me. I was an artsy kid in high school, a creative writing major in college, and a comparative literature student in graduate school, so I have never taken a physics class. As a result, physics feels more to me like a world of magic, mysticism, and philosophy than a world of science. Or, rather, it feels like a world where magic and science become one.

As we move into our analysis of *If Found*, let us hold in mind the generative specter of the black hole. We will find that the game itself, in the interplays between its narrative and its time-based mechanics, exudes a similar spirit of contradiction and impossibility. The game builds a world structured around a mode of trans temporality that defies supposedly commonsense logics of time—resisting normative, linear narratives about transition, disclosure, and acceptance for transgender people. Simultaneously, we will see that *If Found* actually inverts accepted scientific understandings of the operations of space-time. Through this inversion, the game proposes yet another approach to the work of building worlds queerly: by shifting the operational logics not only of gameplay but indeed of the very laws of the universe.

Erasing the World

If Found performs multiple modes of worldbuilding. On its surface, the game appears to engage in worldbuilding primarily through what I have described thus far as more traditional means, such as the development of narrative, characters, and cultural backdrops. Indeed, unlike many of the other video games discussed in this book, *If Found* has a strong focus on storytelling. Admittedly, its science-fictional universe, populated with astronauts and celestial bodies, remains somewhat loosely sketched out.

However, Kasio's world on Achill—a real island connected by a short bridge to the mainland in Ireland's County Mayo—is presented in concrete detail, filling the game with bits of local dialect, depictions of local places, and references to local traditions that contribute to its narrative worldbuilding. In these efforts, *If Found* even goes so far as to include optional footnotes to explain Irish words and other day-to-day elements of life particular to Ireland. "Oiche Mhaith," we learn, is Irish for "good night"; "tea" refers specifically to Irish breakfast tea, highly caffeinated and always drunk with a splash of milk. Touches like these make the world of *If Found* feel believable and tangible without seeming contrived or romanticized. They imbue the game with an autobiographical air, as if the game was itself an animated personal diary from a creator who spent her own formative years in a world much like Achill.[15]

In this sense, *If Found* functions both as a built world and as an invitation into an existing world. The game offers a gateway into a specific place at a specific time as seen through the eyes of a person for whom that world has already been intimately real. To simply dismiss these elements of the game as mere marks of traditional worldbuilding because they are expressions of storytelling (and I am pointing a finger back at myself here) would be to downplay just how deftly *If Found* performs the building of its narrative world. As narratology scholars Cody Mejeur and Chiara Pellegrini explain, trans-affirming narratives and those written by trans creators serve a crucial social function. Such narratives counter dominant, transphobic stories and offer opportunities to "seize control of the narrative operations that are used to construct and limit trans identity."[16] Certainly *If Found* contributes valuably to these efforts by offering a nuanced picture of some of the lived realities of trans life. I would also be remiss not to note how emotionally impactful I myself find the narrative world of *If Found*. If a video game is going to build a world through elements like storyline, character, setting, and cultural ephemera, I say let it be a world of beach bonfires and icy late-night walks to a fish-and-chip shop. Let it be a world where nuns serve as ornery landlords and where scrappy punk rock concerts turn out to be vital places for queer youth to lose themselves in the frenzy of the crowd. Let it be a world that feels as raw and true as this one.

Our focus here, however, is on how the game builds its world through its mechanics—and, more precisely, its mechanics of time. In chapter 1,

I used an analysis of *What the Golf* to map some of the core ways that video games build their worlds. Among these was the design of game mechanics: the specific rules for what a player can do in a game and to what effect. By a certain (admittedly limited) way of thinking, mechanics are the key element of game design because they bring structure to games as interactive systems. Yet mechanics themselves are not simply a matter of formalist concern. Mary Flanagan and Helen Nissenbaum have demonstrated how, across game genres, mechanics communicate cultural meaning by embodying and perpetuating social values.[17] For instance, one set of mechanics in a multiplayer game might emphasize conflict and defeat, while another might emphasize cooperation and goalless play. Mechanics themselves are critical to the construction of video game worlds because they set the rules for how the game world works, what is possible there, and which actions matter. In this way, the values embodied by mechanics establish the worldview of each in-game world.

As mentioned, for the vast majority of *If Found*, the only mechanic available to players is erasing the contents of Kasio's diary. Except for the little flecks of rubber that the act of erasing leaves behind (the eraser-cursor gets gradually smaller as it wears away over time), the player can leave behind almost nothing on each page in order to proceed to the next page. As an illustration of this mechanic, consider the very first pages of Kasio's diary that the game presents to players (figure 2.3). In the upper left, the diary reads, "This book belongs to: somebody . . ." Beneath and beside these words are a series of hand-drawn sketches: Kasio standing at a bus stop, Kasio walking up a country road, the inside of Kasio's mother's kitchen. In the lower right quadrant of the open notebook, we see written, "My name is Kasio." Below this is a list of things for Kasio to remember about herself (refer to figure 2.1). Many of these things are crossed out; over one item, she has written in thick, dark letters, "NEVER."

The game zooms in on each of these areas of the page in turn. First, the player erases the printed text about whom the book belongs to. Next, the player erases the drawings of Kasio as she makes the journey home. Then, the player erases the scrawled marks that cover up the things that Kasio wants to remember about herself. Erasing one set of marks reveals the reminder, "When people stare, just ignore them";

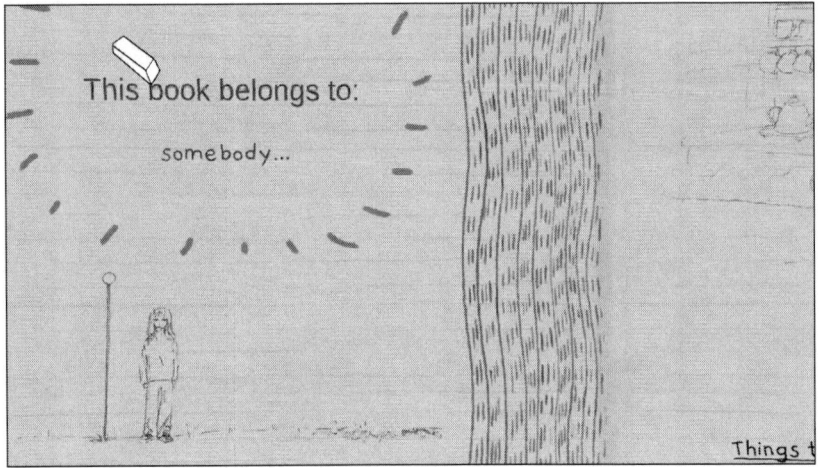

Figure 2.3. The first page of Kasio's diary that the player erases shows Kasio's journey home. (Screenshot by author)

erasing the word "NEVER" reveals the statement, "You don't need to be nice to people who bully you." It is unclear whether the presence of these marks suggests that Kasio no longer wants to remember these things about herself. Or perhaps, in a moment of frustration and defiance, she has simply given up trying to fit her weary sentiments of self-care into tidy lists. In either case, when the player erases the marks that cover these numbered items, they return Kasio's diary to an earlier moment—a moment before Kasio decided to scrawl over them, a moment when she presumably felt these self-directives held value and meaning.

Eventually, after the player has erased the full contents of this page, they run the eraser over the notebook once more, this time to reveal the next set of images and texts. These describe Kasio's first few days back on the island and provide brief profiles of the people she interacts with there: her well-intentioned but close-minded mother, Brid; her bigoted brother, Fergal; her taciturn school friend, Colum; and Colum's bubbly boyfriend, Jack. Once again, the game proceeds through each of these elements in turn, zooming in just long enough for the player to read them and erase them before moving on. In this way, the game's camera turns the pages of Kasio's diary into something like a comic strip, shifting from one image area to the next in sequence. At the same time, the erasing mechanic often functions like a wipe transition (a film technique), shifting the screen gradually from one scene to the next. Now, when the player finishes erasing this second set of pages, the eraser wipes away the notebook itself, revealing beneath it a screen filled with rain. The rain, we find, can also be erased, and doing so reveals a scene inside Kasio's mother's kitchen. From these early moments, the game makes clear that erasing in *If Found* means more than removing information. It also represents a form of transition—foreshadowing the narrative contents of the trans story that will unfold—from moment to moment, place to place, memory to memory, time to time.

There are many ways that we might interpret this erasing mechanic. We could read it as a form of cleaning, an alternative expression of the tidying-up mechanics that Shira Chess has identified as common in feminine-coded, mobile video games.[18] From this perspective, we might interpret erasing as a femme (or more specifically trans femme) mechanic, one that uses the transformative act of erasing to reclaim cleaning as a method for uncovering and thereby laying bare personal stories. Or we might interpret the erasing mechanic as a way to peel back layers—a metaphor for moving deeper and deeper into the heart of a narrative, wiping away its outer skin, and getting closer to the truth that lies in its depth. This kind of insistent pursuit of depth, which calls to mind again the image of the black hole, inherently entails an act of destruction. What has come before is discarded; what lies on the surface is scrubbed away. It is not coincidental that one of the very first things that we erase are the basic facts that Kasio (at least initially) wants to remember about herself. For Kasio, finding herself first means losing herself. Rebuilding her world means first undoing her world. Personal self-discovery, like erasure, is apocalyptic.

Alternatively, we could read this eraser mechanic as a reflection on queer and/or trans erasure, generally understood as the ways in which LGBTQIA+ people are overlooked, undervalued, or made the objects of outright violence that quite literally and heartbreakingly removes them from our world.[19] Here we are, in *If Found*, erasing a trans woman's story. Maybe we, the players, are agents of hegemonic, cisheteronormative society who are wiping Kasio's life from the record books, so that all that remains is a worn, empty notebook full of eraser scraps. Or maybe we are Kasio, who makes the choice to erase away her old life, her old pain, and her old self so that she can draw herself anew. Considered together, these possibilities underscore the productive tensions contained with the erasing mechanic as a metaphor. It conjures up large-scale societal concerns about being erased while also inviting us to reconsider what might be powerful about the right for marginalized people to do their own erasing—to wipe clean the person they have been so that they can be somebody new.

Backward Time Mechanics

If Found is very self-consciously aware of its own interest in time. References to time recur throughout the game. Kasio's stay on Achill is very carefully bounded in time, and each new day in her diary begins with a notation of the date. Even as her weeks on the island go by and Kasio begins to spiral into the depths of depression, she still always has the presence of mind to write down the day of the month. Simultaneously, as the game regularly reminds its players, Kasio seems to be lost in time: unsure whether she will ever make it back out of Achill (roughly halfway through the game, she learns that she has not received the scholarship that would have allowed her to pursue her PhD) or whether her month away from Dublin will transform into an eternity. We might see Kasio herself as representing time; her name is obviously meant to be a play on Cassiopeia, yet it also calls to mind a Casio watch. Meanwhile, in the game's science-fictional secondary narrative, this focus on time manifests itself as a fascination with notions of space-time, which Cassiopeia fears will be ripped asunder by the rapidly expanding black hole. Time is what Cassiopeia is running out of as she dashes across the universe in search of answers that will put a stop to the destructive anomaly, but time is also what Cassiopeia is trying to save.

At a number of moments, *If Found* also nods to the links between queerness and time. After the first of two blowout fights with her mother, Kasio runs off into the cold, wet night and ends up on the doorstep of the crumbling, old Big House ("a common nickname for the houses that belonged to the Anglo-Irish aristocracy in the years before independence," the game explains in a footnote). There, her friend Colum, his boyfriend Jack, and their bandmate Shans have been living as squatters. Shans is biracial, with an Irish father and an Indian English mother, so he too feels out of place in the otherwise seemingly all-white world of Achill.[20] When Kasio asks Shans whether he is bothered by Colum and Jack's displays of affection, Shans says no, adding, "It's legal now anyway." Kasio replies, "About time." Later, Kasio's mother writes her a letter in an attempt to reconcile after a second fight. Her words of support are far from supportive, however. "It's ok if you like men or dress funny or whatever it is," she writes to Kasio, but just "keep it quiet.... What you do on your own time is your own business." In both of these instances, time is linked to same-sex intimacy—whether the intimacy between boyfriends Colum and Jack or the intimacy that Kasio's mother (who misidentifies her daughter as a gay man) envisions that Kasio might have with men. The first reference to queer time is affirming, while the second is insulting, implying that queerness should be kept a secret for Kasio to pursue "on her own time." Yet both moments clearly suggest what the game's structural relationship to temporality will suggest as well: that queerness and time go hand in hand.

It is fitting, then, that the erasing mechanic has its own messy and multilayered relationship to time. At first, the act of erasing appears to allow the player to explore the game's narratives in nonlinear ways. When first presented with a spread of pages from Kasio's diary, packed with text and images, the player is likely to feel a sense of almost disorienting freedom, as if they could proceed through the material before them in any order. Where to begin? Where to go next? How to make sense of it all? Technically, the erasing mechanic does allow the player to wipe away certain elements of images before others. However, it quickly becomes apparent that the game carefully controls the order of the images and text that the player can erase. This sense of freedom to move through the story in a nonlinear fashion is largely an illusion. In *If Found*, erasing quite literally requires moving the cursor around the screen in looping circles and switchbacks, rubbing back and forth in a motion that seems, by nature, to defy the notion of order. Yet, doing so ultimately moves the narrative forward in a surprisingly orderly fashion along a predetermined path. No matter how we erase, narrative time moves forward apace, along a largely straight line. (We will return to this topic of straight versus circuitous movement in chapter 5.)

This does not mean that the erasing mechanic itself has a straightforward relationship to time, however. Instead of scrambling time, this mechanic makes time work *backward*. By this I mean that the act of erasing layer after layer of imagery implies a specific relationship to temporality. It suggests that the whole contents of *If Found* have been stacked on top of one another—or, more accurately, written and drawn on top of one another. The top images may tell the *first* part of the story, but, by this logic, they have in fact been added to the pile *last*. As we erase away, we move back through these layers. Narratively, we progress farther and farther forward into the game's parallel stories. However, within the logic of the erasure mechanic, we are actually moving farther and farther back, digging down, and accessing imagery that lies even more deeply nestled below the images we have seen thus far. Therefore, time in *If Found* flows in two directions simultaneously. Narrative time slides along a forward track toward the game's conclusion. Meanwhile, gameplay time slides in reverse along a track that erases moment after moment, memory after memory, until it returns us to the very beginning.

If Found itself confirms this interpretation of the erasing mechanic as a mode of moving backward in the game's concluding moments. I have said that players can only act by erasing for most of the game. It is in the game's final stretch, after Kasio's story culminates with her mother rescuing her from near death, that this interactivity changes. Following a brief narrative epilogue, the game returns the player to the blank opening notebook page with which it began. Still printed at the top is the statement, "This book belongs to _____." When the player attempts to interact with this page, however, the game takes them to something not yet seen in *If Found*: a character creation system. Character creation systems allow video game players to customize the appearance of a specific character; they are common in games with a primary character who stands in for the player.[21] The character creation system in *In Found* is not dissimilar to other such systems. Selecting from options rendered in the game's characteristic illustration style, players choose different physical elements (eye shapes, hairstyle, clothing) to build an image of Kasio as she appears at the end of her saga (figure 2.4). No longer represented by a loose, black-and-white sketch as she has been throughout the game, Kasio now becomes a fully realized visual character outlined in the style of pen and ink and vibrantly colored in as if with watercolors. This is,

Figure 2.4. *If Found . . .* ends with a character creation sequence in which players build a representation of Kasio. (Screenshot by author)

in one sense, a logical conclusion to her story. Kasio, who has wrestled with her identity throughout, has finally become herself. In each possible iteration of her appearance, she smiles knowingly. It seems that she has found peace.

However, from a structural perspective, the character creation system in *If Found* is unlike such systems in any other video game (at least any other game that I have encountered). Temporally, it exists entirely out of place. Character creation systems are almost always placed at the very beginning of video games. It is common for players to be prompted to create their characters before gameplay proper has even begun. That is, by the normal logics of game design, creating a character is what players do first. In *If Found*, however, where gameplay itself flows backward, creating a character comes last. The implied purpose of the character creation system is also flipped in time. Whereas such systems typically invite players to create the character that they are *about to play as*, this system tasks us with creating the character whom we have *already been playing*. In this way, the implementation of the character creation system at the end of *If Found* serves as a nod to the idea that we have been, in fact, using the game's mechanics to proceed backward through the norms of video game design all along.

Conceptualizing erasure in *If Found* as a time-based mechanic also opens up additional avenues for making sense of its meaning. As many game studies scholars have pointed out, it is not uncommon for video games to play with temporality through their use of mechanics. Numerous mainstream game series and independent games alike, from the *Prince of Persia* (various developers, 1989–2022) to *Assassin's Creed* (various developers, 2007–2023) to *Braid* (Jonathan Blow, 2008) and *Life Is Strange* (Dontnod Entertainment, 2015), structure their gameplay around opportunities to rewind time. Other games allow players to pause, slow, speed up, or replay specific moments. In these games, playing with time is often necessary for accomplishing goals like winning combat sequences, solving puzzles, or progressing correctly through a multipronged narrative. Christopher Hanson, writing in his book *Game Time*, describes these different time mechanics as offering "new modes of temporal control" that players can "master," gaining "agency over that which cannot be controlled in the real world: time." In this way, says Hanson, video games are able to offer "remarkable temporal structures [that] exceed and transcend more familiar temporal experiences."[22]

Other game studies scholars (myself included) are less sold on the supposedly transcendent experience of playing with time that large-scale or otherwise widely popular video games offer. As Steve Wilcox writes, many of the games of the sort that Hanson celebrates seem to break with temporal norms but end up replicating "a linear, cause-and-effect paradigm," enlisting players into bringing to fruition a preset series of often problematic and even violent events. Writes Wilcox, "This limited depiction of time dissuades us from recognizing and imagining alternatives, including non-violent means of resistance that could . . . have helped in the past and may yet be of use in the future."[23] Thus, even as many games with time-based mechanics appear to transcend the limits of the real world, they often reinscribe the occurrences and norms of the oppressive timeline we already inhabit.

Nonetheless, the point remains that video games have the potential to serve as spaces for experimenting with designing—and actively inhabiting—alternate structures of time. *If Found* is far from the only game to deploy game mechanics that resonate with queer experiences of time. Drawing from writing on queer temporality by theorists like Kara Keeling, Elizabeth Freeman, and Jack Halberstam, queer game studies scholars have presented analyses of multiple games that model nonnormative structures of time in ways that do not feed back into the ethical pitfalls of linearity described by Wilcox.[24] Most of these games, like *If Found*, have been made by LGBTQIA+ creators outside the paradigm of AAA production.[25] This work sets a valuable precedent for the idea that time-based game mechanics can challenge the dominant temporal norms of the larger societies in which video games are made and played. Yet the backward time mechanics of *If Found* also differ in critical ways from the mechanics of the other games that this existing work has addressed. Many of these games—like Mattie Brice's *Mainichi* (2012) or Kara Stone's *Ritual of the Moon* (2019)—use looping or repeating mechanics to challenge the presumed linearity of gameplay.[26] By contrast, the mechanics of *If Found* do move in a linear fashion: they move directly and insistently backward. This imbues the world of *If Found*, which takes shape through its time mechanics, with a different set of meanings and ways of resonating with LGBTQIA+ lives.

Moving backward in time, as a mode of gameplay, rejects the temporal mastery promised by video games like those described by Hanson and instead strips almost all agency from its players. The fact that we play *If Found* backward is not a useful strategy; it does not make us feel as if we have the power to control time. Instead, much to the contrary, time controls us. As players, we can do almost nothing but erase (and erase and erase) text that has already been written. We cannot change history. All we can do is remove layer after layer of that historical record, bearing witness to its unfolding. This backward time mechanic also abruptly abandons any investment in a normative figuration of futurity. Complicating cultural narratives of progress for individuals with LGBTQIA+ identities, it moves simultaneously toward the future (through the narrative arc of Kasio's story) and to the past (through the erasing mechanic). It therefore embodies an ambivalent position between futurity and negativity, optimism and hopelessness: literalizing through game design a tension that Heather Love describes, writing in *Feeling Backwards*, as queer people's longing for progress and our inevitable ties to the painful histories of the past.[27] In this way, the game's mechanics, as Jayna Brown writes of Black speculative fiction and music in *Black Utopias*, "radically disrupt the very idea of the future," inviting us to restructure our worldviews by "open[ing] up the possibility for radical temporalities ... not governed by earth time."[28] Alternatively, we might say, *If Found* suggests that earth time may have been something different than we expected all along—not unidirectional but instead multidirectional, reversable, invertible, where the start is always also the end and the end is the beginning.

An Alternative Trans Temporality

Rather than simply offering up *If Found* as one more example of how queer temporality might operate in video games, however, I propose that we think about *If Found*'s backward mechanics specifically as an expression of *trans* time. As I mentioned in the introduction, I am inspired here by calls from trans studies scholars who warn against subsuming the particularities of transgender experience under the broad umbrella of queerness, which can itself often stand in for a set of presumed default (white) cisgender gay and lesbian identities.[29] At the same time, I am mindful of the fact that separating transness out from queerness risks implying that trans people are not already an integral component of queer studies. In shifting tacks to analyze the mechanics of *If Found* through the lens of trans time, I am arguing for an approach that combines these considerations. This approach aims to find unique insights by reading media objects with an eye toward the specific concerns and possibilities that surround trans lives, while also recognizing the importance of bringing these insights to bear on larger formulations of queer meaning. Not all queer video game worlds are trans video game worlds, in the sense that an individual video game might support certain queer identities while perpetuating discrimination against transgender people. Yet any robust, nuanced, and truly inclusive theory of queer worldbuilding must meaningfully account for trans experience.

When I talk about trans temporality, I am referring to structures of time or ways of moving through time that echo the lives of transgender people—whether by paralleling the temporal shapes of those lives or by otherwise translating experiences of transness into time-based forms. As queer history scholars Leah Devun and Zeb Tortorici explain in the introduction to their special issue of *Transgender Studies Quarterly* on trans time, trans studies has turned increasingly toward questions of temporality over the past decade. This work, as Devun and Tortorici write, has posed "challenges to traditional chronology while highlighting the temporal dislocations necessary for self-narrativizing in autobiography, for refusals of settler colonial time, and for identifying echoes of transgender in history."[30] That is, as this existing work demonstrates, thinking about trans identity and time together requires thinking about both trans people's experiences *with* time and the ways that dominant notions of time may be misfit *to* the lived experiences of trans people.

Writing about trans temporality has often grappled with the gulf between the messy realities of transgender experience and tidy dominant narratives about gender transition. For many cisgender subjects, the very concept of trans time cannot help but invoke a vision of transition, generally understood as the movement from one gendered state to another over a bounded period. Trans studies scholar Hil Malatino explains how a growing number of mainstream media representations present "transnormative narratives of transition that are invested in the reification of hegemonic medical constructions of transition as a linear, teleological path."[31] Often in these narratives, trans people follow an established progression: they are assigned the wrong gender at birth; they take steps to alter their gendered appearance; and they arrive at their gender destination, newly minted as beautiful, proud, fully realized trans men and women.[32] Borrowing from Malatino's use of the term "transnormative," we might think of these narratives as modeling a broader *transnormative temporality*. Ironically, transnormative temporality has much in common with what queer studies scholar Jacob Lau terms "cisnormative" temporality, which centers "coherence, linearity, and progress."[33] In direct contrast to the kinds of Black trans temporal movement that C. Riley Snorton describes in *Black on Both Sides: A Racial History of Trans Identity*—"movement with no clear origin and no point of arrival"—transnormative temporality has a clear starting point (the "wrong" gender) and a clear ending point (the "right" gender).[34] Whether it does so quickly or slowly, transnormative temporality can only move in one direction: forward. It walks a straight line from bad to good, from sorrow to joy, from falsehood to truth. It is fundamentally future oriented, moving toward an imagined time when the experience of being trans will have "gotten better."[35]

This transnormative temporal narrative has been critiqued from a variety of angles by trans studies scholars. Jian Neo Chen links the dominant transition narrative to race. Argues Chen, trans activist groups that have "privileged narratives of bodily transition from biologically assigned gender to self-determined gender in alignment" have, in effect, operated "in alignment with the white gender binary" and a white-dominated medical establishment.[36] As Malatino states, the temporal reality of transition is itself often far less straightforward (or conventionally uplifting) than these privileged narratives would suggest. Malatino's own process of transition, he writes, was "circuitous, stop-start, and decades long, mediated by poverty, insurance exclusions, rurality, and a complicated, ongoing grappling with the cultural politics of white masculinity."[37] This suggests a profound nonlinearity to the experience of transition, which can move in circles, stop indefinitely, or simply never reach its destination, if it can be said to have a destination at all.[38] Living a trans life, as geography scholars Max Andrucki and Dana Kaplan write in their study of transmasculine subjects' homes, also commonly means existing in multiple moments simultaneously.[39] Even a person who has followed a linear trajectory of transition is likely to retain innumerable memories and mementos testifying to earlier iterations of their gendered selves. Thus, being trans often means inhabiting a world populated by multiple versions of oneself. In this sense, trans time parallels the time of science-fictional worldbuilding, with its parallel universes and alternate timelines that exist side by side. To be trans is already to be a subject whose mere existence defies the normative logics of time.

These formulations and critiques of transnormative temporality are worth articulating here for two reasons. First, they offer us models alongside (and against) which we can read the time-based mechanics of *If Found*. Second, the robust body of existing work on trans temporality itself repeatedly asserts the pressing need for alternative models of trans time. Clearly, dominant temporal narratives are insufficient for (and often counterproductive to) supporting the lived experiences of trans people. In *If Found*, then, we can look for how time might work otherwise—for a model of how a work of art created by queer and trans people might energize us to envision new relationships between trans life and time.

On multiple levels, *If Found* can be read as a refutation of transnormative time. Even though we might interpret the game's narrative as ultimately uplifting, it remains deeply ambivalent. Kasio's mother finally seems to accept her, but her brother never ceases to be a hateful ass. (As for Cassiopeia, she finds some kind of happiness, but only after functionally bringing about the end of the world.) And Kasio's path to that murky acceptance is anything but linear. Throughout the game, she goes through multiple ups and downs with both her biological family and her chosen queer family. All in the span of a month, Kasio returns home from Dublin, stays briefly with her mother, runs away after a fight, crashes with her friends, sneaks home to steal her own clothes, attends her friends' concert and becomes temporarily mesmerized by two queer women musicians, has a falling out with her friends, gets kicked out of the Big House by the police at the insistence of the nuns who own the property, goes to live with Colum's closeted queer aunt, goes back to her mother's for Christmas, runs away again, locks herself in the Big House with no electricity or heat, and eventually goes home again with her mother. Through these many twists and turns, the player continues erasing, letting the messy realities of trans life wash over them in wave after wave as they wipe the screen clean. The costs at which Kasio finally earns her acceptance also deeply unsettle transnormative progress narratives. It seems that Kasio must reach the point of a dire medical emergency (starvation and a raging fever) before her mother will embrace her. Why, we must ask even while playing through the game's heartwarming final moments, does trans life only merit love and care when it teeters on the brink of trans death?

Just as *If Found* does not fit normative narratives about trans progress, it does not fit normative narratives about transition. Kasio does not change her gender presentation over the course of the game (though we might say she does so once the player reaches the character creation system). Instead, she comes home to Achill already femme-presenting but unsure of how to articulate her gender identity, and she largely remains that way. In an intimate conversation between Kasio and Shans, who is interested in Kasio romantically, Shans asks, "Are you like Colum and Jack?" By this, Shans means, "Are you a gay man?" Kasio responds, as if with a shrug, "I don't know, maybe? Does it even matter." Shans pushes, "And does that mean you like girls . . . or boys?" Kasio, growing weary, replies, "Both? Neither. I like sleeping" (figure 2.5). In a more transnormative narrative, this would be a moment of clarity for both Kasio and

Figure 2.5. Shans questions Kasio about her gender identity and her sexual orientation; Kasio replies with weary disinterest. (Screenshot by author)

her audience; she would give a pained but impassioned speech about how she is finally coming to understand her identity and her place in the world. Instead, Kasio herself remains unsure of how to make sense of her gender or whether to even bother trying. And she is entirely uninterested in linking up that gender with a sexual or romantic interest in others. "Don't you want to kiss me?" Shans tries to insist. Kasio refuses, stating simply, "I don't want to kiss anyone right now."

If Found's refusal of transnormative time also manifests itself through the game's interactive design. The erasing mechanic itself functions as an expression of an alternate trans temporality. Consider the player's interactions with the handwritten letters that Kasio's mother sends her. (Brid sends two, one after each of the fights that cause Kasio to run away from home.) The first letter is deeply misguided, and it opens with an address like a punch to the gut: "My dear son." Brid's second letter, when it first appears on screen, seems poised to be just as hurtful as the last. Parts are covered over with Kasio's furious pencil marks, but the paragraphs that remain immediately visible include lines like, "I'm so sorry if all of this is my fault. I must have raised you wrong." However, when the game's camera zooms in on the first half of the letter, we are met with a surprise. Erasing one dark patch reveals that this letter, in contrast to the last, is addressed, "Dear child." This seems, at first, like progress. Just as quickly, however, the act of erasing upends that progress. Now the game moves the player to the second half of the letter. Erasing the dark marks there reveals the paragraph in which Brid delivers the line mentioned earlier: "It's okay if you like men or dress funny or whatever it is ... [But] you're making life difficult for yourself!" Just as the erasing mechanic reveals discordant bits of the letter in a nonlinear progression, Brid's journey toward acceptance has similarly deviated from a linear path, taking one step forward and two steps back.

Through a combination of the game's narrative and its mechanics, then, *If Found* proposes an alternate vision of trans temporality. In this vision, being trans means always navigating—or perhaps simply accepting—the contradictions of time. Moving forward (as the game's narrative moves forward in time) may necessitate, in some other sense, moving backward. Figuring out a new way ahead in the world likely requires allowing oneself to stand still and dig deeply into the layers of own's own personal past. Our conceptualization of time shapes our conceptualization of the world around us; changing the structure of time also changes the world to which time gives shape. The world of *If Found* operates on a structure of trans time. Rather than trying to fit a trans story to established gameplay mechanics, it creates its own original gameplay mechanics modeled on the temporal experience of living a trans life. In this way, we can say that the mechanics of the game themselves are trans, in that they emerge from the realities of what it feels like to be trans in the world. At the same time, these trans mechanics build a video game world that is trans at the level of its structure. In the world of *If Found*, time is always on the move in multiple directions. The self is always changing, being erased and remade, while still staying the same. Transition is always bound up with loss and uncertainty but also rebirth and creation. Moving through time always means peeling back the layers of oneself, engaging in constant acts of revelation—peering into a mirror, peering into the abyss, waking up and doing it again tomorrow.

Black Holes as Worldbuilders

And here is where we return to black holes. I have just argued that *If Found* offers a compelling alternate model for trans temporality. Yet, in truth, the game aims to reconfigure not only trans temporality but the very fabric of space-time itself. Much as *If Found* frequently tips its hat to its interest in time, the game makes a point of underscoring its investment in astrophysics—and in connecting astrophysics directly to worldbuilding. Both Kasio, the real-life astrophysics grad student, and Cassiopeia, her astronaut double, describe this connection. In one of Kasio's confrontational conversations with her mother, Brid pushes Kasio to reconsider returning to grad school; Brid thinks Kasio should instead take a middle-class job at a local bank. When Kasio insists that she wants to pursue what she is passionate about, her mother asks in exasperation, "Stars and things?" In an uncharacteristic burst of enthusiasm, Kasio proclaims, "Yes! The building blocks of the universe!" In this moment, *If Found* prompts us to see the astrophysics elements of the game as critical for how the game builds its own universe. If stars are the building blocks of the physical universe, then ideas about space-time (another form of "stars and things") are the building blocks of the game world.

However, importantly, not all "stars and things" are created equal in *If Found*. Black holes, it seems, are the true worldbuilders. Later in the game, in the concluding moments of the science fiction storyline, Cassiopeia sits amid the rubble of society, gazing out at the sky. In this contemplative moment, the text on screen reads, "It has been hypothesised that black holes are the seeds of new universes. Cassiopeia can't be sure. Her opinion changes from day to day." In this moment, finally, *If Found* officially gives voice to a notion that has been gestured at throughout the game. The black hole is acknowledged as a figure for creating the world (or many possible worlds) anew. Admittedly, the game proposes this as a hypothetical; Cassiopeia's own opinion wavers on whether the black hole that has ravaged the world is the seed of a new universe. Yet the game, for its part, seems to present its own final sequence as an argument in favor of the worldbuilding power of the black hole. Kasio enters into the black hole of her near total self-destruction, ignoring the friends and family who come searching for her in the Big House and instead resolving to let herself perish alone—and comes out the other side. There, she finds a new world waiting for her, one in which she can finally build a life for herself among the people she loves.

In addition to offering a passageway that characters can travel through to find new worlds, the black hole in *If Found* functions almost as a

Figure 2.6. In the opening sequence of *If Found . . .* , the player erases the mysterious Planet X to reveal a black hole. (Screenshot by author)

character in its own right, a sheer force of nature with its own will and intent. Before we meet Kasio—indeed, before we are even shown the title of the game—we meet the black hole. *If Found* opens by giving the player their eraser-cursor and inviting them to erase away the logos of Annapurna Interactive (the game's publisher) and Dreamfeel (the game's developer). Doing so reveals a starry sky in the depth of outer space. In one corner of the screen appears the image of the astronaut who we will soon know as Dr. Cassiopeia. Now the first text of the game appears, presented in Cassiopeia's voice: "750 million kilometres from Earth. In orbit around Jupiter. I've never been so far before." When the player erases the blanket of stars, the game shifts to a view of the glowing, mysterious Planet X, which Cassiopeia has initially set out to explore. Once she reaches the planet, however, she proclaims, "Something is wrong. . . . I can feel its gravity. How can it be so small when its pull is so strong?" The player now erases Planet X, revealing its true form: a gleaming black circle, big enough to fill up the screen. "This is . . . A BLACK HOLE," Cassiopeia exclaims (figure 2.6). Like the first photographs of a black hole (black hole M87, estimated at fifty-five million light years away from earth and six and a half billion times more massive than our sun), which were captured by the Event Horizon Telescope in 2017, the black hole

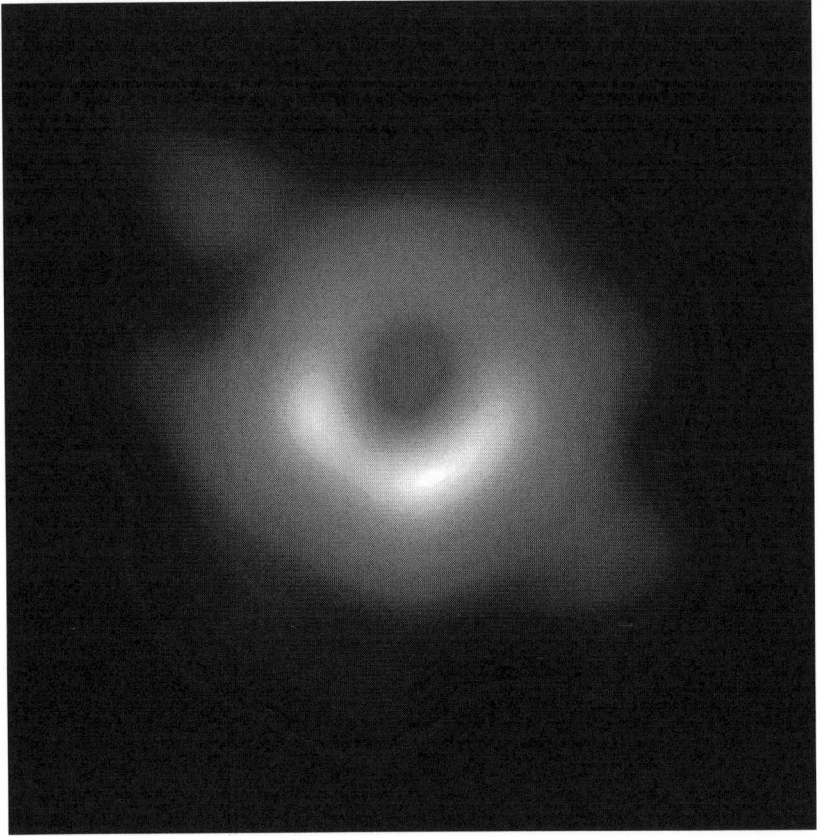

Figure 2.7. A photograph of the M87 black hole taken by the Event Horizon Telescope in 2022. (Image via Wikimedia Commons)

that Cassiopeia now faces appears entirely dark in the center but radiates a circle of light at its edges, as if ringed by fire (figure 2.7).[40] This black hole is, of course, the visual embodiment of contradiction: a place of infinite invisibility made visible by its surrounding, brilliant glow.

Faced with this black hole, the player may try to wipe it away, but, in this moment, they will find that their eraser has no effect. Instead, as if acknowledging the sheer futility of the player's attempts, the game's camera zooms inward into the hole, drawn by its sheer gravitational force. Blackness envelops the screen and, for a time, the eraser remains powerless. When the player can erase again, doing so reveals an outline of Cassiopeia floating through space accompanied by the words, in radiant letters, "If Found . . ." Entering the game, then, requires entering the black hole. Presented in this way, the game's title itself, *If Found . . .* , takes on a second meaning. It simultaneously references the message one might leave on the inside of a diary ("If found, please return to ___") and Cassiopeia's current predicament; floating out in the stars farther than she has ever gone before, she is now lost in space. Will she be found? Her future, contained within that trailing ellipsis, remains uncertain. Because Cassiopeia is a clear stand-in for Kasio, this implied meaning also serves as foreshadowing. Later, Kasio too will be drawn toward a black hole of sorts, become lost, and require finding.

Fittingly, the image of the black hole quickly bleeds over from Cassiopeia's story into Kasio's. On the first day that Kasio arrives on Achill, she worries about how to tell her mother about her gender identity but then erases the note she has written in her diary about her concerns, leaving behind only the phrase "I'm fine." Just behind the phrase looms a sketch of a sphere with lines extending out in concentric circles: equal parts black hole, hazy sun, and bleary, squinting eye. In this moment, the black hole as a visual motif seems to embody a mix of hopefulness and concern, a ball of feeling pulsing with nerves. Soon after, following a conversation that Kasio has with Colum and Jack, the player's view of the journal page shifts to a spot where Kasio has written in large letters, "Maybe the visit [to Achill] will be grand." ("Grand," a footnote clarifies, is used to mean "fine.") Beneath these words is a large black scribble. At first, this moment seems genuinely optimistic, until the player erases the black lines covering the image beneath it. Doing so reveals, once again, the image of the black hole: now a dark, gaping circle in the middle of the page. Positioned alongside the black hole, the sentence "Maybe the visit will be grand" takes on a different air. It becomes ominous, a clear sign that the visit will likely be far from fine. At the same time, the recurring presence of the black hole in Kasio's diary serves as a reminder of the things she loves ("stars and things"), making the black hole both a worrying omen and a familiar, even welcome companion.

Simultaneously, we might interpret ourselves—the players—as the true black hole in *If Found*. After all, our lone role in the game is to hover around the screen and suck up its contents; our cursor is depicted as an eraser, but it could just as easily be the hungry, open end of a handheld vacuum cleaner. Or perhaps, to add another layer to its meaning, the black hole might operate as a metaphor for transness. To transition (or even simply to acknowledge one's own gender), the game seems to suggest, is not entirely unlike entering a black hole. Doing so takes one on a vertiginous journey fraught with peril and offers no guarantees about what life might look like on the other side. Despite this peril, trans identity, like the black hole, often pulls one ever closer with a force that is stronger than human resistance. In this way, through *If Found*, the black hole offers a metaphor for trans life that moves beyond binary poles of optimism or bad feeling. It acknowledges and even embraces the way that being trans commonly means facing immense danger while also planting, to use Cassiopeia's words about black holes, "the seeds of new universes."

Importantly, *If Found* does not want us to pay attention only to what black holes *are* or even what they *represent*. Above all, the game is fascinated with what holes *do*. And what they do, in effect, is create worlds. (Cassiopeia may be unsure whether black holes are the seeds of new universes, but *If Found* itself is not.) Specifically, the black holes in *If Found* create worlds much in the same way that the game's erasing mechanic does: by reshaping the normative operations of time.

To understand what I mean, it is helpful to have a bit of context for the real-life physics of black holes. Black holes, both as depicted in *If Found* and as understood through contemporary astrophysics, distort the fabric of space-time around them.[41] Their gravitational pull is so strong that a person who approaches one—if their consciousness weren't already obliterated when their atoms were ripped apart by overwhelming gravitational tidal forces—would experience time as moving at a very different rate than an observer positioned sufficiently far away would.[42] This kind of temporal distortion can be understood as an extreme dilation of time: the idea that, since time is relative given the conditions under which it is perceived (demonstrated by the theory of special relativity, among other theories), it might be experienced differently by individuals in different situations.[43] This is true for any two entities moving at different speeds or, more precisely, different rates of acceleration. Black holes intensify this phenomenon because their infinite gravity is functionally equivalent to a force of infinite acceleration, sucking material into itself at a precipitously increasing rate. By manifesting time dilation in the extreme, black holes allow us to recognize a broader truth about our material universe: that there is no such thing as one absolute experience of time, only a set of highly relative experiences of the speed at which the world goes by around us.

Fittingly, temporal distortions and time dilations can be found alongside black holes throughout *If Found*. We see this most literally in Cassiopeia's narrative. Once she realizes that the anomaly she is searching for is actually a black hole, Cassiopeia flings herself into the hole to try to take "data readings." Throughout her mission, she communicates over her radio with Control. (Curiously, Control later turns out to be an accountant named Mac, who lives on the mainland in County Mayo.) When she emerges from the black hole, Cassiopeia reports to Control that it only took her a few minutes to collect the information and escape. Control, however, insists, "It has been a week!" Soon after, Cassiopeia enters a series of wormholes that allow her to jump across the solar system. "You travelled 50,000 km in a few days!" Control exclaims when Cassiopeia finishes her jumps. Cassiopeia retorts dryly, "In a second." Control, flabbergasted, replies, "That's an unbelievable distortion of space-time!" In response, Cassiopeia warns, "This is just the beginning. As the black hole expands, the time dilation will only get worse." Time dilation, then, as much as the black hole itself, is the apocalyptic force that supposedly hangs over the game's science-fictional side narrative. This exchange between Cassiopeia and Control suggests that extreme distortions in space-time have the power to destroy the world by causing us (the entities that exist within the world) to perceive time in radically divergent ways. An event that Control lived over a few days, Cassiopeia lived in a second. What makes the black hole so frightening, it seems, is that it unmoors us from a shared experience of time.

Kasio's world back on Achill, a world that orbits ever closer to its own metaphorical black hole, is similarly characterized by temporal distortions. Many of her interpersonal relationships are contorted by what we can understand as interpersonal time dilations. Kasio experiences time at a different pace than many of the people around her do. For her, time seems to be moving extremely slowly. Though she has presumably come home from Dublin at various points during her undergraduate and master's programs, Kasio reflects on her first day of winter break, writing in her diary, "It feels like I haven't been on the island for years."

The whole main narrative of *If Found* takes place over less than a month, from December 4 to December 31, moving ploddingly day by day. One gets the sense that Kasio is proceeding through her life so slowly, in fact, that she is almost standing still: unsure about whether to go back to Dublin, unsure about whether to live in her mother's house, unsure about how and whether to address her gender identity. One evening, she lies in the attic of the Big House with Shans, smoking marijuana and gazing at the stars through a hole in the roof. When Kasio tries to describe the "weird," complex beauty of the ever-shifting universe, Shans asks, "Are you saying we have to make the most of the time we have?" Like any reasonable (and stoned) astrophysics student, Kasio responds, "You're assuming time is even real." For Kasio, the world is inching along against the force of so much temporal resistance that it barely seems to move forward in time at all. For the player too, who must painstakingly erase their way through each moment of this never-ending month, time almost seems to stop.

To the people around Kasio, however, her life appears to be moving incredibly fast. Kasio's mother repeatedly insists that the changes in her daughter's life—by which she means the early stages of her gender transition—have come at breakneck speed. In the second letter she sends to Kasio, Brid writes, "I understand you're not who I thought you were, but I can't believe it. This seems so sudden, there were no signs." Later, when Kasio returns home for Christmas dinner, she ends up pleading in exasperation for her mother to accept her. "What 'me' are you talking about?" her mother snaps back. "The one I've known for 23 years, or the one I've known for two weeks?" Dejected, Kasio cries out, "It's the same me!" Here the temporal distortion portended by the black hole breaks free from the science-fictional side of the game's narrative, bleeding over into the real world. When it comes to Kasio's identity as a transgender woman, Kasio and her mother have wildly divergent perceptions of time. What seems head-spinningly fast to Brid (that her child is suddenly her daughter) simultaneously seems excruciatingly drawn out to Kasio (that she is somehow still in the process of coming out). This reflects a fundamentally different understanding of trans time, specifically. Brid experiences Kasio's transness as brand new, a blip that has only recently appeared to disrupt the much longer timeline of her child's life. Meanwhile, Kasio perceives herself as always having been trans; her identity has no start date. This is indeed, as Control says of Cassiopeia's wormhole jump, a truly "unbelievable distortion of space-time."

In such moments, *If Found* uses the types of time dilation described by astrophysics to give language to the time dilations of trans life, while also illustrating how shifts in experiences of temporality enact a kind of worldbuilding. Indeed, two people living inside such different perceptions of trans time (like Kasio and Brid) functionally live in different worlds. In this sense, the figure of the black hole illustrates one way that worlds are built by revealing divides within the existing world. The black hole, much like the turbulent relationship between Kasio and Brid, makes the very idea that we might all experience a unified vision of time seem improbable, impossible, or even absurd. Inching ever closer to the (metaphorical) black hole, as Kasio does, reveals the universe itself to be already fractured into a million pieces: infinite little worlds of divergent human temporal perception. I am my world. You are your world. For a brief time, if we cling together tightly enough, we might be a world together.

Queering the Operations of Space-Time

Thus far, I have described how *If Found* creates parallels between the real-life phenomena theorized by astrophysics and the lived experiences of the characters in its trans narrative. In this, admittedly, I have somewhat purposefully misled you, saving my own very favorite thing about the game for last—a twist, an inversion, a rebuilding of the world of scientific knowledge. At first glance, *If Found*'s representation of black holes and temporal distortion seems to track accurately with currently accepted understandings of the operations of space-time. However, if we look closer, we find that the game actually *flips* these operations—both through details in its narrative and, even more strikingly, through the mechanics it deploys in the final stretch of gameplay. That is, *If Found* takes ideas from astrophysics and rewrites them, forcing the laws of the universe to function backward, thereby creating a world structured around a queer inversion of the universe's most foundational operational logics. It scrambles the "building blocks of the universe," to use Kasio's phrase, and places them in new positions and new relations to one another. In the process, *If Found* rebuilds the universe itself.

Let me explain. I have said that time, according to the dictates of astrophysics, distorts around a black hole, causing an entity close enough to the black hole to experience time at an extremely different rate than an entity farther from it does. That is true. However, around a real black hole, temporal distortion functions in precisely the *opposite* way that it functions for Kasio and Brid. For the person closest to the black hole (in this case, Kasio, tugged ever closer into her downward spiral), time should be precipitously shortened—that is, the world should go by immensely fast. For a second person observing the first person approach the black hole (like Brid, who watches as her daughter stumbles closer and closer to despair), time should seem comparatively lengthened; the first person should seem to the second to be moving extremely slowly.[44] To state the concept bluntly, without any particular scientific precision, we might say that every second that passes for the person who inches closer to the black hole should feel like a lifetime for the person who observes them. When *If Found* applies this concept to Kasio's life, though, it reverses the effects of temporal distortion. Kasio is the one who experiences time as moving incredibly slowly; the people who observe her from afar experience time as moving vertiginously fast. Therefore, just as through the erasing mechanic, the game creates a world built on a contradictory system of time: a world that looks like our own, and in some ways moves like our own, yet simultaneously also works backward.

Additionally, contemporary astrophysics posits that an entity who enters a black hole should have, in effect, no ability to act.[45] Due to the black hole's infinite gravity, time itself becomes infinitely elongated as one approaches the black hole's center, making the ability to complete any action or enact any change itself functionally impossible. For Kasio, at least, this metaphor seems to hold; as she approaches the black hole at the center of her psyche, she too appears frozen—both figuratively (she holes up in the Big House and cannot bring herself to leave) and literally (the Big House has no heat, and she nearly resorts to burning her notebook for warmth). Indeed, as Kasio descends into the final depths of her emotional black hole, the game enters an apocalyptic sequence, zooming out from the cold, isolated scene of the Big House to show the island of Ireland and Northern Ireland and then the whole globe. The player now erases the Earth, which radiates in psychedelic colors, to reveal once again the glowing black hole, which

Figure 2.8. As Kasio spirals down into her own personal black hole, the player seems to erase Kasio herself from existence. (Screenshot by author)

grows bigger as it swallows up our solar system and eventually the cosmos. Continuing to erase, scrubbing away with the last little stub of the eraser, the player finds Kasio at the center of the black hole, a dark floating silhouette in a sea of swirling static (figure 2.8). Now the player erases Kasio herself, bit by bit, wiping her out of the universe. Once Kasio's body has completely disintegrated, the eraser reveals text hovering in the void: "Time doesn't exist in a black hole. Every moment crushed together, past and present and future in one endless scream. No way to change anything. No way to move. No way to escape." These statements are poetic and gut-wrenching, certainly, but they are also scientifically "correct."

Yet Kasio does escape. On a narrative level, we know this because we see her mother rescue her from the Big House; on the level of mechanics, we know this because the gameplay of *If Found* shifts dramatically in its concluding stretch. As soon as Kasio begins to wake from her feverish, near-death slumber, a critical transformation occurs: the cursor turns from an eraser into a pencil. Now, when players move the cursor around the screen, it draws rather than erasing. Bit by bit, an illustration appears of Kasio held tightly in her mother's arms. The pencil marks reveal the words, "Your Mammy's here now love," then,

Figure 2.9. Rather than being destroyed inside the black hole, Kasio emerges into a new world; she sits in her mother's kitchen surrounded by her friends. (Screenshot by author)

"I've got you Kasio." This moment is full of catharsis, relief, and a sense that a new path back to the world of the living has suddenly revealed itself—in no small part because this is also the first time that Kasio's mother has called her by her name. The player's cursor now scribbles a new scene over this one. In it, Kasio and her mother hug in the kitchen of Kasio's childhood home; around them, sitting with mugs of tea in hand and gazing sweetly at Kasio, are her friends (figure 2.9). Instead of being destroyed by the black hole, Kasio has entered it and survived, emerging into a loving world that the player draws into being. Kasio has once again flipped the script on astrophysics. Instead of losing the ability to act, she can act in ways she never could before.

And, suddenly, the player can act in new ways as well. Now, in addition to drawing, the cursor allows the player to write. As the cozy scene in Brid's kitchen fades away, the game switches into a primarily textual mode, telling a series of follow-up stories about both Kasio and Cassiopeia in the style of a choose-your-own-adventure epilogue. Unexpectedly, the text of this epilogue pours out haphazardly from the pencil's tip, trailing fractured lines of words that point in all directions, depending on where the player drags the cursor. Because space is limited on the page and making these lines parallel is finicky work, it is likely that players will end up with snippets of text radiating out in multiple directions (figure 2.10). These snippets create a cacophony of text fragments, like trails left behind by a pack of disoriented snails. Thus, to read about what ultimately happens to Kasio and her astronaut counterpart, the player must actively participate in the creation of this multidirectional writing process, choosing which way to array the text: a symbol of new opportunities, new forms of agency, and new worlds of possibility, however unusual and messy in form. Once again, *If Found* has taken the operations of astrophysics and inverted them to create its own version of the world. Instead of stripping the player of their already-limited ability to act after they follow Kasio into the black hole, *If Found* bestows on them an unprecedented level of agency.

This inversion of the laws of the universe lies at the core of how *If Found* enacts its own mode of queer worldbuilding. In other chapters, I analyze video games that perform queer worldbuilding yet that do not appear to produce worlds populated by LGBTQIA+ subjects. In this regard, *If Found* is different; its world is full of queer and trans people, even as these queer and trans people struggle against the world around them. Yet *If Found*'s world is also queer in that it shifts, scrambles, destabilizes, and ultimately reimagines what we typically accept as the material truths

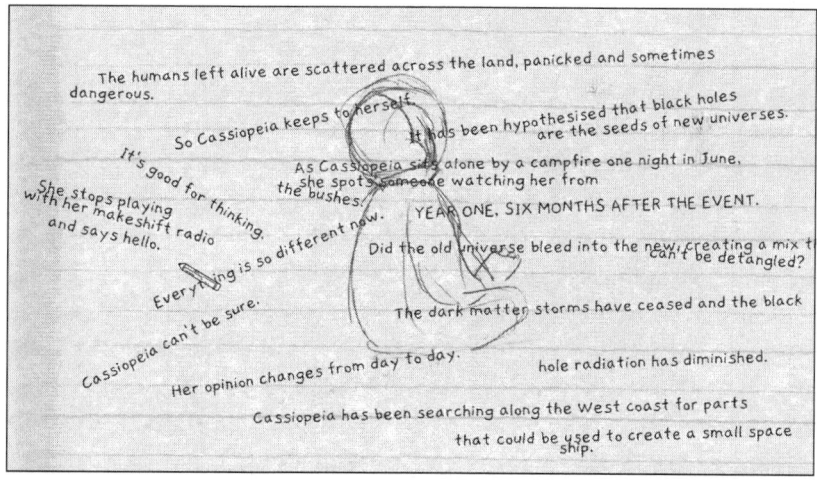

Figure 2.10. The player writes out the epilogues to Cassiopeia's and Kasio's stories in fragments radiating out from the new pencil-cursor. (Screenshot by author)

of our physical universe. What I find so compelling about this mode of queer worldbuilding is its sheer audacity. It aims to queer the universe at the level of its very fabric. In doing so, it proposes a new form of astrophysics, of science, and of the types of worldbuilding that are drawn through empirical observations of the world around us. It takes information generated by scientific inquiry and asks, "How can we, knowing now how the world works, use this knowledge to make the world otherwise?" The world that *If Found* imagines is one where time itself works in the service of queer and trans people. In contrast to the real-life tragedies of our own world, where queer and trans lives are so often cut short, Kasio is offered the chance to live in an elongated present. In effect, *If Found* is an alternate temporal universe where trans people get more time. They have, we might say, all the time in the world.

Let me conclude by contending that *If Found*, along with other video games that use queer mechanics of time, also communicates a message about worldbuilding that is more audacious still. By queering the laws of space-time, *If Found* reveals the inherent queerness of time as it already operates in the world around us. Time, like identity or desire, cannot be contained by normative systems or tidy units of measure—no matter how we might try. It is strange, elastic, and unruly, at least as viewed by the standards of white, Western, rationalizing Enlightenment principles. (I am thinking here about Bliss Cua Lim's writing on the ways that hegemonic clock time has been imposed on societies in the Global South as part of ongoing projects of colonialism and imperialism.)[46] When video games use their mechanics to restructure the operations of time, they shed light on the inherent constructedness of time itself; they reveal that time is not an immutable, incontrovertible truth but a system for understanding how we move through the world and how the world moves around us, a system that could be constructed differently. The laws of astrophysics themselves function much like game mechanics: sets of rules that describe (or, in the case of game mechanics, *prescribe*) how the world works and what actions are possible within that world.[47] Redesigning these mechanics can, in turn, serve as a step toward promoting a more liberatory vision of time both within and beyond video games. If we change the way that time works in video games, we can begin to imagine changing the way that time works in the world. If we change the way that time works in the world, we change whom the world has time for and who is granted the privilege of having time.

Simultaneously, by presenting us with an alternate universe, *If Found* challenges us to shift our perspective on our own existing universe. As queer and trans studies scholars, we have spent so much of our own time arguing for alternative temporalities. Yet, despite the ongoing efforts of cisheteronormativity to tame the unruliness of time and transform it into a weapon to use against marginalized people, maybe time has always been queer. Maybe time has always been trans. Unnatural, odd, absurd—just like us, just like generations of scientists feared. Maybe time, along with the worlds it creates, has always been ours.

3

Queer Bodies in Motion

Game Physics as Worldbuilder in Goat Simulator *and* Wobbledogs

A loose-limbed goat flies high into the air, pausing at the top of his jump, where he seems briefly to float. He is a worldly creature who, if only for a moment, has defied the dictates of gravity. A gaggle of dogs— little more than colorful blocks with wide eyes, pert snouts, and perky ears—amble through a playpen. Their bodies, oddly gelatinous, wobble and bounce with each step. These animals and the unusual trajectories of their movements are expressions of a set of physical laws that underlie their computational worlds. Such animals are the stars of this chapter, as we will see—digital creatures who embody what Jane Bennett, writing from the perspective of the environmental humanities, describes as "the strange ability of ordinary, man-made items to exceed their status as objects and to manifest traces of independence and aliveness."[1] Simultaneously, these animals are more than individual, man-made items. They are also stand-ins, expressions of the deeper systems that give them form and set them in motion: systems of video game physics.

In chapter 2, I presented an example of a video game that builds its world—and, by extension, proposes an alternate structure for our own world—by inverting the laws of physics at what I described as the grandest possible scale: the movements of the stars, the effects of black holes, the very shape of space and time. This chapter too is about physics, which we can understand as a set of rules (like a set of game mechanics) for structuring the physical operations of the world. Yet these physics function on a very different scale. They are not the physics of the universe or the motions of celestial bodies; instead, they are the physics of our immediate, lived, material realities and the motions of our own bodies. Specifically, I am shifting here from contemplating the worldbuilding potential of remaking astrophysics to the worldbuilding potential of remaking software-based game physics. Game physics, as I describe in the next section, are the technical systems that set the terms for how objects act and interact in simulated digital spaces. Commonly overlooked by cultural critics of game as a merely technical matter, game physics in fact serve a critical role in encoding cultural meaning into video game worlds. Often, they do so either by attempting to replicate and thereby reinforcing dominant notions of physical realness or, alternately, by abandoning realness and turning the physical world into a site for unruly, ecstatic, embodied play.

While there are many examples of physics games (video games whose gameplay focuses on interacting with physics systems) that could be or have been interpreted queerly, I focus here on two specific video games. These games, I argue, use their physics systems to rebuild the foundational logics of their worlds in ways that resonate with nonnormative experiences of sexuality and gender. By extension, they construct an alternative vision of physics that I am calling *queer physics*. In this way, these games model yet another possible approach to queer worldbuilding: building a world that begins by reconfiguring typically unquestioned expectations about matter itself.

The first of these video games is *Goat Simulator* (Coffee Stain, 2014), a now-iconic physics game that has spun off many successors in what Marco Caracciolo terms the "animal mayhem" genre. Games in this genre, Caracciolo writes, use "nonhuman-oriented thinking" to enact the "destabilization of anthropocentric assumptions."[2] In particular, I am interested in how *Goat Simulator* plays with the physics of gravity, defined scientifically as an attractive force. The game creates a world characterized by floatiness and, by extension, denaturalizes the accepted operations of attraction.[3] The second game I discuss, *Wobbledogs* (Tom Astle, 2021), is less widely known but equally provocative in its use of queer physics to build its world. Part physics game, part pet simulator, *Wobbledogs* is about breeding increasingly ridiculous iterations of dogs with long, undulating bodies. Whereas *Goat Simulator* models queer ways that bodies can move through space, *Wobbledogs* offers us a vision of how bodies themselves might move queerly by embracing the uncanny, non-Newtonian fluidity of the wobble.

In contrast to most of the other analyses I offer in this book, my arguments in this chapter are drawn in substantial part from a consideration of the game development process itself. When discussing the worldbuilding effects of *Wobbledogs*' physics system, I pull from publicly available documentation about how creator Tom Astle constructed the game, with a focus on his "developer diary" (also referred to as "devlogs" or "dev diaries") forum posts about wrestling with different iterations of the game's physics system. I have found this documentation to be particularly helpful for addressing game physics because it offers a window onto a technical system that can be challenging to accurately deconstruct simply by playing a game as a finalized product. Though Astle's devlog posts feature prominently in the final section of this chapter, attending to the game development process does not necessarily mean centering the role of a human author in the creation of a game like *Wobbledogs*. Ironically, as we will see, Astle's posts suggest that video game physics systems may often enact their own desires about the worlds they want to bring into being.

The Gendered and Sexual Implications of Game Physics

Though physics systems have rarely been included in conversations about worldbuilding, they represent a core component of how video games build their worlds as spaces for player experience. Used in both two-dimensional and three-dimensional games (as well as virtual and augmented reality), game physics refer to the software systems that dictate how an object will interact with other objects or with its environment inside a given game world.[4] These systems "model object properties such as mass, velocity, and friction by means of algorithms derived from physical laws," as photography scholar Eugénie Shinkle explains in her writing about physics-based renderings of nature in video games.[5] They set parameters for gravity, weight, bounce, and the effects of force, among other factors. Game physics determine, for instance, which objects—broadly defined to include any designated entity in the game—will roll down a hill and which will splatter upon impact. I am differentiating here between the terms "physics engine" and "physics system," though the two are sometimes used interchangeably. For our present purposes, a physics engine is a set of software tools for simulating in-game physics that are made available to video game developers, commonly from within a development platform. A physics system, as I am using the term, describes the individual configuration of physical parameters (out of the possible parameters afforded by a given physics engine) that the developers of a specific game have chosen to implement in their world. A physics engine offers possibilities. A physics system represents a set of selections from among those possibilities.

Often, game physics are developed and deployed in ways that uphold dominant norms of video games. Though physics engines may theoretically be modified, repurposed, or remade by individual game developers, many contemporary, widely used physics engines have been constructed by large-scale game studios or software companies. They are now available "off the shelf" as prepackaged parts of larger game development engines, such as Unity. As Benjamin Nicoll and Brendan Keogh explain in their writing about Unity, each "engine has default ways of simulating physics, responding to inputs, casting light, drawing textures, or generating audio."[6] The physics engines contained within these development engines are often advertised as key components of a given engine's preset capabilities. Corporate marketing for these engines—as well as the consumer hype around the games that they are used to develop—typically emphasizes the claim that their new and improved capabilities in the realm of simulating physics will make video games seem more "real." Consider the promotional material for the physics engine contained in the current iteration of the widely adopted (if ironically named) Unreal engine, Unreal 5, which launched in 2022 and has been used to build numerous hit AAA video games in the intervening years. According to the website of Epic Games, the developer of the Unreal engine, Unreal 5 includes a robust variety of sub-engines that compose its suite of physics software. Among these is a sub-engine for real-time fluid simulation, described by Epic as "[producing] realistic effects for things such as fire, smoke, clouds, rivers, splashes, and waves breaking on a beach," and another for "hair physics," explained succinctly as a tool set for "achieving realistic hair and fur animations."[7]

This emphasis on making video game worlds seem more real—in the case of Unreal 5, through the physical movements of the elements that populate a game's environment—has a long history that stretches back across decades of game design and development. As early as the creation of the 1962 game *Spacewar!* (Steve Russel), commonly credited as one of the very first video games, physics simulations have been used to model the physicality of real life.[8] In the game, two spaceships operated by separate players shoot at each other while navigating the gravitational pull of a star: a seemingly fantastical scenario. Yet the game began its life, as its creators have since explained, as a physics simulation, an attempt to replicate the movements of bodies and projectiles in space under a set of specific gravitational conditions.[9] In the intervening years, as physics engines have evolved from rudimentary systems to expansive software packages, each new generation of these engines and the video games that use them have been sold to players through claims that they render simulations of the physical world in unprecedented realistic detail.[10] Video game developers, in turn, often understand their goal in working with physics engines to be the achievement of in-game simulations that most convincingly replicate the physical movement of materials in reality.[11]

This insistence on simulating reality may be frustrating—one more expression of the video game industry's endless push toward "better" tech—but the implication that game physics are inherently tied to questions of realness is important for understanding their role in worldbuilding. Whether or not game physics are realistic, in that they accurately replicate the physicality of the material world outside of video games, they are indeed crucial for making game worlds feel *real*. I mean this in a tangible, embodied, and affective sense. Game physics establish the feeling that players could reach out and touch a game world; they allow players to envision what it would feel like, in a material sense, to exist within a game. Physics systems also structure forms of cultural meaning into game worlds that have direct real-world implications. These systems help establish what Noah Wardrip-Fruin terms the "operational logics" of a game world.[12] How objects move through a given world tells us an immense amount about who and what has power in that world: who can push and pull; who can leave the ground and who is rooted to it; who is granted bodily resilience and whose precarious bodily integrity is at constant risk. As Carlin Wing points out in her writing on the Indigenous and colonialist histories of bounce (itself a key component of physics across both digital and physical games), the meaning encoded into play by varying forms of movement are not absolute. "Logics of bounce," writes Wing, "look different when enacted in different materials and under different social and political conditions."[13]

This perspective on game physics, which understands them as key to both how a game world is built and how that world relates to the wider world that surrounds it, represents a turn away from long-standing scholarly presumptions about the technical components of video games. Writing in 2004, new media theorist Alexander Galloway described how "realistic representation" had already become a central concern in early game studies. Representation in games, Galloway asserted, extends beyond the images that players see on screen, into the actions that players take and the "gameworlds in which [these actions] transpire"—a statement that I certainly agree with.[14] However, Galloway cautions that, in deconstructing the connections between video game representation and reality, we should understand "realistic-ness" and "realism" as fundamentally distinct concepts. (I myself have chosen to use the word "realness" in this chapter, since it sidesteps both "realistic-ness" and "realism" and instead draws from the rhetoric of queer cultures like drag, where the real is always already understood as a socially constructed performance that is open to evaluation and reinterpretation.)[15] Realism, says Galloway, is unrelated to realistic graphics or physics; instead, it describes whether a game can reflect something true about the social and "phenomenological qualities of the real world."[16] Only artistic and activist game designers who follow in filmic traditions of questioning "the real," Galloway implies, can create games with true realism. By contrast, according to Galloway, realistic-ness of the sort promised by software tools like physics engines are merely the stuff of computational modeling and "polygon counts": crude, lowly concerns that are unrelated to the artistic or social meaning of the worlds that video games create.[17]

But Galloway, as well as those who have since adopted his distinctions between realness and realistic-ness, gets game physics all wrong. In truth, Galloway's distinction fails to see past the rhetoric of the industry hype. The companies that sell video games and game development engines may broadcast the snake-oil promise of realistic-ness powered by innovative tech. Yet game physics themselves, as they actually function with game worlds, do precisely what Galloway suggests that only artists can do: imbue a game with the phenomenological qualities of a space that feels real while also offering us opportunities to reflect on the nature of our shared social realities.

What does this look like in practice? Though physics systems are used in a great many video games today, the game genre that makes these systems most visibly—and therefore most readily available for analysis—is physics games. Physics games place interactions with a game's physics systems at the core of their gameplay. They often prompt players to experiment with and even struggle against a game's particular flavor of physics, while ultimately encouraging the player to master the challenges of the physical world. Some prominent examples of physics games include *World of Goo* (2D Boy, 2008), *Getting Over It with Bennett Foddy* (Bennett Foddy, 2017), *Octodad* (Young Horses, 2014), and *I Am Bread* (Bossa Studios, 2015). For these games, which foreground situations in which player-characters must navigate perilous terrain by flinging or splatting or wobbling themselves toward a goal, there can be no game world without game physics.

To date, physics games have primarily interested queer game studies scholars to the extent that such games often emphasize unruly bodies and revel in transgressive play. Software studies scholar Eric Freeman explains that contemporary physics systems typically place the objects they govern in two categories: hardbody (or "rigid bodies," depending on the terminology of the engine) or softbody (or "deformable bodies"). Whereas hardbody objects maintain their physical integrity when acted on, softbody objects, writes Freeman, "are subject to distortion—they are malleable and breakable."[18] It is precisely in this tension between the hard and the soft that others have identified the queer potential of game physics. Amanda Phillips argues that the floppy bodies seen in ragdoll physics games—including explicitly queer games like *Genital Jousting* (Free Lives, 2016)—challenge the hegemonic idealization of masculine hardness in gamer cultures and gay men's cultures alike.[19] By making bodies floppy, physics games also have the potential to manifest a kind of "radical softness," a concept that Teddy Pozo borrows from the artist Lora Mathis. Pozo applies Mathis's concept to both digital and nondigital games as a way to describe the queer affective power of games that abandon hardness (linked to the idea of the "hardcore" gamer) and embrace soft materials and practices of care.[20] The queer potential of game physics, which often render the body simultaneously erotic and strange, can also be seen in the work of queer independent game designers. Robert Yang, for instance, has provocatively described his popsicle-sucking video game *Succulent* as simulating "immersive cheek physics."[21] Similarly, Jimmy Andrews and Loren Schmidt have explained how their game *Realistic Kissing Simulator*—in which player-characters lick each other's faces—was inspired by trying to replicate "tongue physics."[22]

Physics games with clear queer implications, like *Realistic Kissing Simulator* or *Genital Jousting* (a game about wiggling phalluses chasing one another), are often messy by design. They turn video game play from a matter of precision into a spectacle of floppiness. In this way, they invite players to participate in simultaneously making and being what queer theorist Heather Love describes as a "queer mess."[23] Yet explicitly queer physics games like these also prompt us to confront the fact that the domain of video game physics, taken as a whole, is already kind of a (queer) mess. Game physics, as I have said, have been sold time and again on the promise that they will awe players with their graphical prowess. However, historically, game physics have actually drawn more attention from players when they break than when they function properly.

From the time of their early uses in major commercial video games, game physics have been known for their glitchiness. Infamous examples, as well as some more contemporary games, are filled with scenes of physics gone wrong: body parts extending wildly, characters clipping through surfaces. Ari Gass historicizes this phenomenon through their reading of the 1998 *Jurassic Park* video game *Trespasser* (DreamWorks Interactive).[24] *Trespasser*, often cited as the first game to use what we now refer to as ragdoll physics, is best known today not as a pioneer of physics simulation but as a laughable footnote in games history, most famous for the wildly broken physics that controlled the player-character's arm (figure 3.1). A player of *Trespasser* navigates its game world, filled with belligerent dinosaurs, from a first-person perspective. Their arm, held out in front of them, is constantly at the ready to grasp weapons or interact with objects. The result is far from realistic. As recently as 2020, more than twenty years after the game's release, players and games journalism outlets were still uploading videos to YouTube with titles like "The Weird Arm Physics of Jurassic Park: Trespasser": compilations of scenes in which this arm appears to float and contort, bending at the joints in impossible directions, waving guns around with all of the grace of a partially cooked strand of spaghetti.[25] Games like *Trespasser*, silly as they may seem, are not actually historical footnotes; they are the foundational iterations of game physics that laid the groundwork for

Figure 3.1. The player attempts to fend off a carnivorous dinosaur while navigating the game's glitchy arm physics in *Trespasser*. (Screenshot by author)

the physics systems that have followed them. Considered within this lineage, we can see a queer game like *Realistic Kissing Simulator* as parodying not only the act of kissing but also the very idea that a video game might be able to simulate the world realistically at all.

At the same time, the history of game physics highlights just how actively dominant cultural beliefs about gender and sexuality have shaped the evolution of supposedly realistic physics. Much of the technical advancement that has given rise to robust, contemporary physics engines was in fact driven by the game industry's initial quest to create increasingly appealing "breast physics."[26] Starting in the early 1990s, fighting games like *Street Fighter II* (Capcom, 1991) began attempting to render the bounce of women's breasts, with a focus on large-chested characters like Chun-Li (figure 3.2). Chun-Li's character design, which the player views from a side angle, accentuates the jutting prominence of her chest. Even when she stands still, her breasts never stop moving. While she waits for a fight to begin, she breathes heavily, causing her chest to heave rhythmically; when she jumps or kicks, her breasts bounce dramatically in response. In later games, this rudimentary form of breast physics quickly grew more complex. By the late 1990s and early 2000s, more graphically advanced games were quite literally marketing themselves as having superior "jiggle physics," a claim designed to make such games seem simultaneously more realistic and more sexually appealing to straight, male players.[27]

Thus, attempts to replicate the movements of women's bodies (including the bodies of Asian-coded women characters like Chun-Li as well as white women characters, as seen in infamous "jiggle physics" games like *Dead or Alive: Xtreme Beach Volleyball* [Team Ninja, 2003]) triggered a kind of arms race in the development of physics simulation software. In turn, the systems that were developed in response to gamers' imagined desire to watch breasts bounce have since been baked into today's prominent physics engines. As a result, the problematic worldviews that shaped these systems—worldviews in which the motions of femme bodies are envisioned as performances to gaze upon and in-game movement is understood as a vehicle for imparting erotic pleasure to heterosexual men—have been hard-coded into the physics software that is used to build contemporary video game worlds.

As we move into our analysis of the physics systems found within two specific games, we take with us an awareness of this charged yet ambivalent relationship between game physics and queer worldbuilding. On the one hand, game physics systems are ripe with potential for

Figure 3.2. Chun-Li's breasts bounce as she waits to begin a fight with Blanka against the backdrop of a Brazilian village in *Street Fighter II*. (Screenshot by author)

effusive queer expression that destabilizes normative expectations about how bodies move through the world. On the other hand, these same systems have been built on a lineage of sexist beliefs: beliefs about whom video games should represent "realistically," who the audience for these representations is, and what realness looks like in the first place. (The cruel humor of video games that tout their realistic breast physics is, of course, that they usually represent the movement of breasts in laughably unrealistic ways.) How, then, can physics systems participate in building the kinds of alternate worlds we are seeking in video games? How might such worlds break from the discriminatory logics that have shaped their software, repurposing these tools to imagine more radical ways of being in the physical world?

Gravity, Attraction, and "Floatiness" in *Goat Simulator*

One model for this alternative approach to worldbuilding through physics systems can be found in the game *Goat Simulator*. First released as a PC game in 2014, *Goat Simulator* has since been ported to and updated for various platforms. In 2022, *Goat Simulator 3*, the sequel to *Goat Simulator*, was released for Nintendo Switch. (In fittingly ridiculous fashion, Coffee Stain Studio titled the sequel *Goat Simulator 3* despite the fact that there is no *Goat Simulator 2*.)[28] I focus my analysis here on the original *Goat Simulator*, but there is considerable continuity across the series. All of the *Goat Simulator* games, as their name implies, are about being a goat. This is not just any goat, mind you, but a particularly hectic goat, one who passes his days wreaking havoc among humans, ramming himself into obstacles, and, above all, flinging his body dramatically into the air under various conditions.[29] The goat's character design is—let's say, to be polite—distinctive. His yellow eyes, with their disarming rectangular pupils, stare vacantly out from either side of his face; an uncomfortably long and fittingly floppy red tongue dangles from his semi-open mouth (figure 3.3). Once on the move, however, the goat reveals himself to be feisty, fearless, and seemingly indestructible. He can run, head-butt, fling himself off buildings, hijack vehicles, and even launch himself on rockets, all functionally without consequence to his physical well-being. Theoretically, in *Goat Simulator*, the player's primary goal is to

Figure 3.3. The goat in *Goat Simulator* stands waiting to wreak havoc on the human world, his long tongue hanging from his mouth. (Screenshot by author)

explore a series of human-inhabited environments and complete small missions. Mostly, however, the goat's purpose (and, by extension, the player's) is to run amok through suburban and urban landscapes simply because he can.

Goat Simulator itself has a storied history in the physics genre. Though it became a sensation soon after its release—inspiring the creation of numerous other wacky physics games starring playable animals that we might term, riffing off the names of genres like roguelikes or metroidvanias, *goat-likes*—the game began its life as a seemingly silly one-off concept. According to a 2014 blog post written by Coffee Stain designer Armin Ibrisagic, *Goat Simulator* was not originally intended to be developed into a full game. Ibrisagic explains that the concept emerged from a game jam that Coffee Stain ran to help train new programmers. "The initial game pitch was very loose," he writes. "It was basically 'goats are funny, let's make a goat game.'"[30] However, according to Ibrisagic, when he put footage of the project on YouTube, it quickly went viral, garnering news coverage and more than a million views. In turn, says Ibrisagic, this prompted Coffee Stain to pivot and develop *Goat Simulator* into a commercial release. In a sense, then, *Goat Simulator* went from vague concept to an actual game because would-be players who saw this early footage wanted access to the imagined world that this video conjured up: a world where they too could play as an ecstatic, death-defying goat.

In theory, *Goat Simulator* could be described as an open-world game in the spirit of the *Grand Theft Auto* series (Rockstar Games, 1997–2021)—a comparison that links it to Ken Watanabe's *San Andreas Deer Cam*, the subject of chapter 6—or perhaps as a quirky, madcap cousin of 3D skateboarding games like those in the *Tony Hawk's* series (various developers, 1999–2020). First and foremost, though, *Goat Simulator* is a physics game. What animates its gameplay, that spark that made the game an instant sensation before it had even been developed, is the exuberant experience of messing around with its physics. The goat himself is a sheer spectacle of game physics at work, an intentionally messy entity whose design splices together hardbody, softbody, and ragdoll physics.

This spectacular physics garble makes itself most visible when the goat's body leaves the ground. Indeed, the game looks for every possible excuse to get the goat airborne. Consider the opening level of the original *Goat Simulator*. There, the player-as-goat begins in a fenced grassy area surrounded by neighboring houses and yards. Their first task, as they orient themselves to this new game world, is to learn to jump and climb. For a moment, it seems that the goat will not be able to leap over the fence that surrounds this particular patch of backyard grass; when he presses against the fence, his long, rubbery neck spins around, and his head hangs limply to one side. He soon breaks free, however, and clears the fence with a running leap, heading off to find new situations that will send him much higher into the air. In one such moment, he interrupts a backyard barbeque, where he walks over a firework stuck in the ground; the firework promptly shoots off, flinging the goat up over the trees and dropping him onto a set of craggy hills. Tumbling down the hillside, the goat flops and contorts, as if his bones were made of pudding. At the bottom of the hill, his body becomes suddenly rigid again. He stands up and dashes off to create more chaos. In another moment, the goat straps on an enormous jet pack, which takes him careening haphazardly around the level, smashing into buildings, trees, and telephone wires (figure 3.4). In a third moment, he scales an enormous, theme-park-sized waterslide, only to fling himself down. As his body tumbles head over heels on the slippery tile surface, his enormous,

Figure 3.4. In *Goat Simulator*, the goat straps on a jet pack and soars haphazardly through the air. (Screenshot by author)

twisting tongue flops out behind him. Indeed, in both the game's level design and its physics, the whole world of *Goat Simulator* seems created to give players the chance to watch the goat fly through the air in increasingly ridiculous ways.

Yet, if we look closer, we see that there is one particular feature that most strikingly characterizes the physical world of *Goat Simulator* and its longing to launch the goat upward—not the floppy motions of the goat's own body but the larger systems of in-game gravity that govern how that body moves. I have said that *Goat Simulator* is a game about playing with physics; let me be more specific and say that *Goat Simulator* is a game about playing with the physics of *gravity*. Gravity, as Alenda Chang points out in discussing the role of "collapse" in video games (such as ecological collapse or the collapse of societies), is already central to many kinds of play. She writes, "Anyone who has ever played a children's game of pick-up sticks or the wooden tower game Jenga [can] attest [that] gravity is one of the very first constraints we encounter in elementary play. In other words, things fall, be they blocks or civilizations."[31] *Goat Simulator* translates this play with gravity into the digital realm, while also intentionally warping the operations of gravity that players are used to encountering in the physical world of pick-up sticks and Jenga. That is, *Goat Simulator* takes the seemingly self-evident assertion that "things fall" and brings it into question: Must the physical world always function like this? Are there different ways for gravity to operate, different ways to fall?

We can see this emphasis on gravity—as well as this interest in altering its standard operations—if we return once more to the topic of bounce. *Goat Simulator* provides plenty of opportunities for the goat to launch himself skyward, yes, but it provides even more opportunities for him to bounce up and down. As soon as the player begins exploring the opening level of *Goat Simulator*, for example, they find that the town around them is littered with trampolines. Somehow each home seems to have one in their backyard. When the goat hops up onto one of these trampolines, he begins to bounce. He bounces again and again, going higher and higher (figure 3.5). With each jump, the trampoline springs squeak, and the goat soars improbably farther into the air, so high that eventually the whole town comes into view beneath him. At the top of each of these trampoline jumps, something unusual happens: the goat hangs briefly in the air before descending, momentarily buoyant. This gives the goat's jumps a floaty quality, as if each time his hooves leave the ground the world around him shifts into slow motion or as if he has become temporarily untethered from the pull of the earth.

Jumping on trampolines isn't the only action that triggers this midair floating. Each time that the goat leaps up, as he so often does—whether he jumps or is launched upward with a rocket or goes tumbling off a building—the operations of the game's otherwise seemingly realistic gravity simulations suddenly shift. Until the goat lands back on the ground, reinstating the standard laws of physics, gravity loosens its grip on the goat, and he becomes semi-weightless. The effect for the player is a kind of vertigo, a feeling at once delightful and dreadful, like pausing at the top of a roller-coaster ride immediately before a precipitous drop. These moments of pause also give us time to indulge in the sight of the flailing goat, hovering above the Earth, before he returns to the ground.

Yet the meaning contained in these moments extends beyond this dizzying feeling. Let's break down this phenomenon (the sudden loosening of gravity when the goat is airborne) into its two main implications. First, because it briefly gives gravity an overall lighter hold on the game world, this phenomenon imbues the experience of playing *Goat*

Figure 3.5. In *Goat Simulator*, the goat bounces on one of the town's many trampolines. (Screenshot by author)

Simulator with a feeling of floatiness. "Floatiness," as a term applied to video games, is typically used disparagingly to describe a game with so-called floaty controls. Players or reviewers will often label a game's controls "floaty" when those controls feel imprecise or delayed or when they produce unexpected results—such as when a light tap to the joystick causes a character to dart surprisingly far. The opposite of floaty controls are "tight" controls, in which player input and the output on screen feel accurately matched. Admittedly, players and even designers sometimes disagree on the precise definition of floatiness; its meaning, like the experience it describes, is imprecise rather than tight.[32] Above all, floatiness, as it is typically used, is the name for an impression, a frustration, a disappointment, a sense that something is not quite right in the connection between the player and the game. Floatiness is a feeling that the control offered by game controllers is no longer sufficiently in control. Whatever exactly floatiness means in the parlance of games culture, it is not supposed to be a good thing.

Unlike so many other video games, which seek to root out the kinds of technical imperfections that lead to floaty controls, *Goat Simulator* embraces floatiness in multiple senses of the word. First, the game's controls are indeed floaty; they are hard to manage and imprecise.

When the goat runs and then stops, for instance, he slides forward, making it hard to predict exactly where he will end up and what he might slam into. The hit boxes for many items in the game are similarly floaty; when the goat runs into an object, the player never quite knows if he will collide with it or bizarrely clip right through.[33] These moments of imprecision lend themselves to the game's air of mayhem. Simultaneously, of course, the game embraces floatiness by making the goat literally (almost, sort of) float. *Goat Simulator*'s physics system deliberately weakens the forces that would otherwise tether the goat to the ground, allowing him to become partially unmoored from the world as we know it, eerily lightweight, uncanny, unreal—part goat, part astronaut, part feather. Let me reiterate that these simulations of floatiness are not mere flecks of fancy sprinkled throughout the game. They are, I would argue, the very point of the game. Much like *What the Golf* is not actually a game about golf (to call back to a statement from one of the game's developers discussed in chapter 1), *Goat Simulator* is not actually a game about a goat. Instead, it is an alternate gravity simulator in which you happen to play as a goat.

The second key implication of *Goat Simulator*'s gravity system that I want to underscore is this: in addition to making the game's physics floaty, it makes the game's physics *variable*. The laws of physics—and I am thinking for a moment about the science of physics rather than game physics—are described as laws because they are understood as immutable. Their effects may shift under different conditions, but their fundamental logics remain the same. Certainly, there are aspects of physics that physicists currently conceive of as messy and uncertain in their own right, defying human expectations for how the operations of the material world should function.[34] However, gravity (and along with it the speed of light, for what it's worth), we laymen are told, is supposed to be the one true constant: an "inexorable force" that can be diligently measured and calculated, if not explained.[35] Newton's universal law of gravitation, astrophysicist Becky Smethurst explains, "states that every single particle in the Universe attracts every other particle with a force that depends on how massive each one is, and dissipates as they get further away from each other."[36] Gravity, then, is a universal constant, *the* universal constant, that gives shape to the physical world around us at a macro level, a micro level, and every level in between.

Goat Simulator, as a model for how physics might operate otherwise, does not only change the way that gravity functions (making goats floatier than they are supposed to be). It also changes the constancy of gravity. By toggling between floaty and firm gravitational pulls, changing the laws of gravity for the goat in different situations, the game destabilizes the basic premise that gravity is absolute. By extension, *Goat Simulator* forces us to reconsider the very presumption that the laws of the universe are in fact laws; instead, they become mere suggestions, or perhaps incomplete descriptors that fail to capture the multifaceted, contradictory fullness of what it means to exist in the material world. In this way, the game's physics system challenges us to ponder the existence of alternate worlds where our most fundamental physical laws might apply themselves in stops and starts, in fits and bursts, attracting a body to the Earth or letting it float at will. What might it look like to live in a world that had no physical laws or material absolutes, only capricious whims and physical possibilities?

And this is where, I believe, we can locate the queerness of *Goat Simulator*'s physics and its lesson for the larger project of queer worldbuilding. Admittedly, there are many elements of the game apart from its physics that we might read as queer. Thematically, *Goat Simulator* shares a premise with *Untitled Goose Game* (House House, 2019), another video game in which a seemingly harmless animal turns a human town upside down. *Untitled Goose Game* has itself resonated with queer and trans players. As Ana Valens argues, it gives voice to a desire to mess with the tidy status quo of normative society.[37] The goat too could be seen as a queer figure. For instance, Phillips, as part of their discussion of queer physics games, describes goats as an "unsubtle symbol of . . . voracious sexuality."[38]

However, these queer valences of *Goat Simulator* are dwarfed in scope by the sheer queer implications of the game's physics system and, in particular, its construction of gravity. The way that we (scientifically and culturally) conceptualize gravity is inextricable from the way that we conceptualize sexuality and gender. This is because, as mentioned earlier, gravity is understood fundamentally as a force of *attraction*. Physicists Brian Cox and Jeff Forshaw conclude their description of gravity this way: "It only attracts, and in the absence of any stronger counteracting forces, it attracts without limit."[39] Gravity, then, describes what we might otherwise call a boundless expression of desire. In attracting "without limit," it manifests a kind of ravenous, unstoppable yearning for one body with mass to be close to another body with mass. This yearning, which compels matter to eternally long for other matter, is itself already queer. It does not discriminate between bodies, dictating that it is "right" or "natural" for only some bodies to be attracted to other bodies. Gravity is, instead, an indiscriminate, pansexual, polyamorous, polymorphously perverse force that quite literally holds the world together (without gravity, planets themselves would never have formed from the debris of the big bang) by charging our universe with an attraction that extends in all directions. Gravity is the deep, material, *weighty* longing that connects us to the world, that stops us from floating out into space, that prevents us from coming apart at the seams—as a planet, as a society, or as a community—by imbuing us with the unshakable desire to come together.

Goat Simulator, through its physics system, presents a version of this attractive force that is notably queer. In embracing floaty controls rather than trying to optimize for tightness, the game abandons dominant, heterosexual, masculinist, and implicitly sexualized ideals of video game mastery in favor of a feeling of airiness and an erotically tinged relinquishing of control. Because this gravity is also in flux, it also refutes the expectation that attraction should be consistent, predictable, or neatly categorizable by some set of limited, heteronormative metrics. In this way, the operations of gravity found in *Goat Simulator* resonate strongly with experiences of queer sexuality and identity. Of course, being queer does not simply mean that we desire (or love or form intimacy with) people of the same sex. But, additionally, being queer does not necessarily even mean that we consistently desire the same types of people or the same types of sex over the course of our lives. Queer people know that our lived experiences of sexual and intimate attraction, like the gravity in *Goat Simulator*, are variable and ever changing. To echo Sara Ahmed's writing on the "deviant" paths of queer lives, discussed in chapter 6, the trajectories of our longings rarely proceed along straight lines. We may understand our sexual orientations differently at different times. We may understand our gender identities differently as well. We may find ourselves, at certain moments, drawn to particular relationship styles or particular kinks or particular sexual subcultures. These desires, like the gravity in *Goat Simulator*, are likely to change as our position changes in the world.

The gravity in *Goat Simulator* also holds one last queer twist. In what may seem like a paradoxical move, the game's floaty physics actually suggest that, sometimes, the force of attraction between bodies becomes *weaker*. Typically, we equate gravity with weightiness, whether physical (entities that weigh more are more strongly affected by gravity) or conceptual (consider the semantic connection between "gravity" and "gravitas," which describes a weighty seriousness and solemnity).[40] However, by contrast, the physics systems that regulate gravity in *Goat Simulator* are notable, in part, because they often make the goat *light* rather than heavy. For the goat to float, the Earth must relinquish some of its gravitational pull. This represents what we might describe as a weakening of desire. Alternatively, we might say, the goat becomes less receptive to the Earth's longing. Thus, *Goat Simulator* offers us a model for reimagining physics that leaves room for forms of queer sexuality such as asexuality and demisexuality, which themselves productively question what we commonly misconstrue as universal experiences of queer desire.[41] Across these interpretations, the queer physics of *Goat Simulator* serve as a playful yet stirring provocation. What if, in our world too, we could release ourselves from the seemingly unquestionable truths of our material reality? What if we could reconfigure the operations of attraction that not only hold us together but also hold us down?

The Queer Physics of the Wobble in *Wobbledogs*

Just as there are many ways to experience queer desire, there are many ways to envision a world formed around queer physics. A second model for queer worldbuilding through game physics can be found in *Wobbledogs*, a video game that shifts us from one strange animal (the floaty goat of *Goat Simulator*) to another. *Wobbledogs* was developed by game designer and programmer Tom Astle and released in 2021, initially for PC and soon after for Nintendo Switch. *Wobbledogs* describes itself, in pop-up text that introduces players to the game, as "a sandbox game where you can raise your own little hive of mutated pups." Indeed, the focus of gameplay lies in creating, caring for, and ultimately breeding a cast of strange "dogs": creatures with blocky bodies, rickety legs, and

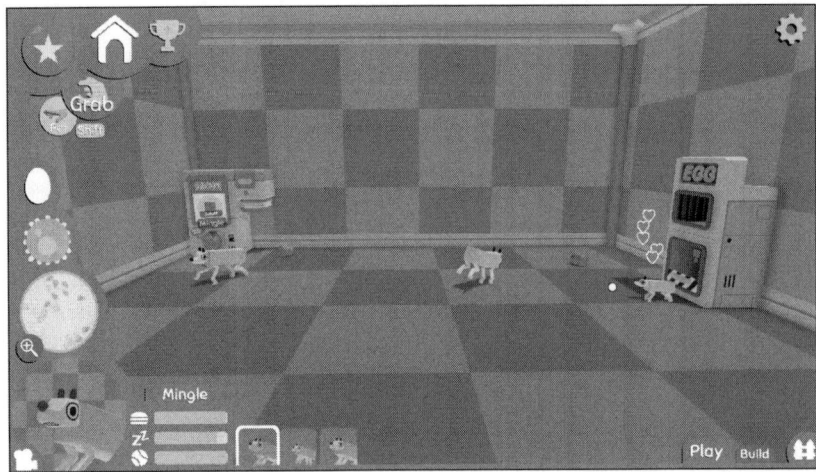

Figure 3.6. A set of blocky, pink and blue dogs wobble around in search of food in *Wobbledogs*. (Screenshot by author)

vaguely dog-like facial features. These dogs live their lives wandering around a brightly colored room (or set of rooms) where they merrily eat, sleep, and defecate (figure 3.6). Here, they wander about with their characteristic wobble, a rubbery flex that torques their torsos and makes their legs wiggle. Because the bulk of their bodies is made up of a seemingly gelatinous pink rectangle (at least until the player morphs their appearance in later dog generations), the dogs also recall squares of rose-water Turkish delight come to life. Technically, their wobbliness has no effect on gameplay. No matter how much the dogs in the player's care flop and undulate, their tasks remain the same: give the dogs food, reward them for good behavior, and make sure they stay entertained. Nonetheless, this wobble, which is generated in real time by the game's tailored physics system, is central to the game.

Wobbledogs may, at first glance, appear to resemble other pet simulators, such as *Nintendogs* (Nintendo, 2005), which scholars have largely analyzed through questions of virtual companionship between humans and digital pets.[42] However, as quickly becomes clear to the player, *Wobbledogs* is not so much a game about pet care as it is a game about pet *reproduction*. *Wobbledogs* itself seems well aware that it probably does not meet the player's initial expectations for a game about dogs. The game opens with a cheeky bait-and-switch. When the player first loads *Wobbledogs*, they are met with the sight of an empty "pen": a room bounded on four sides (three walls and a floor) that resembles a children's play area and floats in a nondescript, sunny ether. More pop-up text boxes welcome the player. "First," they read, "let's go ahead and get you a dog to play with!" In the pen, a hovering cloud bursts into a confetti-like poof, and out pops the very first dog: the magenta rectangle-creature with ungainly blue legs described earlier, to whom the game automatically gives the name "Mingle."[43] Mingle hits the ground with the game's characteristic wobble, flopping over onto the floor, his limbs wriggling as a stream of pink hearts float up from his body. Mingle, it seems, is destined to live up to his name. He is single (a lone dog in an empty pen) and ready to mingle (full of pulsating energy and oozing with love). This should perhaps be our first clue that *Wobbledogs* is more a dating simulator than a pet simulator—a matchmaking game for dogs in which romance quite literally floats through the air.

For a few brief moments, in this opening sequence, it seems that *Wobbledogs* will offer us the chance to interact with this dog, as ungainly and strange as he may be, in a relatively normal way. We are prompted to equip the pen with a food dispenser, which initially pumps out nondescript pellets, and encourage Mingle to eat. However, as soon as Mingle chomps down on his first puppy treats, the text box pops up again and proclaims, "Oh! Looks like your dog's ready to pupate." Excuse me, my dog is ready to *what*? The player is now prompted to select "pupate" from a wheel of possible commands. Doing so encloses Mingle in a large, green pupa clearly designed to resemble the pupa of a caterpillar who is preparing to turn into a butterfly. The pupa is then hoisted up to hang in midair. A moment later, the player is given the chance to "hatch" the pupa. When they do, the pupa cracks open, green goo rains from the cracked shell, and down falls Mingle. This pupa mechanic is one way that *Wobbledogs* enact mutations, which rearrange the DNA of dogs in gradual increments so that these dogs (or, rather, their offspring) can change in color, body length, leg count, and other physical features. Mingle, for his part, looks more or less the same after he has been hatched, with only subtle tweaks to characteristics like his ear

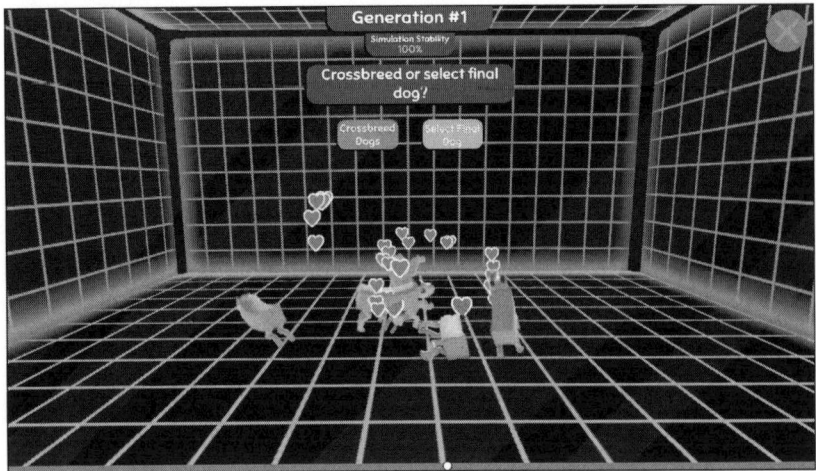

Figure 3.7. In *Wobbledogs*' breeding simulation, players pick two dogs to crossbreed, resulting in a litter of puppies. (Screenshot by author)

color and leg length. Still, it is hard to shake the feeling that he has become something *other*: no longer a simple dog to care for but instead an unknowable, unstable creature, an adorable alien puttering around in (what might just as well be) your living room.

Soon after, we learn that the dogs in *Wobbledogs* also mutate through a second, even more unexpected process. Unfertilized "dog eggs" occasionally appear in the pen. Players are instructed to pick them up and "fertilize" them before placing them in the incubator—a piece of equipment that looks like a cross between a vending machine and Fisher-Price microwave—where they will hatch. To fertilize the eggs, however, players must use the "breeding simulation" system, which injects the eggs with a new, slightly scrambled set of dog genes. Once additional dogs have appeared in the pen, players can select any two dogs to crossbreed in this manner; the dogs are not designated as male or female, so they can be paired without consideration for biological sex. Each breeding session results in a litter of crossbred dogs, who burst onto the screen and flop down on the ground in a wriggling puddle (figure 3.7). From this group, the player selects either a "final dog" to bring back to the pen or two dogs to crossbreed again, rerolling the genetic dice. The breeding simulation portion of *Wobbledogs* takes place in an empty black room crisscrossed by a green, glowing grid, conjuring up the aesthetics of the computer command-line terminal. Don't worry, the game seems to say, this isn't an incestuous puppy mill; it's just a machine for running the genetic numbers.

Once the player does select the official "resultant dog" (the game's own phrase) that they want to bring back to the pen, the breeding process takes an even more dramatic turn. Now, a cinematic cutscene plays, set in a strange white void. Suddenly, the ground begins to shake, and an enormous robot dog with a long, gold tongue and hearts for eyes rises ominously from the floor. The dog lifts up his metallic arms. Resting in his broad, spatula-like paws are the two original wobbledogs from which this new wobbledog will be bred (figure 3.8). Spinning his mechanical, antennae-ears in wild circles, the statue smashes the two dogs together frantically and repeatedly, crushing them until hearts pour out of their torsos and onto a nearby hovering egg. As the dogs' bodies crash together, they make a sound like the high-pitched yelp of a squeaky toy caught in the jaws of a household pet. Abruptly, the cutscene ends, the game chirps with an upbeat notification chime, and the text that scrolls across the screen proclaims cheerfully, "Fertilized egg acquired!" This egg can now be incubated. Once hatched, it will produce a dog that can join the rest of the dogs in the pen: one more member of the multigenerational mutant family.

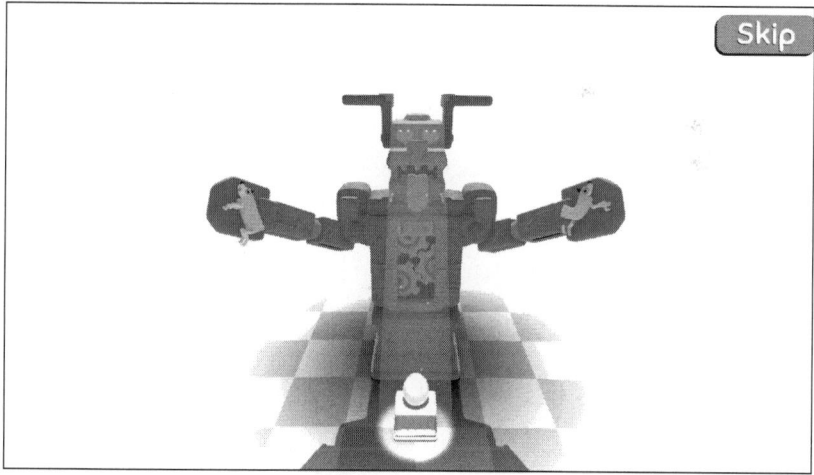

Figure 3.8. In a cutscene from *Wobbledogs*, two dogs are smashed together by a giant metal dog to "fertilize" an awaiting egg and create a new dog. (Screenshot by author)

Though the game does have other mechanics and small-scale objectives (like decorating and expanding the dogs' living space), going through iteration after iteration of this dog-breeding process represents the bulk of *Wobbledogs*' gameplay. The game has no clear endpoint. Accordingly, players who engage with the game for an extended period seem to focus almost exclusively on the creation of stranger and stranger dogs. This is made evident, for example, through the many Twitch streamers and YouTubers who have produced *Wobbledogs* gameplay videos that showcase their own bizarre dog creations or dogs created by their viewers.[44] Here is one with cow spots; here is one with bat wings; here is one with an itty-bitty body and dozens of legs. Many of these "dogs" stopped being dogs long ago, bringing into question the very ontological boundaries that make a dog a dog—or, really, that makes anything anything—in the first place. After all, the game seems to say, what even is a dog? This facet of *Wobbledogs*, in which players push to create increasingly mutated dogs, also gestures toward the erotic and queer valences of the game. We can see in *Wobbledogs* a family resemblance to both a creature-creator game like *Spore* (Maxis, 2008), which players notoriously used to make penis-animals, as well as player experiments like those seen in the Monster Factory video series, which featured bizarre creatures created by pushing character customization systems to their limits.[45]

As perhaps has already become obvious, the breeding system itself represents a notable queer component of *Wobbledogs*. The system entails an explicit reimagining of the operations of reproduction and, by extension, sex and sexuality. In presenting us with dogs that pupate and hatch and robots that fertilize eggs (not to mention appliances for incubating those eggs that look like they should be dispensing cigarettes in the back of a roadside diner), the game uses reproduction to intentionally blur the divisions between mammals, insects, birds, reptiles, and machines. Thus, *Wobbledogs* makes the supposedly "natural" functions of the natural world unnatural, producing offspring from forms of sexual reproduction that (much like queer and trans people's own reproductive practices, as viewed by cisheteronormativity) seem unfathomable and even impossible. Much like Nina Freeman's video game *How Do You Do It?* (2014), in which players smash two dolls together in an attempt to make sense of heterosexual sex, *Wobbledogs* raises the question of how reproduction works largely to propose the idea that reproduction may already be fundamentally bizarre.[46] Simultaneously, by creating a system of reproduction that transgresses divides between entities who supposedly should not reproduce, the game resonates with queer readings of interracial procreative sex, which entails what critical race scholar Brigitte Fiedler describes as a queer "mixed-race begetting."[47] Representing reproduction in this way also places *Wobbledogs* alongside the many science-fictional works of literature and film that imagine futures in which humans reproduce through currently nonnormative means.[48] By extension, it proposes a world in which the mechanics of reproduction are no longer constrained by divisions between species or biological sexes. At the same time, this imagined world is far from idyllic. In *Wobbledogs*, reproduction may be queer, but it is also violent, mechanical, and largely indifferent to the value of individual (puppy) lives.

As tempting as it may be to locate *Wobbledogs'* queerness squarely in its depiction of reproduction, however, my point here is actually to insist on the critical importance of a very different aspect of the game for identifying its queer meaning: the physics of its titular *wobble*. Across all possible mutations and permutations, the dogs of *Wobbledogs* maintain their signature physical quality, that alluring bounce—simultaneously charming and disconcerting. In the following section, drawing from Astle's own step-by-step accounts of the game's development, I talk in more detail about the physics operations behind this wobble. First, though, let us consider the wobble not as a set of behind-the-scenes technical decisions but as a visual and affective phenomenon encountered by the player.

Much as we theorized the physics of floatiness in *Goat Simulator*, we can theorize the wobble. Both floaty physics and wobbly physics describe alternative systems of movement. Yet, whereas *Goat Simulator* shows us a world in which bodies move differently in relation to one another (yanked more or less tightly together by the attraction of gravity), *Wobbledogs* shows us a world in which bodies move differently in relation to *themselves*. The wobble calls to mind many associations at once. It seems, on its surface, strikingly similar to the simulated "jiggle" of breast physics. Yet the wobble found in *Wobbledogs* clearly does not cater to any standard vision of heterosexual male pleasure. Rather than pandering to a normative erotic gaze, the wobble conjures up a feeling that is equal parts intrigue and repulsion. When the dogs of *Wobbledogs* wobble across the screen, their gelatinous bodies recall, rather than the bounce of digitally rendered breasts, the alarming animacy of a substance like Jell-O: a transparent goo that seems utterly thing-like until disturbed by the slightest movement, and then it wiggles itself to life. In this sense, the wobble stands at the intersection of object and subject, life and death, a manifestation in moving form of the racialized boundary crossing between inanimate and animate matter described by scholars like Mel Chen.[49] Bodies that wobble both are and are not hard. They seem, in a sense, to manifest the kind of queer softness that Phillips describes in their discussion of flaccid dicks or, perhaps, to embrace the soft, wiggling motions of fat—that is, to refuse the fatphobic idealization of rigid, unyielding bodies characterized by thinness and muscle, which historian Sabrina Strings has linked directly to lineages of anti-Blackness.[50]

Yet, in truth, as we see in the flouncing bodies of the dogs in *Wobbledogs*, the wobble stands *between* the hard and the soft. I have referred to these bodies as moving like non-Newtonian fluids. Such fluids inhabit a state that alternates between solid and liquid under changing conditions.[51] In this sense, the wobble is not just a queer form of embodied movement, in that it scrambles dominant logics of attraction and desire, but more precisely a nonbinary form of movement. The wobbling body is neither entirely firm nor entirely pliant; it has the propensity to contort itself when put under pressure but also the propensity to bounce back. By extension, the physics of the wobble are a nonbinary physics. They celebrate the contradictory multiplicities of the body and its relationship to the world. And *Wobbledogs* is a game dominated precisely by these wobbly, nonbinary physics. For all the dog care and dog breeding that the player may choose to pour their time into, what takes center stage in the affective experience of playing *Wobbledogs*—the thing that is the most captivating and therefore *affecting*—is the jaunty, unruly, uneasy wobble of the dogs themselves.

Wobble Physics as Worldbuilder

Thus far, I have talked about how the physics of *Wobbledogs* enact worldbuilding by suggesting a world rooted in queer movement. However, I want to pivot and spend the rest of this chapter taking a more concrete approach to discussing the worldbuilding influence of physics on video games. Specifically, I move from *Wobbledogs* as a product—the published video game that can now be played—to a development process. To do this, I draw from materials that Astle published online about his work designing *Wobbledogs*, in the form of forum posts, videos, and GIFs. My key source is the *Wobbledogs* devlog forum thread hosted on TIGSource, a site dedicated to independent video games, as part of its TIGForums section.[52] These devlog threads, of which there are thousands on TIGForums, are places where game creators can post ongoing updates about the development of their new games. Readers of the forum can follow along with these updates and post their own replies.

The *Wobbledogs* devlog stands out among these threads for being particularly extensive, descriptive, and frank about the challenges of the development process. Astle began the thread on February 22, 2016; he then posted relatively consistent updates for five years, adding his last comment to the thread in January 2021, when *Wobbledogs* first became available on the distribution platform Steam. The thread itself spans thirty-seven forum pages, most of which contain multiple posts from Astle as well as dozens of replies from readers. Across this period, especially in the early years of development, Astle regularly posted detailed notes explaining incremental steps in his design and programming of the game (which he completed, for most of the development process, nearly single-handedly), carefully illustrating many of his posts with animated GIFs of his in-progress work (figure 3.9). These bite-sized, looping animations were often presented specifically to capture his experiments with the game's physics system, commonly with a focus on different approaches to setting the dogs' bodies into motion. In some such GIFs, we see Astle iterating on ways for the dogs to walk; in others, we see him tweaking the dogs' bodily proportions or the flex of their joints. Thus, these GIFs and the written posts that they accompany serve as a record of the evolution of both *Wobbledogs* itself and the particular world that it creates through its wobble.

From the start, the *Wobbledogs* devlog thread makes it clear that physics, above all other development considerations, drove the initial creation of *Wobbledogs*. In Astle's very first post from 2016, he writes, "I've been working on this game for just a little under a month now.

Figure 3.9. GIFs created by Tom Astle and posted to the *Wobbledogs* devlog thread on TIGSource show the incremental steps of developing the dogs' movements. (Image printed with the permission of Tom Astle)

The core gameplay is still sort of fuzzy because I'm trying to let the tech drive the specifics and I'm not 100% sure what I'll be able to accomplish and what will be too difficult, but the main idea is that I want to make a monster raising game where you raise these little physics babies."[53] Right off the bat, then, we can see that Astle positions design ("the core gameplay") as a secondary concern; instead of creating software systems to support a specific design vision, he plans to decide on a design down the line, letting "tech drive the specifics." What Astle does seem to know, as far as the actual contents of the game are concerned, is that it should focus on "little physics babies." In early June 2016, after spending more than three months working on (the game that would become) *Wobbledogs* full-time, Astle writes, "I'm really happy with how things are coming along but the project's still way more a collection of tech than a game."[54] Time and again, over the course of these early years in devlog, we see Astle wrestle with how to wrangle this "collection of tech" into a compelling game with functional mechanics and a well-suited narrative skin. For much of the development process, these other elements remain uncertain. Yet the fundamental drive to play around with tech and produce those monstrous little physics babies (who doesn't want a game about physics babies?) stays strikingly consistent.

Every few months, as documented in the devlogs, Astle seems to have a design revelation. For a period, he tries to mold *Wobbledogs* into a dog-racing game. At other times, he plays around with making *Wobbledogs* a game about the economics of pet breeding or a game about raising dogs to star in television commercials. Only after years of self-reflective debate does Astle settle on a version of the game that looks largely as we see it today: a world where your primary purpose is to raise and breed spectacularly wobbly dogs. Indeed, based on Astle's posts, it seems fair to say that, ultimately, Astle's tech drove not only the "specifics" of the game (as he wrote in his first post) but almost the entirety of its design. Just as much as Astle himself, the tech that he developed ended up being an integral cocreator of the world of *Wobbledogs*.

And the vast majority of that tech development, as more than three dozen pages of forum posts attest, seems to have been focused specifically on the game's physics—even more precisely, on the physics of the game's wobbling dogs. In these posts, Astle describes how, by adapting PhysX, the physics engine that comes prepackaged with Unity, he was able to create his own tailored physics system for rendering the dogs' movement. What's more, rather than using premade animations for moving the dogs through the game's three-dimensional space (as would be much more common for a contemporary video game developed in Unity), he constructed the dogs' bodies out of separately configured body parts, like individual leg components connected with unique joints. This meant that Astle then had to develop an ever-evolving set of procedures for getting those body parts to move the dogs effectively across the play space. Since every dog body was composed of multiple parts, each of which functioned as its own physics object, Astle reports spending months of work simply getting his dogs to walk without falling on their faces. In this sense, the devlogs reveal, *Wobbledogs* is a physical world that has truly been built from the ground up. Nothing, not even the act of moving through space, can be taken as a given. Each element of the simulated world has been crafted purposefully, painstakingly, through trial and error.

Following along with Astle's process for building the dogs' physics is revealing, in part, because it pulls back the curtain on the operations of their characteristic wobble. On June 12, 2016, Astle responds to a post from a commentator asking whether Astle has considered using softbody physics for the dogs. Since PhysX itself is a rigid-body system, Astle explains, he cannot simply switch over to softbody physics; instead, he needs to find a "custom solution" to accomplish softbody effects, which will make the bodies of the dogs appear squishy and deformable.[55] Astle's solution, as he describes it, is to think about the torso of each dog not as one physics object but two: a set of "body cubes," each of which can move separately, attached by a hinge at the center. Eventually, as the posts go on, Astle puts mesh renders over the cubes, making them look like one continuous, floppy rectangle (meshes are graphical skins that overlay a digital object's underlying physical structure). However, in Astle's earliest prototypes, we can clearly see the two cubes bobbing about side by side on each dog's body. Even once Astle has gotten his dogs to walk (and jump and eat and sleep), he reports constantly tweaking his physics system to make the dogs' materiality feel *right*. In March 2017 and again in June 2017 and then once more in November 2018, he alters the operations of gravity in the game so that the dogs (in contrast to *Goat Simulator*'s goat) do not feel too floaty. In a November 2018 video titled "Wobbledogs Dogtech Deep Dive," Astle explains that he accidentally made the dogs larger than intended when he first built the game, which in turn made the dogs appear as if they fell too slowly toward the ground. To counteract this, says Astle, "what I did is I have the world's gravity running at three times the normal scale." In *Wobbledogs*, then, even the functions of gravity have been explicitly engineered to guarantee that the dogs maintain their all-important wobble.

Importantly, these devlog posts also reveal that the dogs' physics actively shaped many elements of the *Wobbledogs* world. Sometimes, Astle and his custom physics system seem to have functioned like good-natured collaborators, with the physics system sparking new ideas for other aspects of the game. In a June 29, 2016, post, for instance, Astle describes experimenting with a system for simulating muscle physics that would help control the torque on the dogs' individual limbs.[56] To test out the system, Astle creates the upper body (head, shoulders, arms) of a giant dog, with limbs controlled by springy wires strung between red balls representing connection points (figure 3.10). He then attaches a smaller dog to each of the large dog's arms and, using the push and pull of the new muscle system, has the large dog smash the smaller dogs together. "As one last bit of goofing around," he writes, in describing

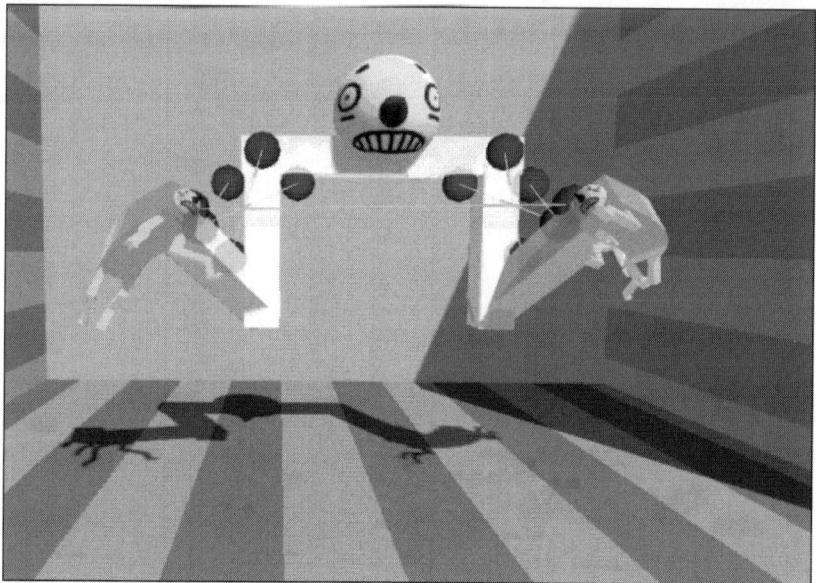

Figure 3.10. A GIF shows how Astle created a muscle physics simulator that inspired the egg-fertilization cutscene. (Image printed with the permission of Tom Astle)

the test, Astle adds a particle effect that makes bursts of hearts explode outward when the two smaller dogs smack together. Reflecting on his "goofy" giant dog prototype, Astle writes, "I'm kinda seriously considering this as a breeding mechanic. I really like the visual metaphor of having the player smash the dogs together like dolls." It's in this moment, then, that we find the origin for the queerly bizarre cutscene of egg fertilization that will later become such a striking feature of the official game. The image of a robot dog smushing together two regular dogs so that they can make babies was, it turns out, not born from some particular idea about the fictional world of *Wobbledogs* or the vision of reproduction that the game sought to represent. Instead, it was born from playing around with physics and, by extension, letting physics dictate the game's (queer) representation of reproduction.

At other moments, the devlogs suggest that the physics system that Astle created, rather than acting as a collaborator, forcibly took over as *Wobbledogs*' primary worldbuilder. On multiple occasions, Astle notes that he is aware, based on feedback from forum readers and playtesters, that the game's "charm" lies in its "goofy physics."⁵⁷ Even as he cycles through different ideas for the game's design, some of which he seems genuinely excited about, he almost begrudgingly acknowledges that the dogs themselves are the real "stars" of the show. Still, he often seems struck by just how strongly viewers and players react to the sight of the wobbly dogs in motion. In a post from September 17, 2018, Astle reflects on his take-aways from bringing a demo of the game to the XOXO Festival. First among these take-aways, he lists, "People loved the graphics. This surprised me but I had a lot of people specifically tell me they hoped I wouldn't change the style."⁵⁸

We can see the sheer force of this goofy charm in a video recording of Astle presenting a June 2017 talk to the indie game collective Glitch City in Los Angeles. Technically, Astle's presentation is supposed to be about how he programmed *Wobbledogs*' genetic algorithm, which determines how dog genes are selected during the breeding and mutation processes.⁵⁹ However, his crowd of listeners has different plans. As seen in the video, Astle has loaded a number of his slides with his signature work-in-progress GIFs, which show the dogs attempting to move forward in variously unsuccessful ways. Each time Astle advances his slides and a new GIF appears, the crowd bursts out laughing—overcome with the sight of dogs accidentally breaking out into a twitchy jig or dragging themselves across the floor on their faces. At one moment, attendees respond with such uproarious glee to a GIF that Astle literally has to shout in an attempt to finish his point about the technical operations of his algorithm. What people want from *Wobbledogs*, it turns out, is not complicated genetic systems. What they want is to bask in the game's strange physics.

There are even moments reflected in the devlogs when Astle himself seems bowled over by the pleasures of witnessing his physics system at work. On August 1, 2016, in a post about combining the dogs' bodies with different tail meshes, Astle includes a GIF of a dog with a long body and an oversized tail that is covered in a mesh of shiny gold. In the GIF, Astle picks up the dog and spins him around in the air, showing off how his gold coloring catches the in-game light. "As always, it's hard not to get caught up with playing around sometimes," Astle writes. "For example, I found this beautiful boy and had to watch him shimmer for a bit." When Astle releases the dog, the dog tumbles to the ground and topples over onto his side. Weighed down by his immense tail, the dog attempts to climb back up onto his buckling, spindly legs; he tries once, twice, three times before finally righting himself. Here Astle reflects, in a moment of uncharacteristic sentimentality, "I [find] myself inspired by these dogs' optimism in the face of adversity."[60]

Ultimately, Astle abandons almost all of his ongoing attempts to steer the design and narrative elements of *Wobbledogs* in new directions. Instead, the physics system is given nearly full rein to decide the shape of the game. This shift plays out in the devlogs over roughly two years. On August 17, 2016, still early in the development process, Astle writes a post about the kind of story he wants to tell through *Wobbledogs*. He insists, "It's very important to me that this game has context and an actual internal world."[61] Across September of that year, we see Astle hard at work building maps for the game, brainstorming heuristics that explain the players' actions, and creating various non-player characters (NPCs) for players to meet as they progress—all traditional staples of video game worldbuilding. Yet, by October 2016, Astle has already begun to unbuild the world he has been busy building. "Done a lot of thinking and I've decided that the best thing for the game is going to be for me to double down on the pen gameplay and cut out everything else," he writes somberly. "The NPCs and the external world are gone."[62] By October 2018, Astle finally seems to throw up his hands and cede creative defeat to his game's physics system. He writes, "Wobbledogs is a pet simulation game. It was always meant to be a pet simulation game. It's going to be somewhat sandbox-y, it's going to be somewhat self-directed, and it's gonna be chock full of the dogs you so desperately crave."[63]

In tracing Astle's process, then, we see a worldbuilding saga unfold. His posts, taken as a whole, tell a story about how the world of *Wobbledogs* was forged through a sort of multiyear wrestling match between a game creator and his physics system—or perhaps, more accurately, between a game creator and the charm of the "physics babies" that his system brought to life. In the end, the wobble wins out. The finalized version of the game that Astle releases to the public three years later fits the description of the game from his October 2018 post almost exactly: it is a self-directed, pet simulation sandbox game chock full, so to speak, of the wobbling dogs that we do indeed so desperately crave. These dogs offer, to circle back for a moment to the concept of gravity, a sort of center of gravity for the game. They create a focal point around which the game turns and make the game relatable, despite its absurdism. We as players are (most likely) not wobbly dogs ourselves, nor have we ever (most likely) encountered wobbly dogs outside of the game. But, thanks to the game's physics, we feel materially connected to the dogs and their world. As we watch them, we cannot help but imagine what it would feel like to reach out and touch them as they wobble.

Like *Goat Simulator*, *Wobbledogs* serves as an illustrative example of how game physics systems—be they queer or otherwise—can serve as core factors in the work of building game worlds. Game physics systems reflect the values and beliefs of the developers who create them. Yet, these physics systems, once engineered and let loose to perform their simulations, also take on lives of their own; they have their own movements but also their own perspectives, desires, and drives. They set worlds in motion, and if that world is queer enough, chances are no amount of careful game design can tame it. In such cases, surface-level worldbuilding cannot keep the sheer disruptive force of a world's underlying physical operations contained. A queer physics always exceeds the bounds of storytelling, but it also exceeds the bounds of reason. A queer physics does not describe the workings of the world; it remakes the workings of the world. It shows us that we, like the floating goat or the wobbling dog, can refuse to accept the normative systems that attempt to dictate how our bodies move. It challenges us to find other ways of being within the material world.

4

Building Worlds through Graphical Depth

The Queer Dimensionality of 2.5D in OlliOlli World

To talk about dimensions is, by nature, to conjure up visions of other possible worlds. The term is heavy with science-fictional weight. Merely invoking the concept of dimensions simultaneously invokes speculative visions of *alternate dimensions*: parallel universes, invisible layers of reality, worlds simultaneously like and unlike our own. In the introduction to this book, I quoted the performance studies scholar Jayna Brown, who, in describing the power of Black alternative worldbuilding, writes that the violence and dehumanization of anti-Blackness situates Black people within a set of "bleak and bloody dimensions we are taught to call reality." In contrast, says Brown, Black worldbuilding, as enacted through art forms like fiction and music, rejects that bleak reality, instead working to build "alternative worlds, in this dimension and in others, and practice alternative ways of being alive."[1] I begin by invoking Brown once again because of her emphasis on the concept of "dimensions," which captures both a sense of the world we inhabit and the possibility that we could inhabit other worlds. It is this sense that worldbuilding and dimensionality go hand in hand—and that radically remaking the world requires pursuing alternatives "in this dimension and in others"—that I explore in this chapter. How might we build new worlds by shifting across dimensions, transforming the notion of alternative dimensions from a speculative fiction into a lived and livable reality?

Video games, it turns out once again, offer an exceptionally productive medium through which to contemplate these questions. In video games, we find alternate dimensions literalized. Certainly, one could envision each video game world as a kind of alternate dimension in the most overt sense, a different possible world that exists alongside our own. But I am talking here about dimensions in another, more literal form: the dimensions of video games as visual, graphic spaces. Most video games are either two-dimensional or three-dimensional—allowing players to move across a single flattened plane (up, down, left, right) or giving them access to an additional plane of depth. As we will see, some video games are (supposedly) four-dimensional, and a few are even one-dimensional. Video games can also occupy hybrid dimensions in between these standard dimensional perspectives. Like the systems of game physics discussed in chapter 3, the ways that video games construct their graphical dimensionality is far more than a mere technical concern. Each of these different dimensional modes serves to build game worlds in a different way, bringing the world into being through a specific mode of seeing and a particular experience of depth (or the lack thereof). Sometimes, the graphical dimensionality of a video game is predetermined by the norms of its genre; however, it is increasingly common to see game developers experiment with shifts in dimensionality across video games in the same franchise or series. Thus, for players, stepping into a new video game or toggling between games often entails stepping into a set of alternate—and *alternating*—dimensions: from 2D to 3D and sometimes even, as we will discuss in a moment, to something called 2.5D.

Granted, video games are not the only media form to operate across dimensions and thus to raise questions about visual dimensionality and worldbuilding. Animation and the generation of computer graphics more generally (from which video games draw heavily) can take on both two- and three-dimensional forms.[2] Cinema has a long history of offering three-dimensional, stereoscopic viewing, while movies screened in so-called 5D attempt to further enhance the viewer's experience by incorporating physical elements like vibrating chairs and water squirters into movie showings.[3] Yet video games remain unique in that they explicitly invite players to step inside their worlds and thereby participate in contrasting modes of dimensional existence. In this way, they transform the very concept of inhabitable alternate dimensions, shifting it from a vision of far-off universes filled with alien societies and concretizing it into an immediate technical reality. By presenting game worlds in varying forms of dimensionality—whether in 2D, 3D, or otherwise—video games offer players different ways of seeing and navigating the world and, by extension, as Brown writes, "alternative ways of being alive."

Here, as one approach to making sense of video game dimensionality and its worldbuilding potential, I focus on video games that operate within dimensions that seem unnatural or illogical and are therefore, as I argue, implicitly queer. These dimensions are truly *alternatives* to reality, in that they do not exist outside the realities of video games. In that way, they serve as the frameworks for creating worlds that could not exist within the inherent dimensional logics of our own—worlds that it would be challenging to even fathom if not for the fact that we can model and experience them through games. Video games offer us opportunities to question what we think we know about depth and how it shapes our world. Discussing *Monument Valley* (UsTwo Games, 2014), a puzzle game that tasks players with navigating M. C. Escher-esque paths through contorted, floating buildings, queer theorist Jack Halberstam describes the game's use of non-Euclidean geometry as producing a kind of "impossible architecture."[4] In *Monument Valley*, disconnected elements of a level that seem to be positioned on different planes of depth, when viewed from another perspective, suddenly connect. Distinctions between what is near, far, deep, and shallow collapse. Therefore, proceeding along logical paths through *Monument Valley* itself becomes impossible. Amid the disorientation of this queer geometry, one's own innate sense of spatial logic loses its meaning. The result, says Halberstam, is "a queer sense of time and space, and an immersion in alternative dimensions that exceed and confound one's expectations."[5]

In what follows, I take this suggestion that video games can create alternative queer dimensions through their engagement with perspective and depth as my starting point. To demonstrate how graphical dimensionality in video games can contribute to queer worldbuilding, I begin by overviewing some of the ways that video games build meaning through their use of space and perspective. I then chart the forms that dimensionality has taken across video games and game genres, with a focus on what is known as 2.5D. 2.5D video games combine features of two-dimensional and three-dimensional graphics, creating what I describe as a liminal, nonbinary, and inherently queer dimensionality. Through a close reading of the 2.5D skateboarding game *OlliOlli World* (Roll7, 2022), I demonstrate how 2.5D serves as a robust yet ambivalent tool for building video game worlds, and queer worlds in particular. As *OlliOlli World* illustrates, 2.5D simultaneously offers and refuses players entry into the depths of its worlds. By extension, *OlliOlli World* prompts us to come to terms with the fact that not all alternate worlds may be ours to enter.

Cultural Meaning in Video Space and Dimensionality

Dimensionality is a key component of how video games construct a sense of space. The approach that video games take to constructing space is itself a central facet of how they build worlds, as Soraya Murray articulates in her introduction to a special issue of *Art Journal* about representations of space and place in video games.[6] Video game spaces give in-game worlds their contours, boundaries, and geographies, but they also imbue game worlds with meaning. Rather than serving as "mere backdrop," as Murray writes, the simulated spaces of games prompt us to ask, "What can be made of these worlds? . . . What do they tell us about ourselves and the world we live in?"[7]

In video games, space takes a number of forms. In addition to the matter of dimensional perspective (whether a game is 2D, 3D, 2.5D, etc.), which I will return to shortly, video games create space through tools like the design of individual levels, the imagining of world maps, the rendering of backgrounds, the use of graphic textures, and the positioning of in-game cameras to create (or restrict) access to specific visual spaces. A growing body of scholarship also investigates intersections between video games and architecture, considering games within a broader "spatial turn" in cultural studies.[8] Such work approaches game worlds as both built environments—a term broadly used to encompass traditional architecture as well as other human-designed spaces—and, drawing from Henri Lefebvre, a set of "lived spaces."[9] Speaking from this architectural perspective, Gregory Whistance-Smith describes video games as "worlds [that] fundamentally offer places to be, ones which are now part of the everyday ensemble of spaces we inhabit."[10] This description of video games as "places to be" resonates with the idea of worldbuilding as finding "alternative ways of being alive," suggesting that video games are *spaces for being* in multiple ways—in the sense that player-characters might temporarily exist within these worlds and in the sense that players might experience alternate approaches to living by spending time inside them.

Prior to this recent turn, scholarship on game space has more commonly focused on *doing* rather than *being*. Much of this existing work has argued for the importance of navigability in conceptualizing game space: considerations of where and how players can move. Mark

J. P. Wolf writes in his essay "Theorizing Navigable Space in Video Games," "Space has always been an integral part of the video gaming experience.... Interaction within and with a space is the means by which space is best understood."[11] For Wolf, interactivity and navigability are critical because they speak to a player's degree of freedom—that is, the options that a game provides for how a player can proceed through the spatial terrain of a game. However, this freedom does not necessarily manifest itself in the same ways for all players. As Henry Jenkins points out in his essay "Complete Freedom of Movement: Video Games as Gendered Play Spaces," the kinds of spaces that video games invite players to explore have long been aligned with the norms of "boy culture," leaving the players of femme-coded games (or, as Jenkins refers to them, using a now outdated moniker, "girl games") cooped up in constrained domestic spaces, like digital depictions of the middle-class home.

Inverting this celebration of the freedom of movement that many game worlds seem to afford, game studies scholars like Oscar Moralde have demonstrated that video games can present powerful messages precisely by restricting a player's ability to move freely through the in-game environment.[12] Through a reading of the game *Dear Esther* (The Chinese Room, 2012), which presents a narrative told in pieces as the player wanders around a seemingly abandoned island, Moralde demonstrates how *Dear Esther* allows the landscape of the game to take control and tell its own story. This valuably suggests, as I will reiterate in discussing *OlliOlli World*, that we might see video game spaces as living entities in and of themselves: not places to visit (a form of digital tourism, calling back to Lisa Nakamura's concept of "identity tourism") or to set up camp within (echoing practices of settler colonialism) but worlds with their own desires that may invite us inside only on their own terms or may refuse us access altogether.[13] Alternatively, as Nathan Thompson describes in his sociological study of sexual play in *World of Warcraft* (Blizzard, 2004), players themselves might change the meaning of a game world by repurposing an in-game locale for their own nonnormative pleasures, enacting one possible mode of what Thompson terms "queering game space."[14]

Spaces in video games—and, by extension, the worlds that game space helps build—are never simply blank territories waiting for players to fill them with their own experiences. To the contrary, as Murray has demonstrated in her analysis of games like *Metal Gear Solid V: The Phantom Pain* (Kojima, 2015) and *Spec Ops: The Line* (2K Games, 2012), the spatial worlds that video games depict and the opportunities they offer players to act within them are intimately bound up with politics and power.[15] Though Murray's point can (and should) be applied widely to games, the specific objects of her critique are mainstream, militaristic video games that often situate explicitly or implicitly white player-characters in dangerous "foreign" lands. These games, writes Murray, use "landscape as a theatre for asserting dominion over space through the player's mastery of gameplay."[16] A similar set of imperialist spatial logics can be seen operating in a game like *No Man's Sky* (Hello Games, 2016), in which players act as space explorers, tasked with "discovering" and collecting specimens from an array of procedurally generated planets. With its constant push to reach new worlds, where players mine for resources and defend against hostile indigenous life forms, *No Man's Sky* clearly embodies what Andrew Reinhard calls, in his writing on the game, "a colonialist attitude towards space exploration."[17] Examples like these demonstrate how the use of space can shape not only a game world but also its worldview, turning play into an act of Western expansion that aims to overtake supposedly uncivilized or undiscovered worlds.

In identifying the cultural meaning of game spaces, we could turn equally to consider the spaces that form *around* games. Not only do video games create bounded spaces that exist within the confines of the play space; they also spark the creation of social spaces built by players and others invested in a game's reception out in the "real world." As I mentioned in the introduction, it is in these second-tier spaces that tensions around race, gender, and sexual identity in gaming culture often make themselves most visible. This has been demonstrated in scholarship by Kishonna Gray on Black lesbian gamers' experiences on Xbox Live, Carly Kocurek on the gendered history of game arcades, Michael DeAnda on drag bingo, and Akil Fletcher on Black players in esports leagues, among many other examples.[18] Some of these community spaces form around physical locations like gaming conventions or bars, while others take shape online. Such spaces are commonly characterized by who can and cannot enter them, who is and is not made to feel welcome within them, what forms of identity are deemed to have a place within these spaces, and which identities are expected to remain elsewhere, in their own separate space.

Yet there is also another critical element of video game space whose cultural implications have gone less frequently addressed. And that, as I mentioned earlier, is dimensionality. As I have said, every video game uses some form of dimensionality to depict its in-game space—whether players are presented with a world that appears flat (i.e., two-dimensional), deep (i.e., three-dimensional), or otherwise. This dimensionality can vary greatly across genres, historical moments, and individual games. Let me illustrate these differences by comparing games from the *Super Mario Bros.* series, since nearly all forms of video game dimensionality have made an appearance in the series at some point in its now roughly forty-year run.

Before the mid-1990s, most video games were two-dimensional, even when they attempted to depict multiple fields of depth. Such games typically represented the play space using either a top-down or side-facing perspective, as we see in the side-scrolling platformer *Super Mario Bros. 2* (Nintendo, 1988) (figure 4.1). In such games, space appears flattened, presenting the game world on one spatial plane—like a scientific cross-section of the Earth's surface or an ant colony behind glass. In the mid-1990s, landmark games like *Super Mario 64* (Nintendo, 1996) marked the beginning of the rise of three-dimensional video games, which allowed the player to move through the game world—either from a first-person or third-person perspective—along additional spatial axes (figure 4.2). Over time, three-dimensional game worlds became the standard for prominent genres like action-adventure games, shooters, and online multiplayer games. While the dominant norms of dimensionality in video games (2D vs. 3D) were largely established by the end of the 1990s, game companies have continued to experiment with additional approaches to representing dimensions. In *Super Mario Galaxy* (Nintendo, 2007), for example, gameplay takes place largely on the surface of spherical planets, adding a new spin on the experience of playing in 3D. More recently, a trend toward augmented reality and virtual reality games has introduced supplemental forms of dimensionality to gameplay, situating players within game worlds that extend outward around their bodies in what is often referred to in marketing materials as four-dimensional space.[19]

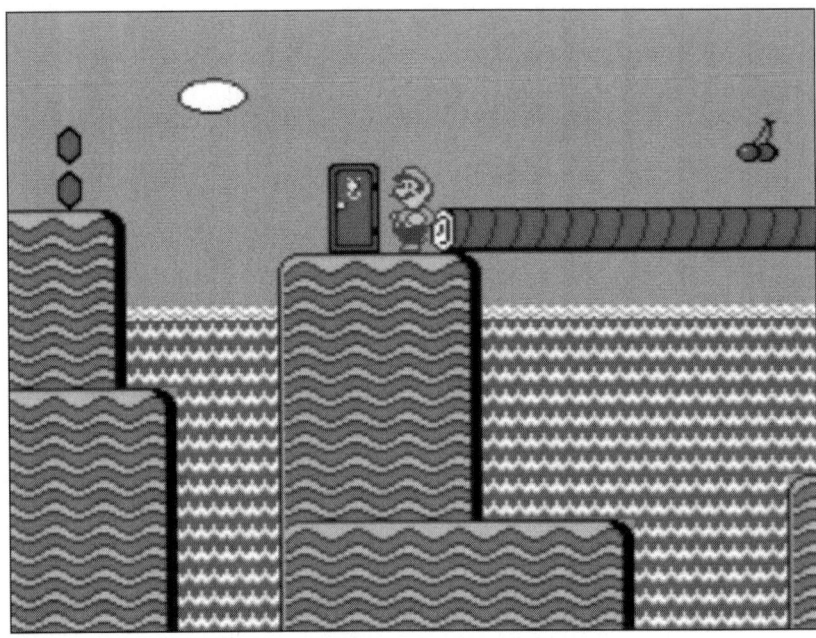

Figure 4.1. The game world is represented two-dimensionally in the 1988 side-scroller *Super Mario Bros. 2*. (Screenshot by author)

Figure 4.2. Mario heads off into his newly three-dimensional world in *Super Mario 64*. (Screenshot by author)

This progression from 2D to 3D (and now to 4D) has been described by some game studies scholars as an "evolutionary process," evidence of an "overall transformation" from the more rudimentary graphical worlds of two-dimensional games to the more complex technical capabilities of three-dimensional games and, eventually, beyond.[20] Hand in hand with this teleological narrative about technological progress has come an assumption that video games have become more *immersive* as they advance in their dimensionality, creating game worlds with increased depth into which players can more fully submerge themselves. (Immersion itself is a game-design value that has been rightly critiqued by cultural studies scholars.)[21] Yet, in truth, the relationship between video games and dimensionality is far more complicated—and far more interesting—than this narrative would suggest. The rise of 3D game development technologies did not, in fact, supersede 2D games. Many 2D game genres, including side-scrolling platformers, continue to be released in droves today. The hype around virtual reality in the late 2010s and early 2020s merely recycled rhetoric from an earlier virtual reality craze in the 1990s.[22] And long before the popularization of augmented reality features on smart phones, Nintendo introduced stereoscopic, augmented-reality-esque game content in 2011 with the release of its handheld console the 3DS. By contrast, what we might describe as the first one-dimensional game (*Line Wobbler*, Robin Baumgarten), a dungeon-crawler played along a single strand of LED lights, was not developed until 2015.

This history demonstrates that dimensionality, far from being a mere matter of linear technological progress, offers a richer and at times productively contradictory set of tools for building video game worlds. The many stops, starts, hiccups, dead ends, and loop-arounds in this history also suggest that the so-called evolution of video game dimensions is in fact a computational poster child for the very kinds of nonlinear queer temporality discussed in chapter 2. In video games today, we find a proliferation of approaches to dimensionality that together model the simultaneous coexistence of multiple alternative dimensions. Thus, video games show us that making the leap across dimensions—in at least one sense—is already within our grasp, as long as we are prepared to abandon the notion that there is one right way for the world to be and one right perspective from which to experience it. Video games remind us that dimensionality is a system for envisioning the world, one that offers and describes a specific perspectival angle on the world. A world viewed from one angle appears flat, simple, reducible. That same world viewed from another angle takes on additional dimensional form, revealing the complexities of its geometries and by extension taking on new meaning.

Video Games in 2.5D

No form of video game dimensionality defies normative views on the world more than 2.5D. 2.5D borrows elements from both 2D and 3D dimensionality. The playable space in 2.5D games is typically viewed from the side (though not in all cases), in the style of a side-scrolling platformer. However, the in-game camera in 2.5D games usually positions the player's view at a slightly higher angle than in a traditional 2D game, so that the player can perceive a greater field of depth in the game space by gazing down on the foreground and background. Asian media studies scholar Andrew Campana has described how this mode of dimensionality was originally developed in the early 1990s, before the introduction of video game consoles with the graphical capability to render fully three-dimensional environments. In order to offer the player a pseudo-sense of moving through a 3D world, says Campana, games like *Super Mario Kart* (Nintendo, 1992) used "a set of graphical projection techniques . . . in which the illusion of three-dimensionality is created by the rotation and distortion of a 2D plane." The effect was that "the sprites of the characters remained flat in appearance, in contrast to a seemingly 3D background."[23] In this way, 2.5D began its life as a kind of hack for infusing a 2D game world with the feeling of 3D dimensionality. Quickly, however, the use of 2.5D morphed from a matter of necessity—a technical work-around—to a matter of deliberate design. Only four years after the release of *Super Mario 64*, a major milestone in the industry-wide adoption of three-dimensional environments, Nintendo shifted a half step backward, in a sense, and released the first *Paper Mario* (2000) game, a 2.5D game that would set a precedent for many 2.5D games to come.

The *Paper Mario* games—there are eight in the series as of this writing—are all about reveling in what Campana terms the "playful mixture" of being 2.5D.[24] They commonly feature characters from the Mario universe

BUILDING WORLDS THROUGH GRAPHICAL DEPTH | 151

Figure 4.3. Characters in *Paper Mario* are rendered like two-dimensional stickers that move through a three-dimensional game world. (Screenshot by author)

presented as two-dimensional, paper-thin sprites that move around a three-dimensional environment (figure 4.3), like stickers standing upright or (to use Campana's analogy) figures in a children's pop-up book.[25] At first glance, *Paper Mario* seems to stand out among 2.5D video games. While later and more recent iterations of 2.5 games have moved toward a subtler juxtaposition of 2D and 3D elements, *Paper Mario* is 2.5D at its most deliberate and bold-faced, an intentionally jarring juxtaposition of dimensionalities. *Paper Mario*'s 2D sprites clearly look out of place in their 3D environment. This intentional clash is likely attributable, at least in part, to the fact that *Paper Mario* functioned as a kind of metacommentary on the move to three-dimensional game worlds that Nintendo itself helped spark with its release of *Super Mario 64*. For gamers who preferred 2D games over (what was then) the new introduction of 3D games—and there were plenty of those gamers—*Paper Mario* offered a tongue-in-cheek concession: here's your 2D Mario back again, just like you wanted.[26] Except that now, in the world of *Paper Mario*, each of the beloved Mario Bros. characters had become strange, frail, and almost tangible: a wafer-like, illogical being trying to make its way through a mismatched dimension.

Despite *Paper Mario*'s unique place within the history of 2.5D video games—as both an inspiration for later 2.5D games and a reflective commentary on dimensionality—the game helpfully highlights a quality that all 2.5D games share, in one way or another: they use their hybrid dimensionality to imbue their game worlds with a sense of materiality. Once we look for it, we readily find a similar emphasis on materiality in many other 2.5D games. *LittleBigPlanet* (Media Molecule, 2008) and *LittleBigPlanet 2* (Media Molecule, 2011), in which players progress through levels using 3D-rendered, knitted plush creatures as avatars, epitomize the materiality of 2.5D. Even though navigating through these levels is still primarily a two-dimensional affair, the game's 3D graphics imbue these squishy, tactile characters (as well as the many familiar, everyday items that populate the world of *LittleBigPlanet*) with the aura of actual, material objects rather than computer renderings. Other 2.5D games exhibit a similar investment in the impression of tangibility. *Puppeteer* (Japan Studio, 2013), *Yoshi's Woolly World* (Nintendo, 2015), and *Unravel* (Coldwood Interactive, 2016) are all examples of video games that pair an explicit focus on playing as an anthropomorphized physical substance (wood, wool, and yarn, respectively) with 2.5D dimensionality. In this sense, 2.5D as a framework for conceptualizing game space jibes with other applications of the term "2.5D." Scholars of contemporary Japanese popular culture, for instance, use "2.5D" (or "2.5 jigen") to describe media cultures that cross over from the page or the screen into the embodied practices of fans, such as through cosplay. In this context, writes Japanese media scholar Akiko Sugawa-Shimada, 2.5D "roughly means the space between the two-dimensional (fictional space where our imaginations and fantasy work) and the three-dimensional (reality where we physically exist)."[27] For video games too, in a different yet related sense, 2.5D enacts a boundary crossing between the digital and the physical worlds.

The example of *Paper Mario* also points us to another notable quality of 2.5D games: their uncanniness. As was the case for the wobbly dogs discussed in chapter 3, something about these games is simultaneously charming and *not quite right*. This not-quite-right-ness often shows up in the places where the design of 2.5D game worlds runs up against our expectations about how the material world should operate. Consider the case of *Paper Mario*'s shadows. If we look again at the way the game situates its 2D characters within its 3D levels (figure 4.3), we notice something strange. Beneath each two-dimensional character sprite, the game has rendered a round, distinctly three-dimensional shadow. Even though Mario, Luigi, Toad, Bowser, Peach, and all of the other characters in the game world look *flat*, their shadows suggest that their bodies are actually spheres (at least, as seen from the top down) that extend out in three dimensions. From a technical standpoint, these shadows are evidence that the game's software actually understands its characters as three-dimensional. This explains why the in-game lighting system, which projects simulated light from above, places shadows beneath the sprites. Yet, simultaneously, these shadows stand as a reminder that video game dimensionality is, first and foremost, a performative fiction. If we see Mario as paper thin, this is only because the game presents us with this graphical illusion. Similarly, in a game like *LittleBigPlanet*, 2.5D dimensionality highlights the constructedness of the pseudo-material world. Each level looks tangibly real, like a little stage set, yet the characters that players control cannot run behind the set or step forward toward the camera and off the edge of the stage. Precisely because these 2.5D worlds feel more tangible, they also feel more limiting, reminding us that a game world, despite its illusion of depth, can only ever go as deep as the game's programming will allow.

In the previous section, I said that video game spaces have commonly been theorized through the opportunities they offer for navigability. For my own part, I too am interested in how games create worlds by providing or foreclosing opportunities for players to navigate space; this is the subject of chapter 5. However, for a little while, I want us to set navigability aside. That is because 2.5D, as we have already begun to notice, does not so much change what a player can *do*. Unlike many of the other aspects of video game worldbuilding discussed in this book, the effect of 2.5D on gameplay itself is often minimal, as the case of *OlliOlli World* will illustrate. Instead, 2.5D fundamentally changes what players can *see*. It is a tool for worldbuilding that operates primarily through visuality and alternate perspectives—perspectives that offer depth while also complicating what it means to see deeply into the world. Dimensionality builds video game worlds; 2.5D dimensionality builds video game worlds that challenge us to question the very act of seeing the world and to reconsider our own place within the worlds that we see.

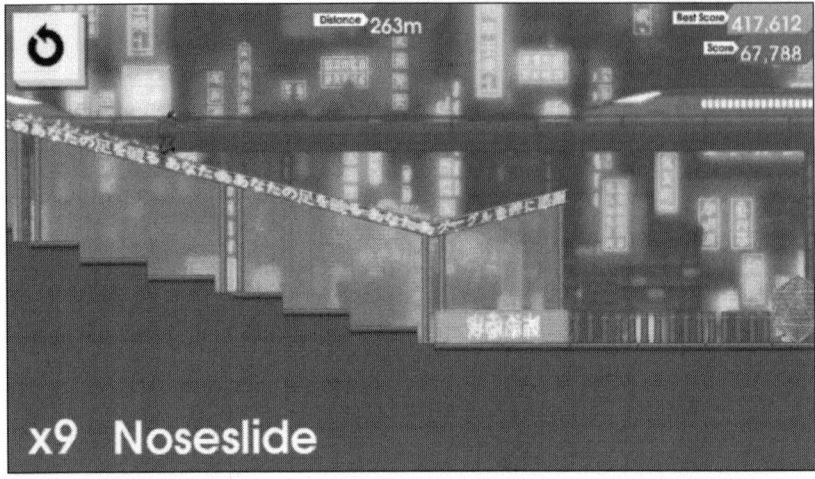

Figure 4.4. The skateboarder in the original *OlliOlli*, complete with a trucker hat, skates through a two-dimensional, techno-futuristic Japan. (Screenshot by author)

Worldbuilding through Depth in *OlliOlli World*

The ambivalent worldbuilding power of 2.5D, as well as its value for queer worldbuilding, are both on display in *OlliOlli World*. *OlliOlli World* is a 2.5D skateboarding game that leans hard into its dimensionality. The game is the third in the *OlliOlli* series, which began with the original *OlliOlli* in 2014 and was followed shortly after by *OlliOlli 2* in 2015. Both *OlliOlli* and *OlliOlli 2* are entirely two-dimensional side-scrolling games. In the tradition of the *Sonic the Hedgehog* games (Sega, 1991–2023), with gameplay that centers on moving rapidly from left to right, these earlier *OlliOlli* games feature a skateboarder who goes careening along a set of elevated 2D tracks (figure 4.4). In the role of the skateboarder, the player works to avoid obstacles and accrue points for increasingly complicated tricks. Despite being relatively small-scale games made by an indie development team, these earlier *OlliOlli* titles amassed a considerable following of fans, including many speedrunners, live streamers, and YouTubers who were drawn to the games because of the challenge of mastering their levels.[28]

Even accounting for this fan attention, I would argue that the first two *OlliOlli* games read as largely *flat*, both literally and figuratively. They are two-dimensional, flattening the playable space and the landscape around it. At the same time, their representational content, aesthetics, and visual worldbuilding all *fall flat*, trading in clichés and pandering to masculine indie gamers with retro tastes. The skateboarder whom the player controls in these first two games is a young white man in jeans and a red trucker hat (never a good sign). In the original *OlliOlli*, levels are set against pixelated backdrops meant to invoke militaristic or "exotic" locales like a US Army base and a techno-futuristic Japan. Admittedly, *OlliOlli 2* smooths out this pixelated look and swaps in less problematic settings, like an amusement park and a palm-tree-lined city street, but it keeps its white male player-character and its two-dimensional gameplay.

Published seven years after *OlliOlli 2*, *OlliOlli World* is a very different kind of game. (It is also much larger in production scale; *OlliOlli World* was released for all major consoles, whereas *OlliOlli* and *OlliOlli 2* were designed for PC and Mac.) As its title suggests, *OlliOlli World* takes the basic gameplay premise of *OlliOlli* and builds it out into a world. The game is set in Radlandia, an island "skate utopia" with five regions, all filled with collections of skateable tracks. In the game's opening sequence, players are told that Radlandia was created by a group of immortal skate gods. Their representative on the earthly plane at any given time is a "skate wizard," a singularly talented skater with the power to master all the skate gods' respective skills. Chiffon, the current skate wizard, is about to retire, and so she and her motley band of skate-enthusiast friends—which include a jovial punk named Gnarly Mike, a camerawoman named Suze, and a skater wearing chinos hiked up above his waist who is just referred to as "Dad"—are running tryouts for the newest skate wizard. Now, needless to say, the unnamed player-character has arrived to try out. Over the course of the game, the player-character progresses closer and closer to becoming the next skate wizard and ascending into the realm of "Gnarvana," a gnarly version of nirvana.

In addition to the inclusion of this fantastical storyline, *OlliOlli World* has shifted in a number of ways from the earlier *OlliOlli* games. Gone are the retro aesthetics; in their place, *OlliOlli World* employs a pastel-saturated, cartoon-esque style in the mode of animated shows like *Adventure Time* or *Steven Universe*. Gone too is the white skater-dude protagonist; instead, *OlliOlli World* offers a robust character creation system that allows players to build avatars with a range of gender and racial self-presentations. The cast of named non-player characters—including Chiffon's crew as well as other local skaters whom the player talks with in new areas—is itself strikingly diverse, with a majority depicted as visibly queer and/or as people of color. Other elements of the series's original racialized overtones admittedly linger. The game has abandoned the vision of a techno-futuristic Japan that appeared in the original *OlliOlli*. However, *OlliOlli World* retains an exoticizing orientation toward Asian-coded tropes. Chiffon is depicted as mystical and wise; her long gray hair covers her face, but her third eye peers out through her purple athletic head band. She is a being of few words, but when she does speak, the game represents her speech with a Simlish-style gibberish inflected to sound like an East Asian language, translating her words into English in a speech bubble above her head.[29] In the game's final sequence, after the player-character has completed the very last level, one of the skate gods congratulates them by proclaiming, "It's time to open up your third eye" and enter "complete Gnarvana." In such moments, the game reveals that, even in envisioning the inclusive world of Radlandia, it retains familiar tropes from techno-Orientalism and enacts its own performance of what Tara Fickle terms "ludo-Orientalism."[30]

However, the biggest thing that has changed about the *OlliOlli* series with the release of *OlliOlli World* is its shift from 2D to 2.5D. What was previously an entirely flat skateboarding game now has depth, allowing players to see (and, to an extent, play within) spaces both farther away from and closer than the skating track. *OlliOlli World* puts the experience of skating in 2.5D at the center of its design. In the game's first area, a beachfront commercial strip reminiscent of the boardwalk in Santa Cruz or Santa Monica, the player-character skates along a wooden path. The 2.5D perspective allows the player to see what lies in front of and behind the path, though the player-character themself can initially only move forward in a straight line. As play progresses, however, the game quickly foregrounds playable depth. In the game's second area, another beachfront boardwalk, the game introduces the "change lanes" mechanic, in which players press the X button to switch to diverging tracks (figure 4.5).[31] Now two tracks run side by side; in toggling between them, the player-character can move back and forth on a plane of depth, rather than simply moving left to right or up and

Figure 4.5. *OlliOlli World* uses the "change lanes" mechanics to allow the player-character to switch over to additional tracks. (Screenshot by author taken from gameplay video by GabeHype)

down. Soon enough, players learn that changing lanes can also, in preset cases, change the skater's direction of movement, acting as a switchback that sends the player-character rolling in the opposite direction when they shift backward or forward along the 2.5D plane.

In this way, *OlliOlli World* uses the depth of playable space afforded by the 2.5D perspective to seemingly *deepen* the experience of gameplay, adding complexity to the basic format of the 2D side-scrolling skating game. In the game's later levels, *OlliOlli World* takes this playable experience of depth even further, moving from engagingly complex gameplay to sheer spectacle. (Here we might think back to the visual spectacle of the high-flying goat in chapter 3.) Following these opening levels, each subsequent set of levels adds more and more parallel tracks, which are eventually stacked side by side in a dizzying display. By the time the player reaches Burntrock, a set of desert levels encountered roughly halfway through the game, the rows of skateable tracks are lined up six layers deep (figure 4.6). Next to one particularly deep cluster of tracks in Burntrock, a gaggle of fellow skaters and anthropomorphic cactus people gather to watch the skater, gazing admiringly as the player-character leaps backward and forward across the tracks. Levels from the

Figure 4.6. In a desert level, the skateable tracks in *OlliOlli World* stretch six layers deep. (Screenshot by author)

final stretch of the game up the ante on this spectacle, positioning tracks so that they curve and intersect wildly, filling up the screen. In these moments, nothing else seems to matter in the game world beyond the vertiginous experience of 2.5D dimensionality: the feeling of moving primarily in two directions (left to right or right to left) while also toggling forward to back. Such moments make clear that *OlliOlli World*'s 2.5D perspective is more than a mere cosmetic shift from earlier iterations of the game. The very point of these levels is to push the implications of playable depth to its limits, creating a space so deep that it threatens to burst forward out from the screen or fall backward toward the horizon.

If we step back and consider *OlliOlli World* more holistically, however, we see that the game's 2.5D perspective serves an even more critical purpose. It builds worlds. This happens in a few different ways. As we have seen in the individual levels of the game, 2.5D adds depth to the playable space, transforming each level from a flat track into an *environment*: a place that players can envision entering into, rather than simply moving along. In this way, the use of 2.5D gives the game its worldliness—its sense that play takes place not just on a surface but within a world. *OlliOlli World* intentionally heightens this sense that the world of the game extends out beyond the skateable tracks. In many levels, tracks are intersected by other environmental elements that cross the player-character's path at a ninety-degree angle. Examples include streams, roads, and railroad tracks, all of which are depicted as originating somewhere back in the distance and stretch forward toward the screen. At times, these visual elements pose challenges to the player; streams, for instance, must be jumped over to prevent the player-character from tumbling off their skateboard. However, for the most part, such elements have no impact on gameplay. Instead, they function simply as reminders of the game world's depth, pulling our eye along the length of a stream or road as it recedes into the distance. Such elements serve as visual encouragements for us to envision this world as one in which a player could go deep, if only they could break free of the confines of the playable tracks.

Simultaneously, *OlliOlli World* makes extensive use of its 2.5D perspective to establish an ambient narrative world: the odd, intriguing, almost-Earth of Radlandia. Because the player is positioned in a semi-face-on, semi-top-down viewpoint, they can see much more of both the background and the foreground of the game space than they could in a typical 2D game. Each level contains terrain and other forms of visual content represented through approximately four layers of background imagery. The boardwalk setting in the game's first area, for example, includes a skating path in the foreground, a stretch of sandy beach immediately behind it, a row of storefronts behind that, a strip of ocean behind that, and far-off islands in the distance. These elements fill up the game world with the impression of life that extends far beyond the playable realm of the skater.

Even more striking than this background imagery are creatures who inhabit that background: the unnamed, unremarked-on NPCs who dot each level, like the film extras discussed in chapter 1. Some of these are human beings. However, a far greater number of the NPCs whom the player-character skates past are absurdist, nonhuman entities doing intriguingly unexpected things. In the game's seashore levels, the boardwalk is lined with banana men: bananas as tall as humans with yellow arms and legs extended out from the skin of their peels. With their hands planted firmly on their hips (such as they are), they thrust out the curve of their bananas like proudly jutting chests and gaze stoically into the distance. Interspersed among the banana men are melty ice

Figure 4.7. The skater in *OlliOlli World* rolls past judgmental banana men and melty ice cream creatures. (Screenshot by author)

cream creatures—thick, squat sugar cones with dripping swirls of soft serve for hair and inscrutably grumpy facial expressions (figure 4.7). Still stranger sights sit in the medium distance of these levels, two or three layers back from the skateable track. There, giant squids rise up out of the sea; an enormous dead narwhal lays beached ashore; and gargantuan inflatable, arm-waving tube men (of the sort used to attract passersby to used car lots) loom like ancient, mythic titans. These scenes build the world of *OlliOlli World* by allowing us, as players, to catch fleeting glimpses of the creatures who populate Radlandia. However we might choose to make sense of these creatures—and whether we attempt to make sense of them at all—they clearly suggest that there is far more going on in this island world than skateboarding.

As for the human NPCs who do sometimes appear in such levels, most of them are fellow skaters. Through these NPCs, *OlliOlli World* portrays a different kind of world: a human social world. The game's 2.5D depth allows us to see that the player-character, rather than being a lone actor in a world built for their sole enjoyment, is actually participating in the day-to-day practices of a skateboarding community. Through its narrative elements—most notably its storyline about becoming the next skate wizard—the game presents the player-character's quest and the quirky individuals who help them along the way as exceptional. However, the elements found in the game's own deeper visual field suggests that the player-character and their friends may not be so exceptional after all.

At certain moments, the player can see other, nonplayable skaters rolling along various levels, either behind (farther from the screen) or in front of (closer to the screen) the actual playable tracks. These skaters are not racing the player-character or otherwise interacting with them; to the contrary, they do not even seem to notice the player-character. (Ironically, the only time an NPC races the player-character, that NPC is not a fellow skater but a large brown bear who floats downstream on a river while relaxing in an inner tube.) As for the other skaters hanging out in Radlandia, we mostly see them going about their lives: trying out moves, walking around carrying their boards, hanging out chatting with friends. They do not greet the player-character or turn their heads to notice the player-character's various sweet tricks. Thus, because the player can gaze up and over the skate tracks, they are able to see that their skater is only one small piece of a larger skating culture, a world that seems largely unconcerned with some quest for a new skate wizard. In this sense, the game uses its 2.5D qualities to build not only one social world—the world that the player-character inhabits, along with their named skateboarding buddies—but multiple social worlds. Like the parallel tracks that players can access through the "lane change" mechanic, these social worlds run alongside each other, intersecting occasionally while remaining apart.

Refusing Access to Video Game Worlds

Thus far, I have been enumerating the ways that *OlliOlli World* uses its 2.5D dimensionality as a worldbuilding tool. Yet, importantly, this same 2.5D perspective pushes back against the player's attempts to access the game's world. Take, for example, those crisscrossing elements of terrain—the streams, roads, and railroad tracks—that I said brought a sense of worldliness to the game when they intersected the skateable paths. These elements conjure up a sense that the game world extends into deeper spaces, but they also function as reminders that players are not actually able to enter those spaces. Players cannot toggle over and travel up these paths; they can only cross over them and pass them by. And what about the layers of background imagery that suggest that gameplay takes place within a rich, surreal, imaginative world? These elements of the game's world are, in their own way, likewise impenetrable. I have been talking about the stern-faced banana men and sun-scorched ice cream creatures as if they were clear and visible to players, who might observe them with curiosity as they play through each subsequent skate track. In truth, the background contents of these levels are very hard to see on a first (or second or third or fourth) playthrough. While skating, the player-character zooms by so fast that these contents become a blur. Indeed, to conduct this analysis of the game's background imagery, I myself had to watch recordings of the game slowed down to 50 percent playback speed, just so that these creatures would not similarly escape my view. Slowing the gameplay footage down revealed a world that, though built into the game, I would never have been able to see in-depth while playing.

Even for players like me who put in the effort to identity what is happening in the space behind (and in front of) the skateable tracks, the world that players find there remains opaque in other ways. Ostensibly, the narrative of *OlliOlli World* is about mastering moves so that you can commune with the skate gods. Yet none of that explains what lies in the depths of the game's levels. What is this world where bananas are people and bears spend their days doing whitewater tubing? The contents of the levels' backgrounds certainly suggest a world, but they also raise more questions about that world than they offer answers. At times, the contents of these backdrops actually distract from rather than deepening (or simply serving as visual background to) the experience of gameplay. In an area called Seaweed Harbor, for instance, the player-character rides along tracks that go past a series of Muscle Beach–esque hangouts for local seagulls.[32] These seagulls have beefy, human-like upper bodies and large, wide-set nipples; they wear serious, bug-eyed expressions and slim-cut jean shorts. Positioned on the side of the skate path, some of the seagulls flex and lift weights, while others lounge, posing suggestively as they stare out from the screen toward the player. If the queer overtones of these butch, *Physique*-ready seagulls were not clear enough, they become even more obvious in a set of tableaux where groups of seagulls sit around streams and waterfalls, like

Figure 4.8. A community of beefy seagulls in jean shorts lounge alongside a skate track, posing seductively or flexing their muscles. (Screenshot by author)

men lounging poolside or visiting a bathhouse (figure 4.8). As a queer player, I found that these seagulls both deepened the game world for me and made me care considerably less about skateboarding. Why am I wasting my time learning skating tricks, I wondered (and still wonder), when I could be hanging out with a community of gay seagulls?

The social world of human skaters—NPCs who pass by in the background without speaking to the player—proves similarly inaccessible. The player-character does not interact with these skaters; since they are skateboarding along parallel routes, the player-character literally does not cross paths with the members of the social scene around them. Honestly, these fellow skaters seem almost entirely uninterested in the player-character's existence. Despite innumerable proclamations from the game's cast of featured, named NPCs (the player-character's actual friends) who assure the player-character that they are an exceedingly talented skating pro, the skaters who mull around in the background do not even deign to look at the player-character as they roll by. Instead, these skaters stand around, wait in line for ice cream, or just skate off to a destination somewhere else in the game world that remains forever unseen. They are the cool kids, self-involved and mildly disaffected, and the player-character is distinctly not one of them. In each of these cases, then, *OlliOlli World* uses its 2.5D dimensionality to build a world, only to then deny the player-character entry into that world. The player can bear witness to these worlds, but only ever from a distance.

Still, in *OlliOlli World*, even this refusal to allow players to access its worlds offers its own form of depth. For example, if we look closely at the unnamed skaters who mull about various levels, we notice that they are uninterested in the player-character, as I have said—but we also notice that, despite the game's racially diverse cast of named characters, seemingly all of these unnamed skaters are white. Whether or not this is an oversight on the part of the game's creators, this fact comes with its own (concerning) implications for the world of *OlliOlli World*. Suddenly the game's seaside skater community comes to look like a very different kind of social scene, not an inclusive band of queer of color misfits but an insular, all-white, mostly male group turning a conspicuously cold shoulder to outsiders. (As a scholar working in Southern California, I cannot help but see a connection to histories of white supremacy as they intersect with skateboard and surfing cultures in places like Huntington Beach.)[33] Like a pair of skateable tracks positioned side by side, then, *OlliOlli World* presents us with a pair of communities: the world of queer skaters and skaters of color who are the focus of the game's narrative and the world of implicitly hostile white skaters that form the larger social context within which that first group must operate. In that way, the simple choice not to include skaters of color in the game's background gives the world of *OlliOlli World* an extra layer of cultural texture. For better or for worse, it makes the game's world feel more like our own world, where the experience of depth goes hand in hand with layers of exclusion, discrimination, and oppression.

Even the gameplay of *OlliOlli World*, which seems to focus so intently on the experience of depth, denies players the opportunity to truly go deep. I have described how the game moves the player through levels with deeper and deeper rows of tracks, where skateboarding no longer means moving in a straight line from left to right (as in the earlier versions of *OlliOlli*) but also backward and forward along a plane that extends into and out from the screen. However, technically, it is more accurate to say that *OlliOlli World* offers the *illusion* of depth. Yes, these parallel tracks are positioned side by side in the 2.5D game space; we can track this by following how the in-game camera shifts forward and back when the player switches tracks. At the same time, the game engages in a kind of sleight of hand, using perspective and foreshortening to make the distance between tracks—and, by extension, the overall depth of the playable space—look wider. In reality, from a technical standpoint, when the player-character moves back and forth across these tracks, they are basically just moving up and down. That is to say, whereas it seems that the player-character is moving along an angled, horizontal plane, they are functionally just being shifted higher and lower along a grid of paths that remain almost entirely vertical and therefore functionally two-dimensional. From a gameplay standpoint at least, the game's rendering of 2.5D is basically just 2D in disguise.

Given this illusion, it may be tempting to dismiss the worldbuilding opportunities that 2.5D offers in *OlliOlli World* as far shallower than they at first appear. It may also be tempting to declare 2.5D, and perhaps video game dimensionality more broadly, a tool for worldbuilding that produces less-than-compelling results. However, despite the ambivalent depth we see in *OlliOlli World*, it would be insufficient and indeed incorrect to say that this game world—or other 2.5D video game worlds that use their dimensionality to similar effects—is shallow. Instead, we would do better to think of these as deep worlds that give us glimpses of their depth without allowing us to enter deeply into them. I have said that 2.5D is a mode of video game dimensionality that functions primarily as a way to build worlds, adding materiality to a video game space. Let me amend that by saying that 2.5D builds material worlds that we, as players, nonetheless often cannot access. 2.5D, like the muscular seagulls whose provocative gaze beckons for us to come closer, presents us with a world and entices us to enter it. But, once we arrive at the world's surface, we find that all we can do is peer at it from the outside. In this way, a game like *OlliOlli World* forces us to confront our own unquestioned, and frankly violent, assumptions that video game worlds—or, really, any worlds—should be available for us to enter, regardless of who we are, simply because those worlds exist. *OlliOlli World* builds a world that we can play inside, but, at the end of the day, that world does not belong to its players.

2.5D as Impossible Queer Dimension

Having talked at length about the ways that 2.5D can be used for worldbuilding, I want to turn, in this concluding section, to consider the queer implications of 2.5D, the worlds that it builds, and how it goes about building worlds. 2.5D is itself a queer form of dimensionality. Neither 2D nor 3D, 2.5D stands between dimensions; it is an impossible, liminal form that can only be made possible in a constructed, simulated space like a video game. This liminality connects 2.5D to spatial experiences of queerness, which often entail existing between social worlds or finding opportunities for creating community in the cracks of dominant society. As geography studies scholar Loren March has written, drawing insights from Jack Halberstam and Jen Jack Gieseking, poststructuralist work from the subfield of queer geography has posited liminality itself as a feature of existing queerly within space.[34] March explains that, in such work, "'queer' is deployed in expansive ways that open time-space to immanent politics rooted in between-ness."[35] To exist in 2.5D is precisely to exist queerly in between. Yet, importantly, 2.5D does not describe one exact way of being in between. To be 2.5D might mean being 2D in a 3D environment (as in the *Paper Mario* games) or 3D in a 2D environment (as is the case, roughly speaking, in the *Little Big Planet* games). In this sense, 2.5D is also not merely liminal, situated between different modes of existing in space. It is also inherently multiple and nonbinary—calling to mind connections with the nonbinary physics of the wobble discussed in chapter 3. The dimensionality of 2.5D is queer, in part, because it embraces this nonbinary state of existence, rife with contradictions, and refuses to resolve itself into being either two- or three-dimensional.

The worlds that 2.5D creates are, by extension, queer worlds. These are worlds charged with desire, invoking a longing for depth while keeping the consummation of that longing infinitely at bay. They are also worlds where queer things happen to the shape of space. Three-dimensional shadows form under two-dimensional objects. Knitted plush avatars rendered three-dimensionally crash against two-dimensional walls. Skate tracks that seem to run alongside one another somehow exist on top of one another, the manifestation of a kind of nonsensical spatial logic that echoes the non-Euclidian geometry evoked at the start of this chapter. These worlds bring into doubt the very idea of a stable dimensionality. By extension, the world (by which I mean the world as we find it in media and the world as we experience it in our everyday lives) begins to seem limitless because the conceits through which it has been delimited become so clear. Put otherwise, once the notion of natural, reasonable, logical dimensions has been denaturalized, we come to realize that the dimensional perspectives through which we view the world could always be otherwise. A world we currently see in two dimensions need not always be 2D; a world we see in three dimensions need not be 3D. Dimensionality is both a graphical and a social construct. Each dimension offers one possible way of seeing the world. 2.5D teaches us that there are always other perspectives through which the world can be seen, some of which are illuminating precisely because they defy the limits of reason.

The construction of these queer video game worlds through 2.5D also resonates with the queer worldmaking practices discussed in chapter 1. These worlds are role models for the kinds of worlds that we might deliberately build as queer people, but they are also metaphors for the kinds of worlds that we are already making through the day-to-day practices of our queer lives. These are worlds that are deep and rich—and, to a limited extent, visible from the outside—yet strive to protect themselves from intrusion. They are worlds where others may occasionally come to play but may not penetrate far beyond the surface. They are worlds for us. We are the strange creatures of *OlliOlli World*. We are the banana men, the melting ice cream creatures, the floating bears, the shirtless seagulls, and the colossal nylon tubes that wave joyfully in the breeze. We are the inhabitants of a world that, to outsiders and sometimes even to ourselves, remains alluring yet mysterious, vibrant yet opaque. This is a world that may be viewed by others from afar. But we queer people are the ones who truly live within it.

At the same time that 2.5D worlds belong to queer people, those who already inhabit 2.5D worlds can be seen as queer. They are themselves liminal, existing between frameworks for conceptualizing space: 2D beings in a 3D world, 3D beings in a 2D world, matter out of place. Seen in this way, 2.5D subjects serve as symbols for queer people's all-too-familiar real-life experiences of feeling at odds with the world. We too are often ill fit to the worlds that surround us. Conversely, we might imagine the 2.5D subject as completely at home in their liminal dimensionality. This subject, like 2.5D dimensionality itself, is nonbinary, refusing to move toward one state or another (man or woman, two-dimensional or three-dimensional). A 2.5D subject is not passing through the 2.5D on their way to a two- or three-dimensional existence. They have taken up residence in the in-between space; they are trans not because they are transitioning toward a binary gendered goal but because they have built a world for themselves inside the *liminus*—Latin for "threshold"—that place between places, the space where one space *transitions* into another. In this way, the 2.5D subject not only inhabits a queer spatial position but also embodies a queer way of *being* in space. For those whose own gender identity is nonbinary, such as myself, a 2.5D world like the one found in *OlliOlli World* becomes a beacon. It is a place where I can imagine what seems, in the world that I currently inhabit, to be otherwise unimaginable: that I might be allowed to exist in between identities while also being in sync with the world around me.

Using 2.5D dimensionality to build video game worlds also represents a mode of queer worldbuilding. 2.5D worlds are built on fundamentally queer logics of depth. Art historian Lex Morgan Lancaster, writing about abstraction in contemporary art, describes how queer art is often "expected to speak directly to nonnormative sexuality and gender politics, often by picturing queer people or eroticized bodies."[36] Queer art, then, is compelled to place its queerness on its surface, offering it up for all to see. Abstraction, by contrast, can be a queer artistic strategy for enacting resistance by undermining what Lancaster describes as "easy legibility" and refusing "ontological certainty." Queer abstraction, in its turn, insists on the importance of materiality and affect, thereby "creating a site to generate alternative spaces and worlds."[37]

We can see the use of a queer dimensionality like 2.5D to create video game worlds as a related strategy of resistance. It too adds material, affective depth to a game world while blurring categories of ontological certainty (Where does one dimension end and another begin? What even is a dimension?) and refusing to offer up the kind of easy legibility that would allow outsiders to readily make sense of its sexual and gender politics. In its refusal to welcome players into its world, 2.5D, like abstract queer art, offers us a powerful lesson for building worlds queerly. Queer worldbuilding is not the work of creating queer worlds for the edification of non-queer players. Queer worlds rarely make sense in any kind of tidy, easily discernible way. Time and again, we have seen this fact manifest itself in the spirit of absurdism that characterizes many of the video games discussed in this book. Queer worlds are indeed often absurd—strange and, to some people, seemingly unknowable. Yet, to others of us, who understand that the world does not need to be logical in order to feel *true*, they make perfect sense.

These queer interpretations of 2.5D also serve as further evidence for one of the core claims of this book: that even the most seemingly technical systems (such as the system of rendering perspective and graphical depth) that underlie video games are always tangled up with sexuality and identity. As Lynda Johnston and Robyn Longhurst write in *Space, Place, and Sex*, sexuality "is constantly being mapped and remapped across various cultural and social landscapes. . . . There are no spaces that sit outside sexual politics."[38] This is true for digital spaces as well as physical spaces: from public spaces like social networks and multiplayer online games to the digital spaces that players step into (or at least attempt to) when they pick up a single-player game like *OlliOlli World*. If there is queerness to be found in the worldbuilding power of 2.5D, 2.5D also prompts us to ask where else queerness might lie in the impossible, liminal spatial worlds that video games can imagine. 2.5D is one alternate dimension, but there are surely many others. What is a 1.5D video game? Or a 3.5D video game? What kinds of worlds exist in the cracks between other graphics dimensions, and what kinds of space do they offer for marginalized people to exist in the world?

5

Straight Paths through Queer Video Games

Overbuilding the World in Gone Home

Writing in *Queer Phenomenology*, Sara Ahmed posits that worlds are brought into being, in part, through our orientations.[1] "Depending on which way one turns," she writes, "different worlds might come into view." Orientation, whether we conceive of it as orientation in space or sexual orientation, describes "how it is that we come to find our way in a world." Our orientation turns us toward certain objects (physical objects, objects of desire), shaping our sense of which elements of our world are imbued with meaning, and thereby "[creating] a ground upon which we gather."[2] Ahmed, returning to the worldbuilding power of orientations in her essay "Orientations Matter," describes orientations as "starting points." It is from these starting points, she says, "that the world unfolds."[3] Once we leave the starting points of orientation and head off into the world, says Ahmed, we bring new worlds into being by taking certain paths. The dominant norms of society instruct us to fall in line and follow a straight path, to move through the world "by not deviating at any point." Queer subjects, by contrast, often forge their own winding paths through life, "deviating" from the straight path and thereby becoming, in the eyes of heteronormative society, "deviant."[4] Yet precisely by cutting a queer path through the world—one that is nonlinear, full of pivots and meandering turns, and decidedly non-straight—queer subjects give form to alternate geographies and enact the creation of their own queer worlds. Moving through the world queerly itself has the power to rebuild the world.

Video games, with their constructed environments and designed player paths, make these metaphors of spatial orientation and movement strikingly literal. Whether the player moves through a game following a straight path or whether they deviate can be seen as an expression of a straight or queer orientation and, by extension, as a starting point for the unfolding of a straight or queer world. This chapter looks at how video games build worlds through the ways they construct orientation and opportunities for players' movement. It does so through an analysis of *Gone Home* (The Fullbright Company, 2013), widely regarded as a foundational queer video game and one that appears, on its surface, to embody queer worldbuilding through both its explicitly queer storyline and its seemingly open-ended possibilities for movement. By critiquing *Gone Home* through the lens of Ahmed's reflections on orientation, this chapter aims to extend and complicate the discussion about the cultural meanings of game space that I presented in chapter 4. This chapter also brings the topic of game space together with questions of in-game movement, which I previously addressed through game physics in chapter 3. Here, we see how video games model the capacity for building alternative worlds by building—or simply offering the option to pursue—alternative ways of moving through the world.

In one sense, this analysis of *Gone Home* suggests that video games might enact their own forms of exuberant queer community-building through movement—as Sami Schalk, writing from the perspective of crip theory, describes experiencing at a disability studies dance, where bodies moved alongside each other to create an "ethos of community and love."[5] At the same time, this chapter also represents a shift in the way that this book thinks about worldbuilding in video games. Rather than simply celebrating *Gone Home* as a positive example of a queer game, as critics have done time and again in the decade following the game's release, I argue that *Gone Home* in fact straightens its queer potential by forcing the player to move through its world "on rails," following a predetermined and strikingly normative path.[6] Therefore, this chapter offers a chance to deepen our reflections on worldbuilding, both by taking into consideration the popular reception of specific video games and by addressing instances in which video games may fail to live up to their queer worldbuilding potential. In the midst of my many proclamations about how video games inspire us to imagine radical new worlds, this chapter points to the potential shortcomings and pitfalls of video game worlds as designed and preprogrammed environments. Though I have argued in earlier chapters that game design can be a powerful tool for building queer worlds, here I offer a counterpoint, contending that some video games may be overdesigned or indeed *overbuilt*, leaving little room for queer expression in their worlds.

However, even as this chapter brings the queer power of video game worldbuilding into question, it also seeks to yet again expand our tool kit for building worlds. It does this by considering, in concrete detail, how the ways that players move through game worlds can contribute to the building of such worlds. In this chapter's second half, I turn from an analysis of *Gone Home* as it has been designed to an analysis of the emergent player practices that have come to surround the game. Specifically, I reflect on the practice of speedrunning *Gone Home*, which became unexpectedly popular during the mid- and late-2010s.[7] Speedrunning, in which players attempt to complete video games as quickly as possible, literally cuts the straightest possible path through the playable space of *Gone Home*. The implications of this practice for queer worldbuilding are—like the implications of so much of the material discussed in this book—ambivalent and messy, as I will explain. On the one hand, we can interpret speedrunning as an example of what Ahmed refers to as a "straightening device," performances and repetitions that turn potentially queer spaces straight by "[getting] stuck in certain alignments."[8] On the other hand, speedrunning constitutes a queering (and, as trans game studies scholars have recently argued, a transing) of the game world by repurposing its space for alternate desires and, by extension, alternate forms of movement.[9]

This turn toward practices of play also brings us back, once again, to the subject of queer worldmaking. I said, in my analysis of *What the Golf* in chapter 1, that video games resonate with concepts of queer worldmaking because their worlds come to life through the performances of their players. Here, I interrogate the contours and boundaries of that premise by examining a case in which play seems to unmake (rather than make) a queer world. Simultaneously, I draw our attention to the fact that the world of *Gone Home* was never actually as queer as it appeared. Therefore, in an admittedly roundabout way, acts of play, even when they seem to operate in service of straightening queer video games, may participate in the building of new worlds by showing us the limitations of the old ones. Sometimes play, rather than being transgressive in and of itself, makes worlds precisely by unmaking other worlds. Tensions between game design and game play, as illustrated through the case of *Gone Home*, remind us that it is never enough to build new worlds or even to build them queerly. We must also account for what people will do with those worlds: what inhabitants will *make* of them and what kinds of lives they will live within them.

Representation, Environmental Worldbuilding, and Queer Movement

Gone Home is an exploration-based game with a narrative that focuses on a young lesbian woman. The game is commonly understood—by game studies scholars, games news outlets, and longtime players alike—as one of the most prominent examples in an upswing of video games about people with specific LGBTQIA+ identities that started in the early 2010s. Released in 2013, shortly before the vitriol unleashed by GamerGate (the online harassment campaign led by reactionary gamers who targeted marginalized game makers and critics) beginning in 2014, *Gone Home* was widely lauded by more progressive sources as a game that promoted diversity, demonstrating how inclusivity in video games was "getting better" and even making homophobic male gamers more empathetic.[10] The reach of the game's positive reception extended beyond the traditional discursive spaces of games culture and into popular feminist and queer publications. GLAAD, *Autostraddle*, and *Mother Jones* all wrote articles in praise of *Gone Home*; *AfterEllen* called it the "beautiful, queer-centric video game of your dreams."[11] *Gone Home* has also been celebrated by queer game creators like merritt kopas, who has described how the game offered her, as a trans woman, a powerful point of identification.[12] Simultaneously, *Gone Home* came under attack by bigoted players, whose disdain for the game is documented in forum threads with titles like "Was Gone Home a Propaganda Game?"[13]

In gaining considerable visibility, from both supporters and detractors, *Gone Home* became a key reference point for the later design of other video games with LGBTQIA+ characters that were aimed toward a similarly broad audience. (I use "LGBTQIA+" rather than "queer" here to signal a focus on individual sexual and gendered identities rather than an interest in queerness as a larger cultural or political project.) Among these are games like *Tell Me Why* (Dontnod Entertainment, 2020), commonly cited as the first AAA video game to feature a trans man as a main character, which itself won a 2021 GLAAD award for "Outstanding Video Game."[14] Thus, as the commercial landscape for such games has widened, *Gone Home* has continued to exert a considerable influence on how queer stories are told in video games, especially those that reach an especially wide base of players.

It is admittedly unsurprising that most commentary on *Gone Home* in the popular press stressed the game's inclusion of queer representation. As the story of *Gone Home* unfolds, it becomes clear that queer experience is central to the game's narrative. Although players play as Katie, an implicitly straight college student who returns from a year abroad to her family's new home in Oregon, Katie's younger sister, Sam, is the real protagonist of the game. As Katie explores the house, picking up items and reading her sister's journal entries, she uncovers the story of how Sam fell in love with her girlfriend, Lonnie. As Dimitrios Pavlounis has pointed out, the game's representation of same-sex romance is also paired with other, nonrepresentational forms of queer meaning. The gameplay of *Gone Home* centers on the gradual discovery of scattered documents, modeling what Pavlounis describes as a queer form of storytelling in which "histories are multiple, intertwined, and always up for interpretation."[15] Kevin Veale writes that *Gone Home* fosters a sense of "affective materiality," which sparks a feeling of nostalgia in the player and builds empathy for Sam and Lonnie.[16] Shane Snyder interprets the space of the family home in *Gone Home* as representative of the figurative closest within which LGBTQIA+ people are often forced to hide.[17] Rowan Tullocha, Catherine Hoadband, and Helen Young point out that *Gone Home* draws on traditions of feminist and queer social action movements (the game includes references to the 1990s riot grrrl scene), while problematically reproducing the racial bias that often characterizes such movements. Indeed, *Gone Home* focuses exclusively on the experiences of middle-class white cisgender women in a monogamous relationship.[18]

In addition to holding a place in what we might describe as the queer games hall of fame, *Gone Home* has also been upheld as an exemplary model for a particular type of narrative-focused worldbuilding known as environmental storytelling. The concept of environmental storytelling is drawn, in part, from longer histories of theme-park design (a connection we will return to later when we discuss dark rides). In theme parks, stories are often told through objects and visual elements distributed around the park space, such as props, lighting, sound effects, and music; the park visitor, rather than being presented with an explicit narrative, pieces together a story from these ambient elements.[19] Similarly, in the context of video games, environmental storytelling describes the practice of telling stories by distributing items, bits of text, and other clues around a game space, allowing players to encounter these as they explore so that the narrative world of the game can reveal itself bit by bit. In this sense, environmental storytelling seems to make good on Mary Flanagan's vision of "navigable narratives," which she described in 2000 as an emerging mode of digital storytelling in which players make and remake a story anew each time they play by "searching and piecing together" different elements of the narrative.[20]

Environmental storytelling constitutes its own form of worldbuilding. Game designer Laura E. Hall, in a talk presented at the 2019 Game Developers Conference, draws from her experience building escape-room games to describe environmental storytelling as a mode in which "the story is told by the world. The set, the objects, everything is speaking to whatever the world is that you're inhabiting."[21] Relatedly, Jess Morrissette writes in his work cataloging soda machines in video games that seemingly unremarkable background objects are in fact often critical for "grounding games in a world we recognize as fundamentally similar to our own" and thereby making the game world feel "real and complete."[22] Many of the games that Morrissette references keep their environmental storytelling quiet; they tuck soda machines, along with thousands of other objects, into their playable landscapes and let the meanings of those objects remain implicit. *Gone Home*, by contrast, places environmental storytelling front and center. The player's one goal, in the role of Katie, is to walk around the house encountering notebooks, photographs, zines, and other scraps of everyday life that, taken together, tell *Gone Home*'s queer story. Just as *Gone Home* has been influential for the design of an ongoing lineage of queer games, it has also been influential for games that build their narrative worlds through environmental storytelling. Notable among these is *Tacoma* (Fullbright, 2017), the next game made by the developers of *Gone Home*. Set in an abandoned space station, *Tacoma* prompts players to piece together the story of the station's mysteriously missing inhabitants through environmental storytelling that the video game press heralded as "groundbreaking."[23]

Gone Home's use of environmental storytelling is also closely tied to the way that the game structures players' movement through its environments. The game is a prominent early entry into the genre referred to as "walking simulators." Elsewhere, I have described the cultural implications of the walking simulator genre, in which gameplay centers on moving through a game space rather than on challenges, competition, or mastery.[24] Originally derogatory, the term "walking simulator" has been used to deride video games that do not fit normative expectations for what makes a game truly a "game" by suggesting that these games entail little more than walking. Ironically, as Aubrey Anable writes in her work on the game *Kentucky Route Zero* (Cardboard Computer, 2013), "the 'walking simulator' rhetoric of contemporary game culture is profoundly ahistorical," since foundational early games like *Colossal Cave Adventure* (William Crowther, 1976) were themselves about exploration.[25] More recently, the label "walking simulator" has been largely reclaimed or simply passed over in favor of newer terms used to describe video games that are similarly non-combat-oriented and invested in cultural issues, like "wholesome games" or "cozy games."[26] Interestingly, the COVID-19 pandemic seems to have introduced a new wave of players to the concept of walking simulators, which have been described as foregrounding "the joy of walking" and offering a "much-needed escape."[27]

The walking simulator genre is inherently bound up with cultural ideas about the relationship between gender, sexuality, and video games. As Melissa Kagen has demonstrated, the concept of the walking simulator is itself highly gendered.[28] Walking simulators are about wandering, writes Kagen, and wandering has historically been associated with women and femininity. Indeed, a large number of video games to which the label walking simulator has been applied feature women as lead characters. In this way, "walking simulator," when used as a negative term, polices what does and does not count as a game along very thinly veiled gender lines. In addition to being implicitly feminine-coded, walking simulators can be linked to queerness through the figure of the flâneur. The flâneur, famously theorized by Walter Benjamin, has been understood by queer studies scholars as a queer (white, male) figure who strolls through the urban landscape, resisting productivity, embracing leisure, and choosing the meandering path over the straight line.[29] Despite the discriminatory attitudes that have given rise to the term "walking simulator," such games prove ripe for reinterpretation and complication through the lens of *flânerie*.[30] Indeed, like the flâneur, the player of *Gone Home* and other walking simulators appear to move through the world primarily by wandering and observing, avoiding straight routes, and instead participating in a form of queer meandering—a literalizing of the nonnormative orientations and "deviant" paths that Ahmed describes as bringing new queer worlds into view.

The (Seemingly) Queer World of *Gone Home*

At first glance, *Gone Home* seems explicitly designed to give players the opportunity to explore its game world without a clear sense of direction. The player, in the role of Katie, begins the game on the porch of the family's new home. Since Katie's parents are out, the front door is locked. Without the option to proceed straight through the door, the player must look around, moving in one direction and then another as they check the various objects on the porch (a potted plant, patio furniture, Katie's backpack) for clues about how to proceed. Eventually, in a cabinet, beneath a duck figurine, the player finds a spare key and is able to unlock the front door—but not without first navigating this dizzying, disorienting experience of spinning around and around to look for a way forward, peering and prodding at odd objects that ultimately serve no purpose.

When Katie does open the front door, the scene that greets the player deliberately communicates a sense of possibility for indirect, circuitous movement. With a wide staircase straight ahead and hallways leading off to either side, the level design of this entryway prompts players to pause, peer around, and question which way to turn: an active attempt to reorient themselves. It seems that they could go left through a door, right through a different door, up the staircase, or even back, deeper into the house. Signaled by these opening scenes, which set the player's expectations for the type of world they have entered, is the promise that *Gone Home* will be a game about finding a way forward slowly along a twisting, uncertain path. In this sense, the game seems to offer multiple possible orientations—so many, in fact, that the player is likely to feel unsure of how to proceed and, by extension, which version of the game world to bring into view. Stated otherwise, *Gone Home* appears to offer an opportunity not only to walk a deviant path but quite literally to get lost within an array of possible deviant paths. Here, inside the house, the player stumbles forward in various directions, easily turned around in the dimly lit space of Katie's new home, where it is often nearly impossible to spot the difference between shadowy corners and awaiting doors. The former lead nowhere, the latter lead somewhere, but all possible paths remain, at first, a mystery.

In keeping with this impression that *Gone Home* will offer a space for nonlinear movement, *Gone Home* also seems to take a circuitous and therefore implicitly queer approach to storytelling. On the locked front door of the family's new home, Katie finds a note from her sister, Sam, that suggests she has run away. Now, the player infers, it is their task to find out what has happened to Sam. "Please, please don't go digging and trying to figure out where I am," Sam's note pleads, yet that is precisely what the player does: digs through drawers, closets, and even bathrooms to find the knickknacks, paper scraps, and memorabilia that have accumulated around Katie's family. Together, these seemingly jumbled bits tell the intimate stories not only of Sam's queer romance but also of the family's life together. This approach to storytelling through dispersed and partial artifacts guides the game's subplots as well as its main narrative. For example, through a series of letters from a family friend, the game reveals that Katie and Sam's mother has had romantic feelings for a younger male coworker. Rather than simply telling the player how this drama concludes, *Gone Home* wraps up the mother's subplot with a final, subtle artifact: an invitation, stuck on the family fridge, to the coworker's wedding to another woman. Thus, following the narratives of *Gone Home* both requires meandering (i.e., exploring to find objects) and creates meandering (i.e., the meandering plot of the story told in pieces). In this way, the game appears to use its storyline as well as its navigable space to build a queer world.

In certain moments, *Gone Home* even seems to explicitly acknowledge the queerness of its nonlinear storytelling. This can be seen most directly in a pair of high school homework assignments that the player finds, one from Katie and one from Sam. While browsing through boxes in the basement, the player comes across a stack of papers. When the player picks up the sheets on the top of the stack, Katie's thoughts from the present moment appear written across the screen: "Oh man, one of my old sex ed assignments." The first page the player sees is a typed sheet with the words "Reproductive System Worksheet 6" at the top and a blank space where Katie has written her name (Kaitlin Greenbriar) and the date (September 10, 1991). Next, the sheet includes a set of directions from her sex education teacher: "Below are two stories. The events are all out of order. Get a sheet of lined paper . . . Then choose ONE of the two stories and rewrite it . . . Put the sentences in chronological order. Make sure the last sentence is a good concluding statement." The "stories" that the directions refer to are lists of steps describing the menstrual cycle and "the life of a sperm cell," respectively. The steps have been jumbled and are printed on the page out of order. The menstrual-cycle list, for instance, begins with, "it travels through the fallopian tube," and ends with, "an ovum starts to develop"—a kind of nonsensical, atemporal tangle of biology.

Next, we see the lined paper sheet with Katie's response to the assignment. She has dutifully followed the instructions, putting each stage of the menstrual cycle in order one by one, beginning with, "an ovum starts to develop," and ending with the (extremely cringeworthy, biologically essentializing) proclamation, copied verbatim from the worksheet, "It is incredible how the female body knows how to prepare for pregnancy!" Katie's teacher has left a bold, red check-plus mark at the top of the page to denote a job well done. Here, the heterosexual protagonist, Katie, has shown her readiness to "fall in line," to use Ahmed's phrase, with both the expectations of authority and normative narratives about reproduction. She has taken a set of bodily operations directly tied to sex and sexuality and diligently placed them in chronological order, unscrambling them and assembling them back in a straight line. By extension, she has also upheld the logics of the US sex-education system—a system, as historians and sociologists have shown, that has its roots in early twentieth-century attempts to protect the sexual and racial purity of white women and continues to be used to direct accusations of promiscuity toward young, low-income women of color, especially Black teens.[31] As a reward, Katie has received an above-average grade.

Shortly after, back upstairs in a new area of the house's ground floor, the player finds a second, identical copy of the reproductive-system worksheet. This one belongs to Sam; she writes her name (Samantha Greenbriar) at the top and adds the date September 9, 1994. Sam is three years younger than Katie, and so, we are left to infer, she has taken the same sex-ed class that Katie took three years later. But Sam's response to the directions, as we see on the lined notebook pages attached to the worksheet, looks nothing like Katie's. Instead of simply placing the stages of the menstrual cycle in order, Sam has chosen to poke fun at the idea of a reproductive "story" by writing her own six-paragraph short story titled "The Menstrual Cycle: A Novella."

Sam's story begins like a work of steamy historical erotica but quickly takes a gruesome turn. It opens with the scene of a woman, Essa Glatz, staring out the window of a train traveling from Vienna to Poland in 1939. Essa's heart races as she thinks about her fiancé, Borislav, a baker from her hometown; in the midst of her daydreams, Sam inserts a line from the worksheet: "The lining of the uterus is getting thick and soft." Borislav is waiting for Essa on the train platform—but suddenly a German bomb explodes in the station, leaving Borislav mortally wounded. Here, Sam adds another line from the worksheet, which takes on a tragic tone: "Essa's egg will not be meeting a sperm. It dissolves." Yet, Sam concludes, Essa "vows to survive," so she joins the Polish resistance and becomes "a daring spy and saboteur," while (as the worksheet states) "another ovum starts to develop in one of the ovaries." Like Katie, Sam ends her story with the same ridiculous proclamation, now turned into a Hemingway-esque reflection on hope in the face of existential futility: "It is incredible how the female body knows how to prepare for pregnancy!" At the bottom of Sam's homework, in an inversion of Katie's good grade, Sam's teacher has written, "See me!"

In Sam's assignment, we find a coded manifesto for the kind of scrambled queer storytelling that *Gone Home* seems to enact. Sam, for her part, has refused to fall into line with the directions of the assignment. Instead of simply putting the steps of the story in order, she has scattered these steps; they have been left for readers to find tucked away between the lines of Sam's own tale. "The Menstrual Cycle: A Novella" responds to the normative and normativizing force of standardized sex education by appropriating the worksheet's contents and integrating them into a whole new narrative world, repurposing its dry biological statements in the service of a far more human story. In contrast to her straight sister Katie's equally straight response to the homework, queer sister Sam has done her homework in an overtly queer way. Why does Sam's teacher write "See me!" rather than simply giving Sam a bad grade for her work? Sam's narrative deviations, it seems, have marked Sam as deviant as well. Yet *Gone Home* itself seems to smirk knowingly at the small-mindedness of a teacher who would chastise a student for writing in this way. By juxtaposing this second assignment with the first, the game also casts a bit of subtle side eye at Katie, whose compliant response to the assignment looks, in comparison to Sam's vibrant story, extremely straightlaced: stilted, unfeeling, and lacking in imagination. *Gone Home*, it appears, is aligning itself with the spirit of Sam's queer storytelling, which refuses to be constrained by the normative structures of straight stories.

Wandering on Rails

Unfortunately, however, the queer freedom of movement that *Gone Home* seems to offer players is, in fact, far more limited than it at first appears. Closer inspection reveals that this invitation to wander is only a veneer over a highly structured gameplay experience in which the player moves along strikingly linear and indeed teleological paths.

Although exploring the house at first seems like a disorienting task that offers players the chance to move in multiple directions, there is actually only one way to proceed at any given time. For instance, when standing in the entryway—facing the wide staircase flanked by dark corridors—the player must go left into the hallway; all other ways are blocked. To turn a seemingly rambling house into a preset path, *Gone Home* uses "gating," an established game-design technique, to prevent players from accessing certain areas of the game world before others. Locked or hidden doors keep the player out of rooms, corridors, and whole floors of the house until they find certain objects or trigger events that allow them to move on to new areas. From the front porch to the foyer, from the foyer to the study, from the study to the living room, and so on: the player's path is already set. Admittedly, this path is not exactly straightforward. It twists and turns through connecting rooms, moving upstairs, downstairs, and finally to the attic, where *Gone Home* ends in the spot that has become Sam and Lonnie's private hideout. Yet, the fact remains that, to progress through the physical space of *Gone Home*, the player must move through areas of the house in a very specific, predetermined order. Exploration is only possible to the extent that it allows players to find the correct way forward. The real task of the *Gone Home* player is to identify, unlock, and follow the singular path that lies beneath the facade of the house's twists and turns.

Similarly, the game's approach to storytelling is far more normative than it at first appears. While it is true that the narratives in *Gone Home* are told through scattered artifacts, those artifacts have been carefully placed by the game's designers in a very precise chronological order. Players who choose to rush through *Gone Home* without stopping to consider all of the objects strewn about the house may miss steps in the game's side stories. Yet none of these stories themselves meaningfully jump around in time. Rarely, if ever, does a player encounter a document that tells them how a thread within the narrative ends, or what it was like in the middle, without first showing them the beginning. The main narrative vehicle in *Gone Home* is Sam's diary, which is read to the player through voice-overs as Katie finds new entries in different rooms. From the very first entry, titled "At the New Home," to the last, "In the Attic," these entries proceed in strikingly chrononormative (and homonormative) fashion.[32] One after another, they tell the next chapter of Sam's time during Katie's year away. The topics of these diary entries progress from how Sam feels out of place at her new school to her growing interest in her friend Lonnie to the relationship that forms between Sam and Lonnie and finally to the circumstances around Sam and Lonnie's decision to run away together. Therefore, much as the player must find the linear path designed into the seemingly twisting architecture of the house, these diary entries create a straight narrative line through Sam's queer experiences for the player to follow. In this way, *Gone Home* ultimately straightens the queer potential of its approach to storytelling. Rather than leaving its narrative elements in a jumble, allowing Sam and Lonnie's romance to remain messy and out of sync, the game ultimately tells a story that is strikingly straightforward in its form, if not straight in its representational content.

We can actually see this kind of straight narrative movement at work if we look again at Sam's response to the sex-education assignment.

Reading "The Menstrual Cycle: A Novella" closely, we find that Sam has in fact followed the directions on the worksheet perfectly—though the result probably looks little like what her teacher had in mind. The instructions direct students to rewrite the story, put the sentences that describe the menstrual cycle in chronological order, and end with a "good concluding statement." Sam has done just this. She has rewritten the story, placed all of the sentences about the menstrual cycle into that story in the correct order (albeit, interspersed with scenes from a tale about a World War II resistance fighter), and even ended with her concluding statement about the "wonders" of the female body. Certainly, we can read Sam's reimagining of the assignment as a satirical send-up or a feminist reclamation, a way of following the letter but not the spirit of the law. But the fact remains that, even in rebelling, Sam has managed to fall in line. Her deviations, those imaginative new elements of her story, end up being little more than minor dalliances that ultimately bring her back to the straight path: an ovum starts to develop; the uterine lining thickens; the ovary releases its egg. The operations of the heterosexual, cisgender body move ever forward, following an orientation from which a decidedly straight world unfolds.

In truth, because the player's movement through *Gone Home* is so structured, the game resembles less a simulation of queer wandering and more a gameplay experience "on rails." In the context of video games, the term "on rails" is associated with a subgenre known as rail shooters. These games, such as the *House of the Dead* series (Sega, 1996–2018), slide the player-character as if on invisible rails through the physical environment of the game, presenting players with a series of enemies to shoot. In their movements through game space, rail shooters exemplify the opposite of queer wandering: these games move players from enemy encounter to enemy encounter, location to location, and narrative beat to narrative beat along an explicitly predetermined and fundamentally linear track. To say that *Gone Home* can be thought of as a game on rails is to directly challenge the notion that the game allows the player meaningful opportunities for meandering, exploring queerly, or moving forward along deviant paths. It also suggests that *Gone Home*, which has so often been interpreted as pushing back against the dominant norms of video games, may have more in common with straight-, masculine-coded genres like shooters than years of celebratory readings of *Gone*

Home would imply. Alternatively, a more generous interpretation of the similarities between *Gone Home* and rail shooters might posit that this comparison points to the relevance of queerness to genres that have rarely been considered through the lens of queer experience.

Much like *Gone Home* can be compared to a rail shooter, it can also be seen as a dark ride. Dark rides are amusement-park rides that take place within enclosed spaces. Riders, seated in cars, are moved through the ride along a track. Of course, many amusement-park rides, such as roller coasters, include tracks. What sets dark rides apart is that darkness makes the track (more or less) invisible, creating an experience of movement that feels freeform but is in fact prescribed and linear. In a traditional dark ride, as theme park studies scholar Suzanne Rahn writes, "a customer rides in darkness through a labyrinth, encountering various surprises. . . . In a dark ride like Snow White's Scary Adventures [at Disneyland], the sequence of scenes is fixed in place—it is the audience which moves physically, in small vehicles, from one scene to the next, literally drawn into the story. The aim is to make the audience feel like participants."[33] The comparison between video games and dark rides is particularly apt because, as Rahn says, dark rides are designed to feel interactive. Much like a dark ride, *Gone Home* takes place in a shadowy interior space that seems labyrinthine but is in fact composed of a fixed sequence of scenes. Seeing *Gone Home* as a dark ride suggests that the tension between the forms of movement that an interactive experience (like a video game or a dark ride) seems to offer and the straightforward path along which it actually moves its participants is not unique to games. It also makes literal the impression that if one were to turn the lights on, in a sense, on the structures of *Gone Home*, one would see not an open space for queer exploration but a singular track.

Admittedly, *Gone Home* is not the only video game that appears to offer opportunities for wandering yet ultimately "straightens" these deviations by setting players on a linear path. Arguably, even though walking simulators are known for gameplay that foregrounds wandering—so much so that Kagen renames the entire genre "wandering games"—almost all of these games could be seen as operating on rails.[34] One example of another walking simulator that plays like a dark ride is *What Remains of Edith Finch* (Giant Sparrow, 2017), in which players explore (yet another) empty and disconcerting family home, progressing from room to room to the house's precariously perched peak. *What Remains of Edith Finch* intentionally plays with the notion that walking simulators, and video games more generally, give players options in determining which direction to take. In a paradox of agency, players of the game have no choice but to participate in flashback scenes that result in the deaths of children. In this way, *What Remains of Edith Finch* points to the underlying straightness of certain game-design logics and techniques, such as gating, that are used widely across genres. Over the past ten years, as we have seen, both proponents and critics of *Gone Home* have stressed the game's uniqueness. However, in the opportunities it affords for moving through both its story and through the physical space of the game world, *Gone Home* is ultimately quite normative. Its engagement with queerness remains surface level; beneath this surface is a game that, to call back once again to Ahmed's terms, falls in line with the spatial orientations of straightness.

The case of *Gone Home* is instructive because it shows us how worldbuilding in video games can—to put it bluntly—go wrong. Despite the fact that *Gone Home* has been celebrated for its more traditional modes of worldbuilding (e.g., the use of environmental storytelling), the world that the game actually builds falls short of embodying the kinds of deviant orientations that would characterize a truly queer world. Ahmed tells us that such orientations are starting points. The orientation of *Gone Home*, and other games structured in similar ways, is fundamentally straight, and thus the game world that this orientation brings into view—no matter how many GLAAD awards such games win—will themselves always be straight worlds. We can also see the case of *Gone Home* as a demonstration of how the tools of video game worldbuilding might be used to make straight worlds instead of queer ones. Game design, here, gives the game world its straight structure. This raises concerns about how queerness might be *built out* of video game worlds. Still, it valuably draws our attention to the fact that a great many video game worlds are already built in accordance with straight orientations in ways we might not otherwise notice, thereby opening the door to ongoing reimaginings of these worlds. My primary purpose in offering this critique of *Gone Home*, therefore, has not been to point a judgmental finger at the game, which has already taken its place in a rapidly canonizing queer games history. My goal instead has been to show how design itself (like the design of the player's path through the house or the design choices behind the careful placement of items) can *build too much*. That is, when video game worldbuilding is overbuilt, it can produce worlds that are structured too rigidly, constraining player experience too tightly and ultimately building away opportunities for the kinds of gameplay that allow queerness to flourish in the world.

Speedrunning *Gone Home*

In addition to the structures of the game itself, there is a second factor that has contributed to the straightening of queer movement in *Gone Home*: how certain players play the game. One play practice that brings questions of movement, straightness, and deviation directly to the fore is speedrunning. As unlikely as it may seem, *Gone Home* was, from roughly 2015 to 2019, a popular game among speedrunners. Speedrunning is the practice of playing video games with great precision in order to finish them as fast as possible, under a variety of possible conditions. Stephanie Boluk and Patrick Lemieux explain that speedrunning can be considered a "metagame," one that uses video games as the raw material for new ways to play.[35] Some speedruns use glitches as shortcuts to reach the end of a game or level, while others focus on 100 percent completion. Although the ultimate goal of this play practice is speed, speedrunning's relation to time is not so straightforward. Training to complete a high-performance speedrun takes considerable time, effort, and persistent attention to detail. In contrast to many other forms of solo gameplay, multiple established communities have formed around the practice of speedrunning.[36] Accomplished speedrunners often live stream their play sessions via Twitch and other platforms, organizations such as Games Done Quick host in-person speedrunning marathons, and websites like Speedrun.com maintain leaderboards for current record times. Many speedrunning communities are built around an ethos of sharing "collective, fine-grained knowledge" of games, as Michael Hemmingsen, a scholar of the philosophy of sports, has shown. This allows the speedrunning community as a whole to achieve faster runs over time.[37]

Of all the video games to be taken up by the speedrunning community, *Gone Home* seems like a curious choice. Through its emphasis on gameplay mastery and competition, speedrunning could be said to have inherent ties to masculinist gamer culture. Admittedly, speedrunning communities are far from monolithic, and a growing number of game studies scholars have drawn connections between speedrunning and forms of queer and/or trans play. Johanna Brewer traces a turn toward what they term "queer conviviality" in speedrunning, led by prominent speedrunners and other community leaders with LGBTQIA+ identities.[38] Madison Schmalzer has argued that speedrunning, as a practice that challenges the established rules of gameplay, can offer a critical lens through which to question "other systems of rules, like gender."[39] Nonetheless, the fact remains that most of the other video games that become favorites among speedrunners are not so-called walking simulators but instead more traditional platformers and adventure games, like those in the *Metroid* (various developers, 1986–2023), *Legend of Zelda* (Nintendo, 1986–2023), and *Super Mario* (1983–2024) series. Compared to *Gone Home*, many other popular speedrunning games have little overt engagement with the politics of identity representation. Speedrunning darlings *Undertale* (Toby Fox, 2015) and *Celeste* (Maddy Makes Games, 2018), which both feature queer characters, are exceptions to this rule, but they are also both notorious for being punishingly difficult, making them well suited to speedrunning's emphasis on frame-perfect gameplay.[40] While it would be unfair to say that speedrunners intentionally sidestep video games with "diverse" subject matter, speedrunning does entail a disengagement from games' representational content. By nature, speedrunning is not about the narrative heuristics of a game or the characters who inhabit its game world; it is about the most efficient ways to play.

Yet, despite being seemingly misfit to the practice of speedrunning, *Gone Home* did, for a period, hold a notable place as a regularly speedrun game. In a recorded session of *Gone Home* speedrunning published on the games news site *Polygon* in 2015—a recording that includes play-by-play voice-over commentary from the journalist Griffin McElroy—McElroy opens by asking, "How much do you know about the *Gone Home* speedrunning community? . . . It's big. It's very active."[41] In the brief article that accompanies the video, McElroy writes, "How much technique, you may wonder, could possibly go into navigating a dark house, scouring its corners for letters and keepsakes? Loads. . . . A proper 100 percent run of *Gone Home* is chock-full of moments requiring nothing less than mastery."[42] Posting in 2018, a blogger for the website *Hardcore Gamer* shared a similar take on the phenomenon of speedrunning *Gone Home*: "*Gone Home* was part of the initial wave of walking-simulators. . . . [It] might seem like the furthest thing from a speedrunning game, but that's exactly what it's become."[43] Indeed, for a number of years after the game's release in 2013, the *Gone Home* speedrunning community continued to play and replay the game, arguably bringing it a new life and lending critiques of *Gone Home* such as the one presented here ongoing relevance.

Setting aside the question of what draws speedrunners to a walking simulator like *Gone Home*, we can find valuable insights about the tensions between worldbuilding and play in videos of *Gone Home* speedruns. These videos demonstrate both how speedrunners play and how they make sense of the particular forms of movement they enact in the game. These two facets of speedrunning *Gone Home*—what tactics players use and how they talk about the game while playing it—shed light on the question of whether speedrunning straightens the potential for queer movement in *Gone Home* and perhaps in video games more broadly. There are dozens of *Gone Home* speedrunning videos on YouTube, and the game has been speedrun many more times on live streams and at speedrunning events. I turn here to McElroy's video as a representative (though by no means definitive) example of a *Gone Home* speedrun. This video is particularly useful for the purposes of critique because McElroy demonstrates a variety of approaches to speedrunning *Gone Home*, all while explaining the tactical rationales and the community discussions behind these approaches.

How does speedrunning straighten movement in *Gone Home*? First, it takes the space of the game world and finds the most direct, straightforward path through it. A standard play-through of *Gone Home* lasts around two hours. By contrast, at the time of this writing, the world record for reaching the end state of the game (called an "any%" run), recorded by the Northern Irish player meneely in June 2021, was forty-five seconds.[44] The record for a "100%" run, in which players collect all of Sam's diary entries before triggering the game's ending, was also held by meneely, with a completion time of three minutes and forty-six seconds. Whereas a first-time player of the game is likely to move slowly through new rooms, opening cabinets, reading documents, and "digging around" (what Sam's letter implores Katie not to do), practiced speedrunners know the shortest routes through the house by heart and race along them.

In his video, McElroy demonstrates how to perform an optimal any% speedrun of *Gone Home*: After entering the house from the front porch, go directly to a nearby wall panel that is actually a secret door, which the player is not meant to access until the final moments of game. "Phase" through the door, using a minor glitch to shave off seconds. Grab the key from the little room behind the door, being careful to walk into the room only just as far as necessary, then head up the stairs to the pull-down attic door. Once in the attic, trigger Sam's final diary entry, and the game is considered (by the standards of the speedrunning community) "done." This constitutes what Rainforest Scully-Blaker has described as a "deconstructive" speedrun: one that "dismantles narrative boundaries by transgressing both the literal narrative and the narrative implied by the design of the gamespace."[45] For a speedrunner who is going for a record time, there is no room for digression; a single step in the wrong direction or a moment of hesitation is enough to ruin a run. Speedrunning *Gone Home* strips the game of all its moments of lingering and disorientation, cutting a predetermined, practiced, and distinctly straight path through the architecture of the game. This forcible and repeated performance of straight movement can even be considered an act of violence, drawing from Scully-Blaker's argument that deconstructive speedruns perform a "violence of speed."[46]

Talking about speedrunning as an enactment of "straightness," far from being from an interpretation imposed on speedrunning from the outside, comes directly from the discourse of the speedrunning community itself. Straightness is a prominent feature in the language that speedrunners use to discuss *Gone Home*. Each video game has its own unique speedrunning techniques; for *Gone Home*, a key tactic is to move as straight as possible through the space of the house. For example, when maneuvering up the main staircase toward the hallway with the drop-down attic door, McElroy explains, "You want to get as straight of a line as possible," since approaching the stairs at an angle will cause the player-character to slow down. Later, McElroy says that, when the player moves through the attic to trigger the final diary, "it's all about straight lines, clean lines, cutting corners."[47] Straightness as a sexuality may well not be what speedrunners have in mind when using this language to discuss their movements through *Gone Home*. Nonetheless, this rhetoric suggests that straightness in speedrunning does constitute an orientation toward gameplay. In this sense, speedrunning can be seen as oriented in opposition to the meandering queer movement that *Gone Home* initially seems to offer its players.

Speedrunning also straightens *Gone Home* by shifting attention away from the game's queer representational elements. In effect, speedrunning reframes the game as an opportunity for players to master efficient movement rather than a queer story. This is demonstrated in McElroy's comment quoted earlier that a "proper" 100% run of *Gone Home* requires "loads" of technique and "nothing short of mastery." Indeed, while queer representation is the facet of the game that has been most talked about by reporters and scholars, that same queer representation seems to be far more rarely discussed in the speedrunning community materials around *Gone Home*. It is tempting to see the popularity of *Gone Home* among speedrunners as a sign that the speedrunning community embraces diverse games, but we could also interpret this phenomenon differently, seeing speedrunning as a practice that transforms *Gone Home* so intensely that it becomes no longer a diverse game. It is striking, for example, that speedrunners deem *Gone Home* "over" before Sam has a chance to finish reading the diary entry in which she voices, breathless and joyful, what might be the game's only true moment of queer movement. She recounts how Lonnie, who was headed to join the army but decided she could not live without Sam, called to tell her, "I want you to pack up everything you can and get in your car and come find me. Let's just drive until we find somewhere . . . for us." Tellingly, the *Polygon* video of the *Gone Home* speedrun fades out just as Sam begins to read this entry. The interactive elements of the game have been completed, and therefore, from a speedrunning perspective, *Gone Home* is over. This telling moment exemplifies how speedrunning, in at least one interpretation, can be seen as straightening the game by presenting its (queer) content as unimportant in the face of its (comparatively straight) gameplay.

Unmaking Queer Worlds through Play

Considered through these questions of movement, we can describe speedrunning as a practice that straightens queer worlds, using play to remake video games along lines of straight orientation. At a number of points in this book, I have pointed to connections between video game play and queer worldmaking. Here, we might say, is a case of queer world *unmaking*. Speedrunning *Gone Home* also serves as a reminder that play can bring an array of different worlds into being, including those that are *not* queer. Players are video game worldbuilders, but the worlds they build are as varied (and, at times, as limiting) as the ideologies that players themselves hold. We see, then, in *Gone Home* a lesson in the ways that video game worldbuilding can be put to use to decidedly non-queer ends, whether by designers who overbuild their worlds or by players who make straight worlds out of queer ones. In this sense, we might think of speedrunning *Gone Home* as a practice similar to other forms of fan response that have effectively straightened a queer game—as seen, for instance, in efforts by gamers to straightwash *Undertale* or videos in which live streamers turn video games about queer sexuality into homophobic jokes.[48] These too are instances in which players have taken the queer possibilities of video game worlds and pivoted these worlds toward very different orientations.

Yet, it is insufficient and even misleading to say that speedrunning simply straightens *Gone Home*—or any video game. As the scholarship on queer and trans speedrunning cited earlier suggests, speedrunning itself can be seen as a form of queer or otherwise transgressive play.[49] Speedrunners, in their own ways, resist the normative spatial and temporal paths that have been designed into video games, rejecting the pace at which games are meant to be played and the ways in which game space is meant to be traversed, instead racing through them at top speed and along alternate routes. As McElroy explains, when *Gone Home* speedrunners run right from the front door to the secret room that triggers the ending of the game, they transform two hours of gameplay into less than a minute of maneuvering—jumping straight from Katie's arrival at the house to the end of Sam's story. Thus, speedrunning cuts new paths through games, reorienting play by blazing its own "desire lines," to borrow a term from architecture: pathways trod through grass and landscaping by the footsteps of people following the paths they wish to take, rather than the ones laid out by the official designers of the built world around them.[50] The term "desire lines" helpfully highlights that desire has its own place in speedrunning, a practice that is similarly driven by a longing to cut corners and find new ways of moving.

Proceeding through the game space at the wrong pace and in the wrong order transforms a game like *Gone Home* from a linear, chronological experience into one that is incomplete and even nonsensical. Speedrunners often make use of glitches to jump between game areas or gain other advantages. Schmalzer writes that discovering and utilizing glitches in speedrunning can be understood as a "trans practice of discovery hinting at other methods of self-determination that also resituate our embodied experiences of temporality."[51] This practice similarly resonates with writing by Edmond Chang and Jack Halberstam, who have both argued that glitches can be seen as queer ruptures within video games and othered computational systems.[52] By embracing glitches like the one that allows *Gone Home* speedrunners to phase through the secret door and unlock the game's final area, we might say that speedrunners perform their own version of what Ari Gass has described, in writing about glitch video games created by transgender artists, as "the glitched body."[53] This embrace of the glitch also potentially positions speedrunners within a larger trans "history of undoing mediation," which Whit Pow describes as an unmaking of computational systems that offers new opportunities for "awareness of how power circulates within and around media technologies."[54] Points of connection like these underscore the ways in which speedrunning is itself an ambivalent practice, straightening games in some ways while also resonating meaningfully with the lived experiences of queer and trans people in others.

In the spirit of Pow's call to conceptualize "undoing" as a practice of increased awareness, we might say that speedrunning does not so much straighten *Gone Home* as it makes visible the straight spatial logics that already lie beneath the game's representational content. Speedrunning emphasizes the linearity of *Gone Home* by demonstrating how a game that has been seen as open and exploratory can be reduced to a few straight lines. One could even speculate that this underlying drive toward straightness is part of the appeal of speedrunning *Gone Home*. As I have said, the game presents itself as a mess, a jumbled archive of interpersonal stories. Perhaps the allure of speedrunning *Gone Home* lies in taking this queer mess and making it tidy—as Pavlounis writes, "straightening up the archive" of *Gone Home*—so that the entire rambling game fits neatly into a few straightforward seconds.[55] In this sense, speedrunning has the potential to help make new queer worlds through video games by drawing our attention to the insufficiencies of the game worlds we are already playing. The practice of speedrunning *Gone Home* inherently raises the question, What makes a video game speedrunable, and what would a video game look like that could never be speedrun?

Even *Gone Home*'s failure to provide meaningful opportunities for queer movement can be reframed as a kind of resistance. I mentioned that Sam begs Katie not to go rummaging around in the intimate details of her relationship, yet that is the very premise of *Gone Home*'s gameplay. What does it mean for the player, in the role of a straight person, to uncover and consume (in the sense of media consumption) a queer person's story against her wishes? Even if *Gone Home* did allow players to enact the kinds of queer movement it seems to promise, would these movements represent an embodied appropriation? To an extent, it is fitting, then, that Katie, a straight character, can only move in straight ways through the queer mess that her sister has left behind. Perhaps the limits that *Gone Home* places on queer movement appropriately constrain the player's orientation toward the game. Seen from this perspective, the game's limitations transform from sites of lack into strategies for protecting against the straight appropriation of queer experience. The world of *Gone Home* may be a queer one after all, but it is a world that straight players can only access by falling in line and letting the world unfold around them.

6

Unplayable Worlds

Queer Posthumanism and the End of Agency in San Andreas Deer Cam

It is a sunny day in the city of Los Angeles. People stride down the sidewalk wearing tank tops or cargo shorts, passing the motley lineup of souvenir shops and tattoo parlors along the boardwalk of Venice Beach. Nearby, on the wide-open stretch of sand that meets the lapping waves of the Pacific Ocean, other people lie out on towels, tanning or reading. A woman on a cellphone can be heard attempting to graciously accept the news that she has been turned down for an acting part; another woman on another call complains about how unrealistic beauty standards are here in LA compared to the Midwest. To a Southern California resident such as myself (a transplant from the East Coast to the Bay Area and then, not without reluctance, to the greater Los Angeles area), everything about this scene seems normal: one more day of perfect weather in which Californians worry about California problems. Except that this scene is, in fact, far from normal. First of all, this is not Los Angeles. It is San Andreas, the extensively re-created faux Los Angeles from the *Grand Theft Auto* video game series (Rockstar, 1997–2013). And, more importantly, the protagonist that I am following on screen is not actually a person—one of the player-characters or NPCs who populate *Grand Theft Auto* games—but rather a wild deer (figure 6.1).

This is *San Andreas Deer Cam*, a 2016 piece of video-game-based online installation art made by the new media artist Brent Watanabe. To create the piece, Watanabe modded *Grand Theft Auto V* (Rockstar Games, 2013), a large-scale, single-player game that received considerable press coverage at the time of its release both for its overwhelming popularity and for the supposedly unprecedented control it gave players over its elaborately rendered in-game world.[1] In Watanabe's *San Andreas*

Figure 6.1. The deer in *San Andreas Deer Cam* stands on the streets of San Andreas. (Screenshot by author)

Deer Cam, however, the city of San Andreas is no longer home to the human protagonists who would normally sit at the center of a *Grand Theft Auto* story, nor does it allow players to enact agency over the game. Instead, the deer-cam project transforms San Andreas, and *Grand Theft Auto V* along with it, into an open playground for a distinctly nonhuman subject: one lone deer, who roams the city according to a set of preprogrammed, semi-randomized choices. The result is an epic yet aimless journey, a real-time exploration by the deer of the game's urban landscape that is simultaneously poignant and chaotic. In the original *Grand Theft Auto V*, this deer appears briefly on the fringes of San Andreas—one more example of what Alenda Chang, in her book *Playing Nature*, describes as "the legions of charismatic and not-so-charismatic fauna and flora who litter the playful world of games."[2] Watanabe's mod plucks the deer from the sidelines, remaking this game celebrated for its realism into an absurd yet powerful spectacle. Simultaneously, *San Andreas Deer Cam* prompts viewers to move beyond the well-worn debates about violence and misogyny that have long surrounded the *Grand Theft Auto* series and instead to ask, How do we make sense of video games that cannot be played?³ And what happens to video games when their players, be they animals or algorithms, are no longer human?

Though *San Andreas Deer Cam* has, to date, largely been interpreted as comedy—a kind of modder's prank—I argue in this chapter that Watanabe's piece can be read as a work of posthumanist worldbuilding.⁴ Specifically, I contend, *San Andreas Deer Cam* models what I refer to as a *queer posthumanism*, which has a unique potential to take shape in video games and game-related art. By "queer posthumanism," I mean a version of posthumanism that embraces the resonances between posthumanist visions and intersectional understandings of gender and sexual nonnormativity, rooting itself in the body and exploring nonhuman desires while seeking to move beyond the dominant and often-oppressive norms of society. In *San Andreas Deer Cam*, the queer valences of posthumanism are both representational and structural, manifesting themselves as breaks from heteronormative standards often found in game systems as well as in game content. This reading of Watanabe's piece demonstrates how a queer posthumanism might emerge through video games but also how video games themselves serve as particularly rich media objects for exploring the queer implications of life, agency, and play both after and beyond the human.

In what follows, I begin by contextualizing *San Andreas Deer Cam*, describing my approach to analyzing the work, and situating Watanabe's piece within a longer lineage of game design and game art. I then discuss the relationship between posthumanism and video games, with an emphasis on articulating a queer posthumanism. Springboarding from this background, I present an analysis of *San Andreas Deer Cam* itself, first by drawing out its posthumanist elements and then by demonstrating how these elements can be interpreted as queer, with an attention to the ambivalent picture of queer posthumanism that the piece offers. I conclude by widening out from *San Andreas Deer Cam* to consider how Watanabe's piece prompts us to rethink human agency in video games, identifying the broader queer potential in video games that cannot be played. Ultimately, as I show, the deer cam brings to life the radical act of refusing—rather than doggedly pursuing—the supposed capacity of video games to offer players agency and to place humans in control.

To an extent, this chapter challenges much of what has come before in this book. Over the course of the previous five chapters, I have talked extensively about how video games build worlds that invite players to enter into them and experience them through interactivity—a mode of engagement that is commonly equated in game studies with the promise of agency (more on this in a moment). My focus on player interaction has taken many forms, from an emphasis on designed game mechanics in chapters 1 and 2 to an interest in navigable paths in chapter 5. I have also talked at length about how play constitutes a critical element of video game worldbuilding, bringing game worlds to life. In each of these cases, I have approached the worldbuilding power of video games through the presumption that games themselves are playable and that the worlds they create offer human players meaningful opportunities to enter into them—to experiment with the operations of the world and thereby to reflect on how their own world might be otherwise. In this sense, much of my own description of video game worldbuilding has hinged on the assumption that players can *act*: that video games are worlds built for humans to play and that human experiences imbue those worlds with meaning.

San Andreas Deer Cam offers us a very different vision of what it means to build worlds in and through video games. The piece clearly creates and depicts a world: a specific bounded place (the pseudo–Los Angeles) with its own environments, atmosphere, population, architecture, infrastructure, and more. It is also a world that, like so many of the video game worlds we have considered thus far, is steeped in cultural meaning. However, unlike the other worlds we have considered thus far, this world is distinctly not for *us*. It cannot be played by human players. Its player is the computational algorithms that control the deer; its player is also the deer itself. As humans, all we can do is witness the unfolding of the digital world from outside. In this way, *San Andreas Deer Cam* serves as a response to questions that we asked earlier in this book about game worlds that partially resist the players' access to them, like the intriguing yet opaque worlds depicted through 2.5D dimensionality in *OlliOlli World*. *San Andreas Deer Cam* pushes this resistance and unplayability to its limits. It offers us a glimpse of what video game worlds look like when they are built for nonhuman players, modeling alternative and future worlds that no longer center human beings and our ongoing attempts to enforce our will on the world. Through *San Andreas Deer Cam*, we can add new depth to our thinking about worldbuilding by acknowledging that worldbuilding goes beyond ourselves. We can use video games to envision the worlds that come after our own or to open our eyes to the worlds (worlds of animals, plants, objects, substances) that have existed alongside the human world all along.

A Deer Roams the Streets of Los Angeles

The premise of *San Andreas Deer Cam* is simple: Mod *Grand Theft Auto V* to remove the human player-character who would normally be at the center of the game and replace him (all of the game's playable protagonists are male) with a three-dimensional model of a deer. Rather than being controlled by a human player, have the deer's movements be decided by a computer, giving the system parameters for randomly cycling through different forms of movement, like standing still, wandering, and sprinting. Then set the deer loose on the cityscape of San Andreas, allowing it to roam the environment and trigger interactions with various NPCs, and see what kinds of scenarios and encounters result. Let the deer stroll by the many sights and neighborhoods of this pseudo–Los Angeles: the Santa Monica Pier, the strips along Sepulveda and Westwood Boulevards, the forest of tall office buildings in downtown LA. As time passes, both in and out of the game world, allow day to turn to night and night to turn back to day—all while the scruffy-haired, dewy-eyed deer (a doe in most versions of the broadcast, a buck in others; I refer to the deer here with the gender-neutral pronoun "it") runs through or lingers in various corners of the city, stumbling into scenes of everyday human life and triggering altercations with the short-tempered inhabits of San Andreas. And, of course, live stream the whole thing on Twitch, so that viewers can watch and comment on the deer's escapades as they unfold in real time.

San Andreas Deer Cam is part video game, part artificial intelligence simulation, and part live performance: a spectacle of serendipity that plays itself. It is inspired by a series of short sequences in *Grand Theft Auto V* in which the main character ingests peyote and hallucinates being a variety of animals, including but not limited to a mountain lion, an orca whale, a seagull, a variety of dogs, and, of course, a deer. (This is the buck that Watanabe uses in some broadcasts, whereas the doe is a nonplayable animal pulled from a scrubby mountainside at the edge of the city.) However, the deer cam drastically reimagines and extends this premise. It transforms San Andreas from a world where animal agency is just human agency in disguise—that is, a world of men tripping on botanical hallucinogens who briefly imagine what it might be like to be nonhuman—to a world that belongs, first and foremost, to an animal. By centering the nonhuman, the deer cam transforms the cityscape into an example of what Chang refers to, in a manifesto for environmental game design, as a "rambunctious garden": an ecologically inflected game space that "[sloughs] off the illusion of control" and embraces, in its place, a spirit of the "unpredictably lively."[5] *San Andreas Deer Cam*, in direct contrast to *Grand Theft Auto V*, is all deer, all the time.

Watanabe's piece ran on Twitch intermittently between February and April 2016 and was watched by more than two hundred thousand viewers.[6] For a brief period, *San Andreas Deer Cam* became something of an internet sensation. Multiple news sources, mostly from the games media but also broader pop culture reporting, excitedly described the charming spectacle of the AI deer.[7] This reporting stressed the slapstick elements of Watanabe's piece. Due to glitches in the mod, the deer would occasionally "teleport" from location to location, suddenly appearing in unexpected locales. It would also get stuck on objects, causing it to flop or twitch in a manner unbecoming of an otherwise majestic creature. Most commonly remarked on in these write-ups, however, was the deer's functional invincibility: the fact that it could not be harmed or killed.[8] When the deer crossed busy highways, cars stopped in its path; if the deer wound up walking through a gunfight, bullets whizzed through its body. Some viewers seemed particularly enamored with the charmingly improbable deer, going so far as to create a set of short-lived social media accounts for the deer itself.[9] Other viewers, I suspect, tuned in to see just how much abuse a digital animal roaming a notoriously violent video game world could take and still emerge unscathed.

Far more than being the mere stuff of internet buzz, however, *San Andreas Deer Cam* can be situated within multiple traditions of game design, game art, machinima, cinematics, and nature media. Chang herself, who has written briefly about Watanabe's piece, describes the deer cam as part of a growing phenomenon of "animal gameplay": video games that feature an "animal perspective, in which as players we are joined with other species in a kind of deterritorialized becoming-animal."[10] Chang also highlights the piece's tongue-in-cheek send-up of both typical mainstream video games and digitally mediated depictions of nature, such as live animal webcam feeds broadcast from zoos and parks. Fittingly, the website for Watanabe's project boasts a pseudo-official National Park Service logo at its top, as if the deer cam were simply real-life footage of an animal in the wild.[11] Watanabe also brought his piece directly into dialogue with politics when he created a follow-up work in 2017, the *San Andreas Community Cam*, which followed human NPCs in *GTA San Andreas* who walked around the city crying in the wake of Donald Trump's election and inauguration.[12]

San Andreas Deer Cam could also be compared to other works of game-based new media art in which, as Alexander Galloway writes, "any conventional sense of gameplay is obscured."[13] Such works have often been created with the goal of reflecting on what happens when human agents are removed from video games (as in Cory Arcangel's 2002 *Super Mario Clouds*) or what forms of agency are enacted onto human bodies through games (as in Peggy Awash's 2001 *She Puppet*). With its cervine protagonist, we might alternatively group *San Andreas Deer Cam* with other video games about deer—like the bar arcade game *Big Buck Hunter* (Play Mechanix, Inc., 2000–2018), the massively multiplayer online game *The Endless Forest* (Tale of Tales, 2005), or the physics game *Deeeer Simulator* (Gibier Games, 2000)—as well as games about other deer-like animals, such as Coffee Stain Studios' 2014 *Goat Simulator*, discussed in chapter 3.[14] In addition, *San Andreas Deer Cam* holds a place alongside projects like Twitch Plays Pokémon (2014) that have similarly experimented with alternate manifestations of interactivity through live streaming platforms.[15] Relevant too is Watanabe's choice to use *Grand Theft Auto V* as the object of his intervention. Given the long-standing prominence of the *Grand Theft Auto* series in the landscape of AAA video games, this choice might be viewed equally as intervening into mainstream video gaming or serving the sensibilities of hegemonic gamer culture.[16]

Admittedly, analyzing *San Andreas Deer Cam* poses challenges. Because the piece was a live simulation that ran for a limited time, it exists today only as secondary documentation, including videos and screenshots, most recorded and maintained by Watanabe himself. For this reason, the primary media objects I draw from for my analysis are two videos of the deer-cam feed. The first runs slightly over an hour and was captured on February 29, 2016. Since shortly after the completion of the live broadcast, it has featured on the website for *San Andreas Deer Cam* hosted by the artist; in this way, it serves as a sort of official record of the project.[17] At roughly thirty minutes, the second video is shorter. This video is not publicly available but was graciously shared with me by Watanabe in January 2021 for the purposes of this analysis. While these videos only represent a partial archive of the activities that took place in *San Andreas Deer Cam*, and while they cannot replicate the experience of viewing the deer's adventures live, they capture many important elements of the piece. I also recognize that basing this analysis on Watanabe's video footage means that my own analysis is skewed toward those elements of the deer cam that the artist himself deemed most notable. In a sense, however, no human analysis of a project like *San Andreas Deer Cam* can ever be complete or comprehensive. The procedurally generated nature of its content means that the deer's escapades always exist as a set of possible occurrences rather than a specific or finite media object.

In part, my analysis of *San Andreas Deer Cam* is informed by but also seeks to break away from existing scholarship about NPCs. The deer at the heart of Watanabe's piece is, in effect, a non-player character gone "wild": a preprogrammed artificial intelligence agent who has become the protagonist of its own video game. To date, scholarly discussions of NPCs have largely—though certainly not exclusively—focused on technical questions about how to make them seem "believably" human.[18] By contrast, *San Andreas Deer Cam* is radically uninterested in believability, and its relationship to the human is messy at best. The deer is not human, but it lives in a human world; it lingers on the edge of ontological humanness. This is partially a matter of projection. Players frequently humanize non-player characters, projecting onto them a sense of autonomous subjecthood and forming interpersonal bonds across the human and nonhuman divide, a practice that has been regarded by some researchers as curious or even pathological.[19] Here, instead, I embrace this projection as both a feature of *San Andreas Deer Cam* and a method for analyzing it. It would be impossible for me, as a human viewer of Watanabe's piece, not to project human traits onto the deer, reading the deer's escapades as weighted with intention and feeling. To an extent, this is precisely the point of *San Andreas Deer Cam*. In Watanabe's piece, computation and randomization manage to produce a nonhuman entity that is simultaneously ridiculous and surprisingly human.

Queer Posthumanism and Posthuman Video Games

Posthumanism is a generative, varied, and at times problematic area of thought with ties to both video games and queerness. Though the nature of posthumanism has itself often been contested, it is worth pausing to briefly outline some of its core tenets so that we can identify them in *San Andreas Deer Cam*.[20] First, posthumanism decenters human beings, focusing instead on other forms of subjecthood and animacy, as represented by machines, animals, plants, and even materials like rock and metal.[21] It seeks to move past an anthropocentric view of the world by challenging the assumption that humans are exceptional or that meaning should be made, first and foremost, from a human perspective.[22] In this sense, the posthuman is always also about the nonhuman.

Second, posthumanism questions what it means to be human. Even as it moves beyond the human, posthumanism remains invested in human beings, in that it seeks to destabilize the category of "humanity." This can be seen, for example, in the recurring interest in posthumanist scholarship and fiction in technological augmentation (e.g., cyborgs) and monstrosity: adaptations, transformations, or "perversions" that move the body "beyond" its current form.[23] Lastly, posthumanism reflects an anxious relationship to technology, "progress," and the future. Science and technology are recurring concerns in posthumanism, with many posthumanist thinkers lauding visions of high-tech advancements and others cautioning against the "shallow optimism of advanced capitalism," which often "market[s] as unproblematic the current postanthropocentric turn," as Cecilia Asberg and Rosi Braidotti write in describing feminist approaches to posthumanism.[24] Posthumanism is simultaneously energized by visions of a world to come and mobilized by a fear of that same world: a post-apocalyptic sense that we may need to envision other, nonhuman ways of being because the human world as we know is quickly coming to an end.

The relationship between queerness and posthumanism is a complicated one. Queer studies scholars and scholars of race have lodged much-needed critiques against posthumanism. In "Has the Queer Ever Been Human?," their introduction to the 2015 "Queer Inhumanisms" special issue of *GLQ*, Dana Luciano and Mel Y. Chen describe the "palpable resistance by many critical race, feminist, and queer thinkers to posthumanism and/or the nonhuman turn." This resistance is founded on important concerns that posthumanism's universalism overlooks issues of identity and racialized power, "neglect[ing] generations' worth of scholarship on gender, race, and sexuality" and demonstrating "an uneven attention to race and related axes of dehumanization."[25] As Zakiyyah Iman Jackson has argued, writing about long-standing cultural attitudes that have positioned Blackness as less than human, when posthumanism calls for a movement "beyond the human," it is imperative to ask, "What and crucially *whose* conception of humanity are we moving beyond?" Jackson explains that there is something "amiss in the call to move 'beyond the human': . . . an attempt to move beyond race, and in particular blackness, a subject that . . . cannot be escaped but only disavowed or dissimulated."[26] A parallel argument could be made about the implications of posthumanism for queer people. Any uninterrogated call to move beyond the human risks "disavowing and dissimulating" queerness, rather than attending to the particularities of queer experience. Already in game studies, as Aubrey Anable has noted, certain prominent scholars have used a seemingly posthumanist emphasis on platform, code, and object ontologies to turn scholarly conversations away from identity.[27]

At the same time, other queer studies and trans studies scholars have embraced posthumanism—or what we might understand as a queer interpretation of posthumanism—arguing for a connection between the posthuman and the queer. Eileen Joy writes, "The posthuman and the queer are, and always have been, importantly enmeshed with, and even coeval to, each other."[28] For Joy, the connection between queerness and posthumanism can be traced to a normative cultural sense that queer people are themselves nonhuman. To reclaim posthumanism, then, is a response to this dehumanization, says Joy; it means engaging in a radical act by which one rejects humanity itself. She explains, "So many marginalized groups have always been 'less than human' and there two ways . . . to deal with this: one is the activist path where you fight back for more rights as a fully fledged human, and the other is the (perhaps) more theoretical-academic (and risky heterotopic) path where you decide to take the marker of 'less than human' as an opportunity to finally bid the human adieu."[29] This decision to "bid the human adieu" also has parallels in writing like Susan Stryker's "My Words to Victor Frankenstein above the Village of Chamounix" and Donna Haraway's "A Cyborg Manifesto," texts that have proven foundational for contemporary trans studies. These works locate trans and feminist power in accepting one's position as nonhuman, sparking ongoing work that is making ties between posthumanism and transness increasingly explicit.[30]

This second approach to posthumanist thought, which recognizes its pitfalls but nonetheless values its resonances with experiences of gender and sexual nonnormativity, characterizes what I am referring to as *queer posthumanism*. The tenets of queer posthumanism are related to the tenets of posthumanism more broadly, but they also differ in key ways. First, queer posthumanism remains invested in the body, even as it seeks to explore possibilities that lie beyond it. It rejects posthumanism as a deracialized, "narcissistic exercise in abstraction," as Noreen Giffney and Myra J. Hird write in their introduction to *Queering the Non/Human*, instead attending to the cultural particularities of power and privilege that are bound up in the body.[31] Additionally, queer posthumanism is drawn to questions of nonhuman desire, intimacy, and relationality, exploring interspecies connectivity. It revels in acts of what José Esteban Muñoz has described as queerly posthuman forms of "being-with" radically incommensurable, unknowable others.[32] Above all, rather than seeking to move beyond the human in some universalized sense, queer posthumanism seeks to move beyond the norms of human society. The "post-" in queer posthumanism is post-heteronormative, post-hegemonic.[33] For this reason, queer posthumanism often entails envisioning alternative worlds. This positions queer posthumanism alongside Afrofuturism and other forms of liberatory speculation. Once again, we find that the worldbuilding (and worldmaking) powers of video games are uniquely suited for bringing the visions of queer posthumanism to life.³⁴

On the surface, the relationship between posthumanism and video games seems more straightforward than the relationship between posthumanism and queerness. As mentioned, posthumanism has long been fascinated with the technological, and video games—along with related technologies like virtual reality—have often been the go-to media form for illustrating how the digital might allow us to move beyond the constraints of our physical forms.³⁵ Video games appear to offer players opportunities to become posthuman, to recall N. Katherine Hayles's turn of phrase, but video games can themselves also be understood as posthuman: exhibiting, in Chang's words, "nonhuman agency as a manifestation of software, hardware, and infrastructural processes . . . that go far beyond the human and even the living."³⁶ Indeed, we might ask, playing off the title of Luciano and Chen's article ("Has the Queer Ever Been Human?"), Have video games ever really been human?

Yet, to understand video games as simply posthuman would be to overlook many of the cultural factors that complicate the interplays between posthumanism and video games. Even as video games seem to move "beyond the human," they are still commonly conceptualized as fundamentally human, in that they are seen as machines for the enactment of player agency. Video games also complicate the very divide between the human and nonhuman, as Paolo Ruffino describes in his writing on "nonhuman games": games "made and played by nonhuman actors" that often "play by themselves" using artificial intelligence. Such games, says Ruffino, reframe the medium of video games itself, challenging "false myths of agency, interactivity, and instrumentalism, and the masculinism inherent in these notions."³⁷ In the analysis that follows, I take up this provocation from Ruffino—that a video game that plays itself might disrupt dominant norms related to gender and power—as a jumping-off point, demonstrating how a game that cannot be played becomes not only posthuman but also queer.

San Andreas Deer Cam as Posthuman

San Andreas Deer Cam offers a distinctly posthuman vision of video games. As I have stated, posthumanism decenters the human and recenters nonhuman subjects. Watanabe's piece takes this tenet to heart. It quite literally moves human beings—in the form of both players and player-characters—out of the spotlight and instead swaps in a creature that is part animal, part machine. This is true when it comes to both what happens in Watanabe's piece and how we see what is happening. Whereas *Grand Theft Auto V* positions the in-game, third-person, over-the-shoulder camera behind its human protagonists, *San Andreas Deer Cam* makes the deer the point of visual focus, guiding viewers through the cityscape of San Andreas with the deer always highlighted in the frame. *San Andreas Deer Cam* likewise decenters human agency through its play with visuality, transforming people from players into spectators who could interact with one another (via Twitch's chat function) and who could choose to interpret the deer's actions in various ways (as I myself am doing here) but who could not affect the deer's progress. In *San Andreas Deer Cam*, the deer becomes its own player or even its own live streamer: a posthuman figure who has no need of people. In this way, *San Andreas Deer Cam* crucially differs from other video games in which human players are invited to *play as* animals, partaking in what Marco Caracciolo, like Chang, describes as an act of "becoming-animal."[38] Such games, arguably set out to blur the divide between animality and subjectivity, as Tom Tyler has written in his work on representations of animals in video games.[39] These games can even, in Debra Ferreday's reading of animal play in video games as a kind of "nonhuman drag," be seen as trans experiences that queer the human/nonhuman binary.[40] Yet, in *San Andreas Deer Cam*, the human does not become animal. Instead, if anything, the animal takes over the realm of the human.

The deer's newfound centrality in *San Andreas Deer Cam* also transforms the human beings around the deer. In contrast to the deer's silent, watchful skittishness, the human NPCs who populate San Andreas seem almost like hordes of extras in a zombie horror film (calling back, once again, to the extras discussed in chapter 1): humans who are not quite human. Consider one such moment in Watanabe's recordings. Standing at the edge of the beach, the deer waits hesitantly before entering the city, as if weighing the pros and cons of stepping off the quiet shoreline and into the bustling streets. Human characters stumble by, shouting or talking to themselves. A police siren wails in the distance.

Figure 6.2. The deer watches a plane land at sunrise. (Screenshot by author)

In the low light of the nighttime, all the figures seem shady, dangerous, unpredictable—an implication that is clearly racialized by the preponderance of characters of color (especially Black and brown men) who amble by. At other moments, the deer's presence curiously reframes the human world by drawing out human beings' own status as animals. The deer wanders around San Andreas observing people in their "natural habitat," like an ecotourist strolling through a wildlife park. NPCs working out on outdoor exercise equipment repeatedly call out, "See you at the gym!" Their looping utterances, a common trait of NPCs, recall the repeated chirps of mating calls. Later, the next morning at daybreak, as the deer stands on the beach watching the sunrise, an airplane flies overhead, preparing to land at (what would be) Los Angeles International Airport (figure 6.2). In this context, with the figure of the deer juxtaposed against the airplane midflight, the scene stirs up its own questions. Who is the "wildlife" here, the deer placidly watching the sky lighten or the massive, bird-like machine soaring overhead? At moments such as these, *San Andreas Deer Cam* has the quality of a nature show, silently narrated by a deer, in which the human inhabitants of Los Angeles are the nature.

Like posthumanism more broadly, *San Andreas Deer Cam* brings into question what it means to be human. The deer is a nonhuman figure, and its power seems to come from being unlike the human NPCs around it. Being nonhuman grants the deer immunity, even immortality, since the game world (driven by its underlying code) does not recognize and react to the deer (which has been coded by the game's developers and then recoded by Watanabe) in the same way it would a human player-character. Yet, in other ways, the deer seems strikingly human, heavy with feeling. In one scene, standing in an empty parking lot as the sky turns to black, the deer gazes up at the glow of lit windows in a nearby apartment building, as if longing to connect with the warm, intimate lives of the people inside: a tableau of mournful, interspecies desire. In another scene, this one in broad daylight, the deer navigates a busy city street. Curiously, rather than darting across to get to the other side (cars in *San Andreas Deer Cam* cannot hit the deer, so why not?), the deer trots gingerly to the crosswalk and waits for the light to turn in its favor, just like a human pedestrian obeying the laws of traffic (figure 6.3). In such moments, the deer's actions read as an attempt to pass for human and, by extension, to find human companionship. Scenes like these also serve as a reminder that *San Andreas Deer Cam*, despite its unruly and occasional slapstick scenes, does not truly fit the mold of the "animal mayhem game," to use Caracciolo's term for video games in which animals wreak havoc in urban spaces.[41] The mayhem here comes not from the deer, who is often careful and still, but rather from the human world around it.

These attempts to build interspecies connections inevitably fail, however, and at times quite dramatically. When the deer walks through crowds, it is constantly confronted with the challenges and minor cruelties of everyday human social interactions. Inevitably, in its algorithmic meanderings, the deer veers too close to one person or another, brushing past a shoulder or standing in someone's path. "You touched me!" shouts one NPC incredulously. "You're not worth my time," another exclaims with disdain. No one seems to find it odd that a deer is walking down the street; they interact with the deer, as a coded object, much as they would interact with another human being. What bothers them is the prospect of someone (or something) not doing humanness right—breaking the boundaries of normative social etiquette and getting too

Figure 6.3. The deer waits at a crosswalk like a human pedestrian. (Screenshot by author)

close. In such moments, the deer seems both simultaneously particularly nonhuman and particularly human. It fails to blend into the crowd, looking more ridiculous than ever in contrast to the "normal" people who surround it. Yet, the upsetting experience of attempting to connect with others and being bitterly rebuffed is one that many humans can relate to. In this way, *San Andreas Deer Cam* blurs the divide between the human and the nonhuman through affect rather than simply through the visual representation of difference. It presents us with a nonhuman entity having a decidedly human experience.

Posthumanism's anxiety toward technology and the future is also made manifest in *San Andreas Deer Cam*. In an interview from 2016, given shortly after the project's release, Watanabe articulated how the piece comments on the environmental effects of technology: "To see this hapless deer wander in this gigantic environment, none of which is designed for it, I think is kind of sobering. . . . The piece touches on universal themes like longing and suffering . . . and what technology and human progress are doing to other creatures on Earth."[42] Certainly, this rings true. Yet *San Andreas Deer Cam* also reflects an even broader concern about the world to come—or, perhaps, a world that is already here—which manifests itself through the work's post-apocalyptic undercurrents. To read *San Andreas Deer Cam* as not only environmentalist (in the sense that it serves as a commentary on what humanity is "doing to other creatures on Earth") but in fact post-apocalyptic may seem strange. After all, the piece appears to be very situated in the present: set in an urban landscape designed to look like present-day Los Angeles and broadcast live. Yet, in other ways, *San Andreas Deer Cam* is set in an uncertain tomorrow: a world where animal-computers play video games and humans have become little more than set dressing.

Bolstering the piece's post-apocalyptic implications are the many references to the end of the world, whether textual or visual, that dot Watanabe's recordings of the deer cam. In one sequence, the deer stands by a row of handball courts in Venice Beach; the tall cement wall at the back of the courts has been graffitied with bold, black letters that read, "THE CLIMATE IS NOT CHANGIN. FACT!!" (figure 6.4). The deer lingers here, as if gazing at the words on the wall, which both call to mind and forcibly disavow the looming apocalyptic realities of climate crisis. At other times, the deer seems to inhabit a world that has already ended. Often, depending on the time of day, the deer ends up wandering through parts of the city that are eerily empty. From a dark beach, without a soul in sight, the deer looks out across a distant city skyline; later, trotting along a deserted boardwalk, the deer meanders alone under flickering streetlights. Such moments spark a strong sense of kenopsia, defined as "the atmosphere of a place that's usually bustling with people, but is now abandoned and quiet, . . . an emotional afterimage that makes it seem not just empty but hyper-empty."[43] This is hyper-emptiness on a grand scale, like the set of a post-apocalyptic film where a vast US city sits suddenly, hauntingly vacant, still, and silent. Sometimes, in Watanabe's piece, the streets of San Andreas feel far too full, overflowing with people and cars. At other times, though, it feels as if the deer is the last living creature on Earth. The posthumanism of *San Andreas Deer Cam* is bittersweet. For the deer, moving "beyond the human" is lonely work. It requires leaving the world as we know it behind to find another world that comes after, paradoxically embedded in scenes of the present.

Figure 6.4. The deer pauses next to graffiti that reads, "THE CLIMATE IS NOT CHANGIN. FACT!!" (Screenshot by author)

An Ambivalent Queer Posthumanism

While we can read *San Andreas Deer Cam* as an expression of posthumanism, the piece also moves beyond general posthumanist tenets, coming to embody a form of posthumanism that is decidedly queer. *San Andreas Deer Cam*'s queer posthumanism—as well as the queer posthumanism of other game works that similarly resist normative expectations around player agency—is twofold, emerging both through what the piece depicts and also through how the piece is structured.

As outlined earlier, one key tenet of queer posthumanism is its ongoing investment in the body. *San Andreas Deer Cam* heavily features one body in particular—and what I read as a queerly erotic body at that—the body of the deer itself. The deer's body remains front and center in all the deer-cam footage, as mentioned. Because the artists who designed the deer's character model never intended it to be used as a player-character for an extended period of time, watching *San Andreas Deer Cam* means watching the deer from an angle at which it was not

Figure 6.5. The deer's backside is a point of visual focus. (Screenshot by author)

intended to be seen: from behind. Since the in-game camera points in whatever direction the deer faces, the deer's rump is pointed squarely at the viewer at all times. As a result, the deer's backside, with its high haunches and its swooping round curves, becomes an ongoing point of visual focus (figure 6.5). It twitches sensually as the deer trots; at its center, there hangs a thick, fleshy, phallic tail that wags gently, always just quite covering the dark area at the top of the deer's legs where its anus would be. I do not mean to suggest that we should ourselves find this deer butt sexy but rather that *San Andreas Deer Cam* itself, in effect, presents it as such, coloring the piece with a kind of queer embodied erotics that are triggered by the sight of the plump, swaying, luscious, decidedly nonhuman backside.

Queer posthumanism is also invested in desire, intimacy, and relationality that bridge the divide between human and nonhuman. These too are recurring elements in *San Andreas Deer Cam*. One of the curious side effects of wandering through the world of *Grand Theft Auto V* as a deer, it turns out, is a proliferation of moments of sexual misrecognition. The game is full of human NPCs walking around talking to themselves, primarily represented diegetically as people chatting loudly on their cellphones. When these NPCs move within a certain radius of the deer, their voices are suddenly projected at full volume. Often, it sounds as if they are addressing the deer directly—before it becomes clear, sometime later, that they are actually on the phone. In these moments, the inhabitants of San Andreas say some surprisingly sexual things. A woman in a pink string bikini calls out in a sultry tone, "Hey, stud. How are you doing, honey?" She moves closer to the deer, only to walk on past, the phone pressed against her ear now visible. Elsewhere, on the sidewalk, a man strides up close to the deer from behind, hollering out, "What's that? You're super wet? I'll be there in ten, babe!" The deer stops in its tracks while the man, like the woman on the beach, walks by to reveal that he has been talking on the telephone. This is, nonetheless, a jarring moment. These comments are technically intended for someone else, but they read and feel very much like catcalls: humans on the street cooing sexual innuendos at the deer, calling it "stud" and asking if it is "super wet."

Such moments imbue *San Andreas Deer Cam* with an aura of queer sexual desire, a kind of "inappropriate longing," to draw from Mel Chen's definition of queerness, that ruptures the divide between the human and the nonhuman.[44] These moments are "mistakes," in that the NPCs' comments are not actually intended for the deer, but they are also not mistakes, since they have been triggered precisely by the deer's presence. Encounters like this make the streets of San Andreas into a sexually charged space: queer in its longings, perhaps, but also abrasive and rarely consensual. Indeed, the same preprogrammed instinct that leads some NPCs in *San Andreas Deer Cam* to make sexual exclamations in the deer's vicinity are also the ones that lead other NPCs to call out threats. Whether its presence sparks sexual excitement or a longing for violence, this deer seems to get everyone riled up.

In *San Andreas Deer Cam*, we also see the drive of queer posthumanism to move beyond dominant norms of human society. This manifests itself in Watanabe's piece, for example, through reconfigurations of the "wild." Jack Halberstam, in his book *Wild Things*, describes wildness as disruptive and implicitly queer: "a chaotic force of nature, the outside of categorization, unrestrained forms of embodiment, the refusal to submit to social regulation."[45] Notions of wildness are also explicitly linked to the erotic—a sense of "going wild" and acting with sexual abandon. Who and what is wild in *San Andreas Deer Cam*? In a piece that features a deer walking around a major metropolitan center, the answer might initially seem obvious. The deer in Watanabe's piece is an interloper in the human world, familiar yet alarming, the nonthreatening cousin of the real-life mountain lions that regularly wander out of the mountains to prowl Los Angeles's various hillside parks. The deer in *San Andreas Deer Cam* is also wild in a computational sense: it is the result of a glitchy, if functional, hacked mod that, in its own way, embodies an artist's unwillingness to "submit to the social regulations" that dictate the forms of mainstream AAA video games. In these ways, *San Andreas Deer Cam* can be seen as representing something like the return of the wild. The animal emerges from the forest to reclaim the developed cityscape. The polished, black-box code of the original game goes feral.

Yet, as wild animals go, the deer in Watanabe's piece is pretty damn tame. Maybe, living as it does alongside the human world, it was never wild at all. Its diminutive face shape and fluffy fur make it look, at certain angles, less like a deer and more like a long-limbed sheep. For its part, the deer appears entirely unperturbed by the presence of people: far more domesticated or even domestic than wild. By contrast, the deer's unflappably chill demeanor often makes the humans who populate San Andreas seem wild. They are the ones who hurl insults, who wield guns, who furiously honk car horns when they encounter the shortest delay. For this reason, even as *San Andreas Deer Cam* appears to push beyond various societal norms, such as the norms that divide the human from the "wild," it pauses to reflect on where chaos really lies. In effect, by casting the human inhabitants of San Andreas as wilder than its wildlife, the piece suggests that so-called wildness may not be so transgressive as queer studies is prone to think. What we often call "wild" may in fact already go hand in hand with heteronormativity and hegemony.

Indeed, ultimately, *San Andreas Deer Cam* proves itself to be deeply ambivalent about the radical potential of queer posthumanism. The deer, as a queer posthuman figure, is simultaneously powerfully transgressive and tragically powerless. This becomes painfully clear at the end of the longer of Watanabe's two recordings of the deer-cam live stream. Here, we are confronted with an alarming final sequence that drives home both the importance of queerness for making sense of *San Andreas Deer Cam* and the precarity that goes along with that queerness. The sequence begins when the deer, having walked too close to a passing NPC, triggers a response loop. As a result, the NPC, a young white man with short-cropped hair, gets angry and tries to initiate a fight. He shouts at the deer, clenching his fists and rocking back and forth on his feet, preparing to throw a punch. Meanwhile, by some fluke of the randomized algorithm that tells the deer when to pause and when to run, the deer stands stock still. In fact, the deer will remain entirely motionless from this moment until the end of the video—a total of roughly thirteen minutes, by far the longest "scene" in the recording. Because the deer neither moves nor responds (as a human player would), the NPC too gets stuck, continuing to taunt and intimidate the seemingly paralyzed deer.

Shortly after the first NPC begins to antagonize the deer, another passerby also gets caught up in the loop: a second young white man, this one in a red baseball cap (figure 6.6). He too wants to fight, but, unlike the first NPC, his programming allows him to lash out without the player-character throwing the first blow. He punches the deer repeatedly: in its side, its neck, its head. Technically, the deer cannot be harmed, but little splatters of blood still burst forth each time the NPC's fist connects with the deer's body. Meanwhile, the NPC throwing the punches shouts homophobic insults at the deer, calling the animal "cocksucker" and "you fucker" and howling at the deer to "get fucked." This hate speech, spit out in a venomous mock "gay" voice, is repeated ad infinitum as the scene goes on and on for what seems like an impossibly long stretch of time. In the game world, with its sped-up internal clock, broad daylight turns to sunset, which turns to night; then morning breaks, and it is day again. The whole time, a steady flow of witnesses stride by on the sidewalk. They see the deer being attacked, hear the homophobic slurs, look down at their cellphones, and keep walking. In the world of *San Andreas Deer Cam*, human characters continually prove themselves to be something other than human: cruel, inhuman attackers and indifferent bystanders whose inaction is shockingly inhumane.

This brutal scene is made all the more brutal because, I suspect, it is supposed to be funny. Here, the implicit queerness of the deer is made

Figure 6.6. Two NPCs attempt to fight the deer, throwing punches and hurling homophobic insults. (Screenshot by author)

explicit by the words and actions of the gay-bashing attackers, whose haircuts and clothing call to mind white-supremacist hate groups (and, viewed somewhat anachronistically, MAGA supporters). Though the sequence has been randomly generated by the interplay between a set of computational conditions, to a queer person, it feels all too real. No one helps the deer, and the NPCs' broiling anger seems infinite. It lasts so long that the clip eventually just fades to black, leaving the viewer to wonder whether this anti-gay abuse would have gone on forever if the artist had not intervened (or simply stopped recording). What I find particularly upsetting, as someone who admires *San Andreas Deer Cam*, is that this specific footage was chosen to be featured on Watanabe's website as representative of the project. This act of selection and framing transforms the scene of algorithmic gay-bashing from an unfortunate random occurrence into a homophobic joke. It becomes one of the "crazy," laughable things that can happen when an AI deer is unleashed in the streets of San Andreas. I began by saying that *San Andreas Deer Cam* is often misinterpreted as simply comical. Perhaps it is more accurate to say that it would be a mistake to read the piece as comical without stopping to reflect on the nature of its comedy. If *San Andreas Deer Cam* is funny, that humor comes at whose expense?

And yet, there remains a glimmer of queer possibility even in this sequence. By staying insistently still for the full thirteen minutes, the deer enacts a kind of pacifist resistance. In a fittingly posthuman vein, we can see the deer take on a radical objectness: abandoning its algorithmic animacy and becoming-*thing* (to call back to the notion of becoming-animal), unmoving and unmovable. When we read writing by queer studies scholars like Luciano, Chen, and Muñoz about queerness beyond the human, we might envision this scene. For queer subjects, there is no such thing as going fully "beyond the human," in part because living a queer life means coming up against the day-to-day human realities of discrimination and suffering (as well as community and joy) that are part of queer experience. The queer posthuman subject, exemplified by the deer who seems to transcend the game world even as it endures a violent attack, likewise does not have the luxury of abandoning the material present. It does, however, have the opportunity to reimagine what it means to live in that present, transforming oneself into the nonhuman and thereby setting oneself apart from an unjust human world.

After Agency: Video Games That Cannot Be Played

To conclude this chapter, I want to return to the unplayability of *San Andreas Deer Cam* and highlight its implications for queer posthumanist worldbuilding in the medium of video games more broadly. Much of what makes Watanabe's piece posthuman, queer, and queerly posthuman lies in the tensions it sparks around interactivity and agency. I have said that *San Andreas Deer Cam* fosters queer relationalities between human and nonhuman entities—for instance, by presenting scenes in which human characters appear to proposition the deer for sex or by drawing visual focus to the deer's own body in a way that eroticizes the relationship between the deer and its viewers. At the same time, *San Andreas Deer Cam* fosters a kind of queer nonhuman relationality between viewers and the "game" itself. By making *Grand Theft Auto V* unplayable, Watanabe turns the original video game into something hard, impenetrable, unknowable. It requires those who view the piece to engage in a queer form of being-with, relinquishing the expectation that they can interact with the work or enter into its world and instead only accessing it through the surface of its image. The unplayability of the piece is precisely at the core of *San Andreas Deer Cam*'s queer posthumanism. In this way, Watanabe's work inspires us to reconsider what a video game is, why we assume that human agency is central to the definition of a video game, and what queer possibilities lie in games that either are designed to be unplayable or refuse to be played—or, at least, to be played by *us*.

San Andreas Deer Cam both is and is not a video game. It hinges on this tantalizing, infuriating tension, which simultaneously teases and forecloses on opportunities for human interaction and control. In Watanabe's piece, what was once a playground for humans (the original *Grand Theft Auto V*) has become something other: a display of agency not so much lost as transferred, human agency rendered posthuman. At the same time, since the deer's decision-making parameters have been preprogrammed, its own agency remains questionable. Does the deer decide its own path, or should its choices be chalked up entirely to randomness? Or is there a third option, a kind of animal or even computational agency that is, as Muñoz suggests, unknowable to human beings? Whichever way we interpret the deer, *San Andreas Deer Cam* prompts us to reconsider the most fundamental thing we think we know about video games: that they are interactive, that they welcome players into their worlds, that they give players control, and that that control has a clear meaning. I have described the posthumanism of Watanabe's piece as post-apocalyptic. Yet, we would do well to understand the piece as offering not so much a vision of the post-apocalypse *in video games* as a vision of a post-apocalypse *of video games*. In *San Andreas Deer Cam*, the end of the world as we know it is synonymous with the end of video games as we know them. If video games are a medium defined by agency, this is agency's end. If playing video games is a mode of worldbuilding, this is the end of building worlds.

In this sense, *San Andreas Deer Cam* takes us not only beyond the human but beyond play itself. The deer—a queer, defiant, Bartleby-esque figure who would simply "prefer not to"—often refuses to act at all. It inhabits *Grand Theft Auto V*, but it does not play through the original game's narratives or missions. It has full access to all of San Andreas (which is rendered around the deer in bits and pieces as he moves), yet the deer often chooses to stand still. Above all, the deer refuses to "work" in the ways that an animal in a video game is supposed to: to work like a bit of computation should, functioning as intended within a larger machine; to work as a set piece in a world designed for the human players of a video game that epitomizes the dominant norms of AAA video games and their imagined straight, cisgender, male audience.

If *San Andreas Deer Cam* is a video game, it is a video game after the collapse of video game culture. It is a vision of a time when deer roam the parts of the Earth that once belonged to humans and when computational media themselves no longer care about the people for whom they were created. Certainly, *San Andreas Deer Cam* is far from the only example of a video game that cannot be played or of what Sonia Fizek calls "self-playing games": games that, in one way or another, play themselves.[46] Yet, this impulse to refuse player control becomes all the more potent when it surfaces in a game world that has been designed to give players the utmost control, the utmost agency. By turning *Grand Theft Auto V* specifically into a video game that cannot be played, *San Andreas Deer Cam* models how the very medium of video games can become fodder for challenging the centrality of the human: a deeply queer endeavor.

This queer posthumanist reading of *San Andreas Deer Cam* also offers us new ways of finding meaning in other game-related art designed to be intentionally unplayable. In addition to pieces such as those by Awash and Arcangel, cited earlier, we would do well to think here of more conceptual works created by game designers, like the "game ideas" of Pippin Barr (2015–2018) or Mattie Brice's *EAT* (2013): design propositions intended as poetic thought experiments that would be impossible to play, recalling Dora Garcia's list, scrawled on the walls of the Louvre, of "100 words of impossible art" (2007).[47] These games are all, in their own way, posthuman. By being games, they hail the human, suggesting that people might play them; by being unplayable, they rebuke the human, becoming sovereign entities unto themselves. The value of *San Andreas Deer Cam* as I have interpreted it lies, in part, in its capacity to draw attention to the queer potential of moments when the medium of video games, typically defined by its very interactivity, becomes insistently non-interactive. Video game developers and players have long held as self-evident and sacred the expectation that the medium should strive to make game worlds more real and game players more powerful within them. *San Andreas Deer Cam* models a different way forward, a queerer way, one in which dominant norms are upended, control is relinquished, agency becomes unknowable, and the nonhuman creatures who populate our game worlds come to claim those worlds for their own.

Conclusion

How to Queer the World

I began this book with the claim that video games can help us envision new ways of building the world—not so much because video games build worlds in the traditional sense of presenting us with narrative worlds (some do, some don't) but because video games *are* worlds: places we can step inside, simulations of other ways of being, experiments in structuring the world around us differently. Through science fiction and speculation, authors, filmmakers, and other kinds of artists have often constructed visions of alternate worlds and parallel dimensions as a way of reflecting on the dimensions we currently inhabit.[1] Yet, in a sense, those alternate worlds are already here; those parallel dimensions are right in front of us. They are our video games: the ones that already have been built and the ones we can build. Video games are models for building (and unbuilding and rebuilding) the world from its very core, rewriting its fundamental operational logics. In this sense, video games are precisely the "objects of scrutiny" that we need in the present moment, to borrow a term from Judith Butler's reflections on the COVID-19 pandemic with which I opened this book.[2] They show us that, to build the world otherwise, we need to tackle systems, opportunities for interaction, and the material conditions of our being. Nothing short of a true redesign will meaningfully change our world.

The kinds of worlds that we can envision through video games are bold, defiant, and often irreverent—and therefore have greater potential to be transgressive and queer—because they challenge us to imagine the seemingly impossible. This is what I mean when I refer to the kinds of worldbuilding that video games inspire as "radical." Relatedly, it is no coincidence that I have described so many of the games discussed in this book as "absurd"; the absurd undermines the hegemony of logic and takes pleasure in refusing to make sense along normative lines of reason.

After all, the pleasure of the absurd is the pleasure of living inside a world, even if temporarily, where the constraints of reason have become unbound. It is similarly no coincidence that I have described many moments in these games as "spectacles." A spectacle is at once a performance and an experience, a hybrid moment of expression and awe that exists between the world as it is enacted and the world as it is perceived. By transforming gameplay into spectacle, these games construct worlds that inhabit a similar liminal zone, blurring the divide between the world as constructed and the world as felt. Such games become engrossing, overwhelming, and, above all, *spectacular*, pushing the very limits of what it is possible to behold or even to endure. We too—as players, as spectators, as worldly beings entangled with acts of worldbuilding—begin to come undone when we enter these worlds.

Fittingly, the video games that I have analyzed here invite us into worlds where the fundamental truths of the universe (the operations of space and time, the laws of gravity, the very notion of ontological permanence) have been reshaped or discarded. The science fiction titan Ursula K. Le Guin, in her acceptance speech for the 2014 Medal for Distinguished Contribution to American Letters, explained the critical importance of speculative worldbuilding for upending such fundamental truths. "I think hard times are coming when we will be wanting the voices of writers who can see alternatives to how we live now," said Le Guin. "We will need writers who can remember freedom. Poetics, visionaries. The realists of a larger reality." Denouncing the commercialism of contemporary book publishing (and we could think here, certainly, of the commercialism of the video game industry), Le Guin issued this proclamation: "We live in capitalism. Its power seems inescapable. So did the divine right of kings. Any human power can be resisted and changed by human beings. Resistance and change often begin in art."[3] I would extend Le Guin's rousing words by saying that, if we are looking for such seeds of resistance and change in art, we should turn our gaze toward the worldbuilding power of video games. Video games have always been worlds, but today we need these worlds more than ever. They show us what our world might be like if we could, answering Le Guin's call to action, question the seemingly fundamental and escape the seemingly inescapable, if we could change the seemingly unchangeable, if we could remake our world and resist.

In that spirit, I want to pivot in these final pages from my more theoretical claims about video game worldbuilding to speak about how we might translate these claims into actionable steps for worldbuilders. I have said that video games show us modes of alternate worldbuilding—as well as concrete models for the sometimes nebulous concept of queer worldmaking. So how can we put these insights *into action*? How can we distill these analytical interpretations of video games into a tool kit for those who are already invested in building new worlds in video games and beyond? And, in particular, how might these insights help those who are engaged in building worlds that support queer lives (whether through activism, community leadership, or social-justice-minded scholarship) to do so using methods that are themselves rooted in queer ideologies and cultural investments?

To conclude, let me offer the following set of lessons and provocations for worldbuilders of many kinds. They are designed to be pragmatic but also brazen and even contradictory, suggesting multiple possible processes through which we might build new worlds. These lessons are numbered to correspond with the chapters of this book and are therefore drawn primarily from the analyses that I presented in those chapters. However, for every lesson, I have also offered an additional example of a video game that illustrates how these same worldbuilding principles could be applied differently. There is no one right way to build alternate worlds or to build worlds queerly. For queer people, who wrestle daily with the larger world around us while fighting to make our own worlds, the vision of hope that video games offer is one in which we are always imagining another possible world, and another, and another.

Lessons and Provocations for Worldbuilders

1. *Always be building and rebuilding the world.* Establish rules and goals in order to rapidly discard them. Do not allow expectations to cement themselves into norms. Let no dominant mode of being or doing or wanting settle in. Destabilize identity. Make identity multiple. Embrace the vertiginous experience of confronting a new world again and again. Build worlds by building surprises. Be ridiculous. Push a premise to the brink to find the place where the world ends.

In *What the Golf*, the focus of chapter 1, these principles played out through the game's proliferation of thousands of levels, each with its own combination of challenges and win states. *What the Golf*, as a golf game that constantly rearranges the basic elements of golf, consistently changed its terms of play: whom the player played as, what they could do on a level, and what goal they were trying to achieve. The terms of each new version of the game world only became apparent when the act of play set the world in motion. Through its individual mountain-top holes, *What the Golf* illustrated the central notion that video games are worlds. Its long lineup of such worlds also offered valuable opportunities for comparisons between worlds, revealing how changing the rules of a game changes the meaning of its world. For video game worldbuilders, *What the Golf* proposes a provocation to take the games we think we already know well (like golf) and rebuild them, questioning their basic premises and scrambling their elements. For queer worldbuilders, *What the Golf* reminds us to make space for identities and desires that are multifaceted, shifting, and molten. As queer people, we know that our own forms of being and longing do not fit within tidy, immutable categories. The worlds we build must allow for us to change and then to change again.

For another model of how this ethos of multiplicity might drive worldbuilding, we could look to the game *Everything* (David O'Reilly, 2017), a simulated world made up of procedurally generated landscapes in which players can toggle between three thousand different forms of being. They may begin by playing as a bear in a forest, then jump into the form of a bird that flits past the bear, and then switch to being a blade of grass on the forest floor. Players can zoom in to become dust mites and microbes or zoom out to become land masses, planets, and galaxies. Everything is playable—all forms of life, all forms of matter—and everything is connected. Kat Brewster, in her review of the game, notes that the world of *Everything* turns increasingly surreal when the game is idle, which switches *Everything* into autoplay mode. "Left to its own devices," writes Brewster, "*Everything* will do absurd things. It will plop tubas into lakes, it will bring pieces of pizza the size of suns into space. The game becomes larger and larger, leaving flowers and moons behind to fold into earths, into ringed planets, into irregular galaxies. . . . Or perhaps it will simply parade a group of multicoloured tents around a fire pit, and let that be that."[4]

In *Everything*, as in *What the Golf*, we find a game that refuses to allow identity to stabilize, inviting players to rapidly and repeatedly change their answer to the question, "Who are you when you play this game?" Yet, even as this element of the game parallels *What the Golf*, *Everything* takes the provocation to always be rebuilding the world in its own directions. Rather than proliferating out a seemingly endless array of separate levels, each its own world, *Everything* is designed to drive home the message that, no matter whom or what we play as, all the worlds we inhabit are in fact the same: one interconnected ecosystem that is always disintegrating and reforming. Whether this world we share looks like a stable world or a world in flux, the game implicitly argues, depends on how you look at it and who you are when you do.

2. *Rewrite the laws of the universe.* Question the structures of space and time. Construct alternate temporalities. Think backward. Model the logics of the physical world on the experiences of those whom that world has pushed to its margins or shoved off its edges. Build meaning through mechanics of interaction. Look to the forces of destruction as forces of creation. Be hubristic. Nothing is too big or too true. Nothing is sacred.

In chapter 2, we saw how *If Found* modeled this mode of worldbuilding through its backward mechanics, which tasked the player with telling the story of Kasio by erasing the contents of her diary. Combining the forward-moving story of Kasio's return to rural western Ireland with backward-moving gameplay, the game offered a vision of temporality shaped by the lived experiences of trans people—a vision that stands in marked contrast to transnormative narratives of time. *If Found* also took on the task of queering astrophysics and the science of the universe at a grand scale. It used the figure of the black hole as both a physical phenomenon and a visual metaphor to suggest that the destruction of worlds and their rebirth may be one and the same. Ultimately, *If Found* inverted the operations of space and time itself, a move that it translated into gameplay by giving the player agency to write Kasio's story only in the game's final moments. For video game worldbuilders, *If Found* offers a model for using design to rethink the basic operations of the world itself. It also serves as a provocation to abandon long-established design norms and instead draw inspiration from the complexity of lived experience. For queer worldbuilders, the game issues an impactful reminder that our worlds must resist renormativization, as might happen through a problematic embrace of tidy transition narratives. Simultaneously, it reminds us that we can and should dream big, destroy big, and put no limits on what is right or reasonable when it comes to rebuilding the world.

To find an alternate model for this approach to worldbuilding, which combines the design of nonnormative mechanics with reconfigurations of the cosmos, we might look to *Noby Noby Boy* (Namco Bandei Games, 2009). In contrast to *If Found*, which emphasizes the story of Kasio's personal journey and is largely set in the realist world of 1990s Ireland, *Noby Noby Boy* presents itself as wacky and intentionally unrealistic, with minimal gestures toward narrative. But the gameplay of *Noby Noby Boy* too is structured around the repetition of a singular, unusual task: moving around the game space as a stretchy, tube-like creature called "Boy." The player's goal is to grow Boy's long, rubbery, and increasingly unwieldy body by gobbling up items and creatures in Boy's path. Though *Noby Noby Boy* is a single-player game, it is also a uniquely collaborative endeavor. From the game's release in 2009 until December 2015, players of *Noby Noby Boy* could submit the points they earned by stretching Boy in their individual games to an online database that kept track of players' shared overall stretch distance.[5] This distance was then used to stretch a second character, GIRL. As players earned more points, GIRL's body grew upward toward the stars. From her starting point on Earth, she stretched out to the moon, then past all the planets in our solar system, eventually turning around to loop back past the sun and eventually all the way to Earth (figure c.1). Each time players returned to the game, they could check on GIRL's progress; GIRL's journey was officially complete once players had submitted so many points that she made a complete circle, with her face returning to meet her tail end, which remained planted on the Earth.

In *Noby Noby Boy*, we find a very different vision of what it might mean to restructure time and rewrite the physical conditions of our universe. The time that matters in *Noby Noby Boy* is the time of the body: how long it takes players to stretch their own personal Boys, how long it takes one giant, shared GIRL to wrap herself around the solar system. *Noby Noby Boy* delights in the celestial sights of our solar system, but the game also impishly revels in imagining ludicrous ways of moving

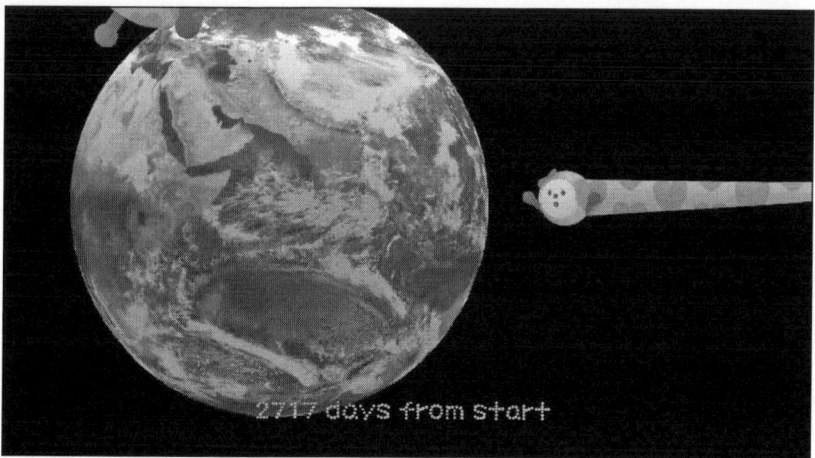

Figure C.1. In *Noby Noby Boy*, players pool their collective points to stretch GIRL through the solar system; here GIRL, having stretched to Pluto and back again, passes by the Earth on her way to the sun. (Screenshot by author)

between them. At the same time, the game raises real questions about the world, which sit beneath its goofy facade: How do we face the vast void that lies between the Earth and the world beyond? What is the role of collective play—and, indeed, collective action—in reaching new worlds, whether they be actual planets or simply other worlds of being? The cacophonous colors and eccentric character designs found in *Noby Noby Boy* are also not inconsequential. Confronting the deep truths of human existence sometimes necessitates being deeply ridiculous, allowing the pleasure of the preposterous to overwhelm the sacredness of reality.

3. *Change the world by changing the nature of matter.* Reimagine the material conditions of the world: how bodies move, how masses attract, what happens when physical entities collide. Abandon the instinct to simulate the real and question how commonsensical notions of embodied realness encode oppression. Build worlds in intimate collaboration with your tools. They have their own desires, other ways they long for the world to be.

Goat Simulator and *Wobbledogs*, the games discussed in chapter 3, drew our attention to how software like physics systems can shape both the material form and cultural meaning of video game worlds. Though game physics have historically been used to simulate realness, they also have the potential to imbue game worlds with alternate material realities. In *Goat Simulator*, we saw how changing the operations of gravity also changed logics of attraction, making the game world "floaty." *Wobbledogs* demonstrated how the body's own movement, exemplified by the gelatinous wobble of the dogs' torsos, can act as a worldbuilding force; the "charm" of the wobble, as Tom Astle described in his developer log, ultimately determined both the game's design and the narrative elements of the game. In both cases, physics did not serve as secondary elements in support of narrative visions of the game world. Instead, the physics systems of these games represented the central, driving force behind the construction of their worlds. For video game worldbuilders, these examples offer inspiration to play with, tweak, and intentionally make strange the software tools that now commonly come preset as defaults in contemporary development engines. Queer worldbuilders can extend this notion, experimenting with tools and systems of many kinds that build the material world around us. These games also remind queer worldbuilders to attend to embodied experience as a force for building worlds. At the same time, they prompt us to seek opportunities to work *alongside* rather than *through* nonhuman technologies.

The game *Nour: Play with Your Food* (Terrifying Jellyfish, 2023) offers a different vision of worldbuilding through game physics. Instead of changing the nature of matter by making it float or wobble, *Nour* uses physics to make the material world into a delicious, indulgent visual extravaganza. The game—which describes itself in promotional materials as an "absurd food art playground" that facilitates the creation of "culinary chaos"—consists of levels in which players can chop, sprinkle, drizzle, plate, and generally toss around components of different dishes.[6] In one level, players drop pancake after pancake into a towering, fluffy, buttery stack; in another level, they launch a barrage of tapioca balls and wide plastic straws at cups of boba tea. Though the game's designer, T. J. Hughes, describes *Nour* as an art and music game rather than a physics game, the pleasures of its gameplay lie in messing around with its physical world, where legions of toasters shoot burning toast high in the air and rainbow sprinkles rain down onto bathtubs filled with ice cream.[7]

In many ways, the world of *Nour* shares a worldview with a game like *Wobbledogs*. Both are structured around providing the opportunity to

Figure c.2. In one level of *Nour*, players control a floating, undulating mass of donuts. (Screenshot by author)

interact with nonhuman animacies in motion. Both use game physics not to create realistic simulations but to experiment with reality. While *Nour* does not have an element equivalent to the distinctly nonnormative dog-breeding mechanic that lent *Wobbledogs* its clearly queer flavor, the game does use its materiality to infuse its world with a kind of queer, multisensory intimacy. Because players are probably familiar with the food items they are tossing around in *Nour*, they can envision touching them, smelling them, tasting them, even cleaning them up off the kitchen floor. This feeling of sensory realness clashes with the unrealness of *Nour*'s physical world, where the ingredients in a bowl of ramen can fling themselves upward in slow motion and a collection of assorted donuts can clump themselves together in midair, undulating in one rotating mass, like a new form of doughy sentient matter come to life (figure c.2).

4. *Shift perspectives to reveal alternate dimensions.* Change the direction of your gaze and thereby change the world that you gaze upon. Seek out opportunities to inhabit impossible, liminal spaces. Be a creature ill fit to the world to better understand your place within it. Make worlds that are deep, layered, and tangible and then refuse others entry to those

worlds. Build worlds that only some people can penetrate, only some people can live inside.

In chapter 4, we looked at how video games build worlds through their graphic dimensionality. Through an analysis of *OlliOlli World*, we homed in on the case of 2.5D video games, which create worlds that exist in between two- and three-dimensionality. *OlliOlli World* illustrated how the unique perspective offered by 2.5D dimensionality allowed for the creation of game worlds with a distinct sense of depth, giving players the impression that they could reach out and touch—or even enter—the overlapping physical and social worlds of the game's fictional setting, the island of Radlandia. Yet, *OlliOlli World* also demonstrated how 2.5D simultaneously resists players' attempts to enter its worlds, using its camera angles to offer a glimpse of the world that exists in front of and behind the playable space without permitting the player to access that world. For video game worldbuilders, this example serves as a reminder to think about not just what world a game presents but also what perspective—both literal and figurative—a game offers on its world. For queer worldbuilders, *OlliOlli World* reminds us that the worlds we make do not need to be worlds that are designed for all people equally. Even as neoliberal narratives about diversity and inclusion push us to create media worlds "for everyone," opening up queer communities to straight and cisgender participants, we are entitled to make worlds that are just for us.[8]

A shift in perspective may also mean shifting the subject position from which we see the world—finding new dimensions within the dimension we already inhabit. Or, alternatively, it might mean approaching the world at a different level of magnification, different scales, changing the terrain around us until the things we thought were insignificantly tiny become enormous and the things we thought were enormously important become a distant backdrop. Both of these approaches to worldbuilding are exemplified in the game *Shumi Come Home* (SomeHumbleOnion, 2023). *Shumi Come Home* is an exploration game about being a small, red-capped mushroom navigating an unfamiliar forest. Players play as the mushroom, who stands only a few inches high. The game world around them is proportioned accordingly. Dainty flowers tower over the mushroom; small streams become wide, swirling lakes; lady bugs hover around like eager, airborne dogs.

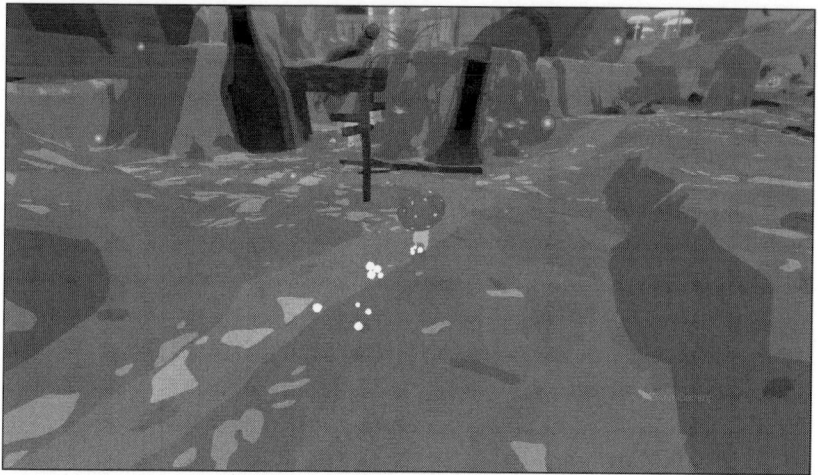

Figure C.3. The mushroom in *Shumi Come Home* passes by glass bottles stuck in the ground. (Screenshot by author)

Because we see the world through the eyes of a mushroom, the world itself changes. The game takes familiar natural landscapes and presses us so close to them that they become both wondrous and disorienting. Traces of the human world that have been strewn about the forest, viewed from this intimate and vulnerable vantage point, seem particularly out of place: glass bottles, half buried in the dirt, protrude from the ground (figure C.3); a set of tea pots bob in a mossy pool of clear, fresh water. Yet these items also seem surprisingly nonthreatening, as if the peaceful world of *Shumi Come Home* is also a post-apocalyptic world, one where mushrooms, plants, and small woodland creatures happily live their lives surrounded by the unassuming detritus of some long-ago human existence.

Thus, *Shumi Come Home* inhabits its own liminal dimensionality. It invites human players to step inside an experience of being distinctly nonhuman and to do so within a world where the human is no longer particularly relevant. The mushroom is imbued with an impossible fungal animacy. It has detached itself from the forest floor, has grown a pair of zippy legs, and now makes its own way through the world. Despite the game's lush, sylvan aesthetic, which would seem to set it apart from desolate scenes of our present global ecological crisis, *Shumi Come Home* resonates with concepts from anthropologist Anna Lowenhaupt Tsing's *The Mushroom at the End of the World*. Tsing writes that mushrooms can spark our curiosity about other forms of life on our planet—curiosity itself being "the first requirement of collaborative survival in precarious times." Says Tsing, "The uncontrolled lives of mushrooms are a gift—and a guide—when the controlled world we thought we had fails."[9] Operating similarly as a guide, *Shumi Come Home* offers us an opportunity to envision a new world by changing our vantage point on the world we already inhabit. When we play as a mushroom, we take steps toward abandoning our human drive to situate ourselves at the center of the universe, participating instead in a world where alternative forms of life (including ones we rarely even stop to think about as alive) are themselves now guiding the way.

5. *Build ways of moving through the world, but do not overbuild them.* Create spaces that allow for meandering, wandering, getting lost. Abandon linearity. Give up hope for telling a story in order. Make meaning and then let it go. Avoid the creation of constricted, linear paths that predetermine experience or use them to reflect on the nature of such limitations. Embrace deviation. Become deviant.

I opened chapter 5 by talking about Sara Ahmed's writing on queer paths and the way that hegemonic straightness attempts to force queer subjects into line. In the acclaimed game *Gone Home*, we saw an example of how a playable space might allow for queer meandering. Yet, upon closer inspection, we found that *Gone Home* serves more as a cautionary tale. The actual opportunities for movement that the game affords—in terms of both movement through space and movement through narrative—are severely limited. We complicated this reading of straight movement in *Gone Home* by considering how players interact with the game, focusing on the practice of speedrunning. On the one hand, speedrunning seems to further straighten the game by cutting the most direct path through its playable space; on the other hand, speedrunning represents its own queer practice of deviating from intended paths. For video game worldbuilders, *Gone Home* warns even those who are invested in constructing diverse story worlds that those worlds can be renormativized by structural design decisions. It is critical to allow players the opportunity to find their own orientation in a game world. For queer worldbuilders, the case of *Gone Home* enjoins us to make space for our community members to move through the world in different ways. There is no one singular right, clear path through queer and trans life.

In contrast to *Gone Home*, which unintentionally overbuilds its world, a video game might build its world rigidly on purpose. A game world characterized by overly constrained opportunities for movement could comment on the highly restrictive options that marginalized subjects have for navigating the world around them. Consider *I Am Fish* (Bossa Studies, 2021), in which players attempt to find a safe path through the human world as a lonely goldfish rolling along in a glass fishbowl. The fish, who has been separated from his fish friends, is wide-eyed and eager for company, but the world around him is—in effect—a hostile obstacle course, making failure always imminent. Players must identify linear and often narrow surfaces along which the fish can travel, such as electrical wires, drain gutters, and metal scaffolding. Rolling slightly askew means falling off these paths and tumbling to the ground below, where the glass bowl will likely shatter and the fish will be left flopping and helpless. From the perspective of the fish, there is no room in this world to be deviant; deviance is equivalent to death. Moving in this way fundamentally shifts how players experience the design of the quaint, seaside city in which the game takes place. In a different sort of game, this might have been the setting for a cozy experience of wandering, exploring the town's European-style architecture or pausing to gaze out at its sparkling ocean vistas. In *I Am Fish*, these possibilities are *built out* of the game world, leaving the fish (and the player) to reflect on what it feels like to attempt to move through a social space that leaves so little room for deviation that the smallest step off the established path means destruction.

6. *Relinquish control.* Decenter the human. Build worlds that take on lives of their own; build worlds and then set them free. Rebuild the world as we know it by showing it through a different set of eyes, while simultaneously resisting the urge to appropriate that perspective so that human beings can make it their own. Use existing worlds as raw material for creating new ones. Nest worlds inside worlds. Accept that building worlds goes hand in hand with unbuilding worlds. Build worlds that render humans obsolete or lay bare our obsolescence.

In *San Andreas Deer Cam*, the digital art piece made from *Grand Theft Auto V* that was the subject of chapter 6, we saw a model for building video game worlds that cannot be played. The piece took two worlds that many viewers were perhaps already familiar with—the in-game world of San Andreas and the real-life world of Los Angeles on which San Andreas is modeled—and repurposed them, creating a world that revealed itself through the explorations of a computer-controlled deer. *San Andreas Deer Cam* productively complicated our discussion about video game worldbuilding by challenging the presumption that game worlds are structured around interactivity, that they must give players agency, or that these worlds should have any place for players at all. Ultimately, the piece modeled how worldbuilding goes hand in hand with world unbuilding: the toppling of one version of the world in order to establish another version. For video game worldbuilders, *San Andreas Deer Cam* serves as a push to question interaction and agency. Is it true, as the games industry and games culture commonly presume, that the quality of a gameplay experience is measured by the power that it gives players to enact change in the game world? What happens when gameplay becomes an experience in losing rather than gaining control? For queer worldbuilders, *San Andreas Deer Cam* is likewise a reminder to question our assumptions about the value of agency and power. Simultaneously, it provides us with an uncomfortable nudge to confront our own obsolescence: the inevitable fact that our queer worlds will pass down to new generations, whether or not we are ready to let them go.

An alternate model for unbuilding the world lies in the game *ALIEN CASENO* (Grace Bruxner, 2016). In *ALIEN CASENO*, players peruse what is essentially a museum of human society, which floats in the depth of outer space (figure c.4). The museum is staffed by an eclectic array of grinning, geometric aliens; other, visitor aliens arrive regularly via a boxy, intergalactic shuttle. A sign in the building's entryway reads, "humens on planet G97 known locally as ERTH have built big things called 'Casenos.' When We visited G97, we liked them a lot and then decided to build our very own 'caseno' on this old meteor." Inside, players encounter more than just a replica casino. They find the aliens' attempt at worldbuilding: a comical re-creation of the human world, dispersed across a handful of galleries. The humor of these galleries lies in the fact that they represent humanity incorrectly while also accurately capturing

Figure C.4. *ALIEN CASENO* invites players into a replica casino that functions like a museum of human society. (Screenshot by author)

the existential weirdness of being human. In one room, aliens gather around a table to try their hand at a game of "ponker." A nearby sign explains that, in ponker, players "sit in a circle and hide cards from each other. . . . The objective is not yet known." In a reconstructed pizza restaurant, aliens play at having a romantic human dinner by staring at each other unblinkingly over lit candles and waiting for slices of "peetzer." The next room is a replica bar; explanatory text on the wall describes how the museum creators constructed the replica so that visitors could have the experience of "eating liquids then making loud noises." Here, alien visitors stand around high-top tables with half-empty bottles in front of them. No one drinks; they seem sufficiently tickled just to pretend to partake in the curious rituals of the beings known as "humens."

Whereas *San Andreas Deer Cam* centers an animal perspective, *ALIEN CASENO* unbuilds and rebuilds the human world from the perspective of creatures so nonhuman that they do not even inhabit the Earth. These aliens have observed the human world, have deconstructed it into some of its visible components, and are now attempting to reassemble its pieces. This act of rebuilding shows us our own world in alternate form, making the norms of our society seem alien even to us, the human players. (Bars really are just places where we eat liquids and make loud noises, aren't they?) At the same time, our encounter with the "caseno" forces us to engage in critical self-reflection. It serves as a biting send-up of a long, deeply problematic tradition of white, European world-rebuilding through institutions like museums of anthropology. Historically, these institutions—there are innumerable examples, but I am thinking of Musée de l'homme in Paris or branches of the British Museum—have often similarly attempted to re-create the daily practices of peoples and cultures who are presented as being intriguing, enigmatic, and, in their own way, alien. Like *San Andreas Deer Cam*, *ALIEN CASENO* uses the stuff of existing worlds as raw material for building new ones. Yet, the new worlds that the *ALIEN CASENO* builds are also old worlds: the worlds of our own troubling and often violent cultural pasts, the worlds of today that those pasts continue to shape and structure.

We Are Never Done Building the World

As a queer game studies scholar and a queer human being trying (like all of us) to make my own way through the world, I hope that these provocations will provide a starting point for others to take up the alternate approach to worldbuilding I have advocated for throughout this book, whether by building video games or by creating any number of other possible worlds. At the same time, I want to stress again a point that I made in the introduction: when I call for us to use video games as tools for envisioning how we might change the world, I do not mean that we are simply changing the world for the better—or, at least, not in accordance with dominant, capitalist, heteronormative notions of what "better" means. Queer people, especially those with multiple marginalized intersecting identities, know that simplified calls to build a better world are highly questionable at best. Such calls commonly serve the goal of more fully integrating diverse people into systems of labor exploitation, socioeconomic hierarchies, normative romantic coupling and family relations, and racialized notions of lawfulness and social advancement. When we hear calls to make the world better or to heal our broken world, we need to ask, Who benefits from healing the world in this way? Who sets the term for what makes a world better?

At numerous points throughout this book, I have posed questions of this sort—evidence, perhaps, that the video game worlds I have analyzed raise more questions than they provide answers. Yet this too serves as a powerful mode of speculation: not the building of specific speculative worlds but the embrace of speculating itself as a radical, endless (and radically endless) process. Ultimately, the video game worlds presented here, as well as many others, serve as inspirations. They provoke us to consider how we might change our world in ways that we may not otherwise have even imagined. But that does not mean that the worlds they inspire us to build will be perfect or unwaveringly just. Building and unbuilding and rebuilding the world is ongoing work that is never finished. The goal of queer worldbuilding is not to fix the world and certainly not to fix it once and for all. The goal is to build the world again and again and, in doing so, to find new ways of living (and loving and desiring and connecting and being) within it. Every choice that goes into the creation of a video game is an act of worldbuilding; every decision we make about how to structure the world around us changes that world. Video games and the modes of worldbuilding that they can inspire contain immense potential. Yet they also carry immense responsibility. This is the responsibility that comes along, as Muñoz writes, with "nothing less than the creation of whole worlds."[10]

ACKNOWLEDGMENTS

Sitting down to write the acknowledgments for a book can feel, in my experience, strangely overwhelming. The final stretch of preparing a manuscript for publication is often a relatively solitary endeavor, undertaken alone in a room, combing through line after line of one's own text on a screen. And then, just before you send the revised manuscript off to the press, in that moment characterized by equal parts relief and exhaustion, you pause to reflect on all of the people whose labor and love have made this moment possible. If you are like me, you realize—in a vertiginous rush—just how many people there are, just how many individuals and groups are rightly owed your thanks, and suddenly the world outside those four walls comes flooding in, filling up the room with the sheer depth and reach and richness of its worldness. It feels as if your book owes its existence to nothing short of the entire world and every person in it, and, though this is technically incorrect, it is also true.

So let me embark on a world tour of thank-yous—in what is surely, inevitably, and fittingly (for all the talk of circuitous queer movement found in this book) an imperfect order. First, thank you to my reviewers. This includes the three anonymous readers who provided feedback on this book project as a whole; your help was invaluable, and, whoever you are, I hope you see your guidance reflected in the final version of the book. This also includes the reviewers who donated their time and insight in reviewing the original articles on which chapters 5 and 6 are based. Chapter 5 builds on my 2018 article "Straight Paths through Queer Walking Simulators," which appeared in the journal *Games and Culture*. Chapter 6 builds on my 2022 article "After Agency," published in *Convergence*. Thank you to Tanya Krzywinska and Helen Kennedy, current editors of *Games and Culture* and *Convergence*, respectively, for granting me permission to reuse and expand on my earlier published work, as well as to everyone at those journals whose efforts contributed to the publication of my original articles. My *Convergence* article was part of a special issue titled "Politicizing Agency in Digital Play after Humanism," so my thanks also go out to the guest editors of that issue, Aleena Chia and Paolo Ruffino, who provided detailed feedback that significantly strengthened this piece.

Next, thank you to my editors at NYU Press, Eric Zinner and Furqan Sayeed, as well as the rest of the members of the press team who have helped (and will continue to help) bring this book into being. It has been a pleasure to work with NYU Press for this project as well as my 2019 monograph *Video Games Have Always Been Queer*. Eric, I truly appreciate both your unwavering support for my work and the pointed feedback you provided when this project was in the proposal stage. That feedback was critical for shaping the project—in both its core arguments and its intersectional political investments—into the form it takes today. Thank you as well to those from outside the press whose expertise contributes to the production of this book, most notably Cathy Hannabach and her coworkers at Ideas on Fire, who have proven, time and again, to be the best indexers and proofreaders that an author could ask for. Thank you to Llaura McGee and the Dreamfeel team for your amazing work on the art that graces the cover of this book. It was a pleasure and a true honor to collaborate with you.

Thank you to my colleagues at the University of California, Irvine (UCI), who have supported me in a number of ways as I have gone through the multiyear process of conceptualizing, proposing, drafting, and revising this project. To my fellow faculty in the Department of Film and Media Studies, who welcomed me with open arms back in late 2019 when I transitioned out of a STEM department and returned to the humanities, I appreciate all of your intellectual open-mindedness, your interpersonal warmth, and the inspiring clarity of your political investments. To the graduate students whom I advise and mentor in the Film and Media Studies, Visual Studies, and Informatics programs, being part of your intellectual journeys has been a profoundly rewarding experience that has been central to my own growth as a scholar. Thank you especially to Aaron Trammell, with whom I co-run the Critical Approaches to Technology and the Social (CATS) lab and co-advise a number of doctoral students. It has been invaluable to have such a close colleague and friend as a constant collaborator—sometimes as a much-needed voice of encouragement and sometimes as a helping hand with grad student care when I have disappeared into the bowels of book writing, as I admittedly do not infrequently.

A special thanks to Jonathan Alexander, Tamara Beauchamp, and Amalia Herrmann, the team that has led the 2022–2026 cycle of UCI's Humanities Core (HumCore) program. HumCore is a yearlong course that enrolls upward of seven hundred freshmen annually. It is taught by nine lecturing faculty, as well as an extremely impressive crew of lecturers and other teaching faculty who lead sections. Each of these nine faculty members lectures intensively for three weeks on a topic under the general theme of the course, which rotates in cycles. I have had the honor of serving as one of the lecturing faculty for a HumCore cycle with the serendipitous theme "Worldbuilding." Though I have been interested in how video games build worlds for the better part of two decades now, it is lecturing for HumCore that challenged me to give true shape and substance to my thoughts about the relationship between video games, queerness, and worlds. If not for HumCore, I surely would not have produced this book.

Thank you to the National Endowment for the Humanities for awarding me a 2023–2025 "Dangers and Opportunities of Technology" grant. The course releases that this grant affords me gave me much-needed time to draft the full manuscript of this book. Thank you to my department chair, Lucas Hilderbrand, for your support in my use of this funding, even as our department's teaching needs continue to grow. Thank you to the UCI Humanities Center, which has graciously provided funding to help with the expense of indexing and proofreading. Thank you to the masthead of the *Journal of Cinema and Media Studies* and especially my co-editor in chief Elizabeth Ellcessor, for your support at moments when I have needed to turn my focus toward book tasks. I am delighted to be part of such a thoughtful, dedicated group.

Thank you to all of the scholars whose writing has guided this book—especially to the fellow game studies scholars (and friends) who have thought deeply and critically about the work of building worlds through video games. Alenda Chang, Soraya Murray, Cody Mejeur, you will find that your names pop up many times in these pages. Thank you to Cass Zegura; advising Cass's master's thesis on queer game engines helped inspire me to dig deeply into the technical elements of video games, an interest that surfaces most clearly in my discussion of game physics in chapter 3. My thanks as well to all of the colleagues and students who have introduced me, over the course of years, to different video games and theoretical concepts that have become ingredients in the alchemical brew that is this book. Thank you to Spencer Ruelos for your patience when I asked you, in exasperation, "But what *is* queer worldmaking?" Thank you, Kat Brewster, for showing me the game *Everything* (David OReilly, 2017). Thank you to those whose more recent work has helped productively complicate my own thinking around speedrunning, discussed in chapter 6, including P. S. Berge, Madison Schmalzer, and Johanna Brewer.

Thank you to the many academic interlocutors who have provided thoughts and feedback in response to earlier iterations of this work. In 2023, Danny Snelson kindly invited me to speak to the Text/Tech lab associated with UCLA's English Department. This was the first time that I presented the material that would become chapter 1 of this book. Also in 2023, I was invited to serve as one of the keynotes for the Queer Directions conference at the University of Toronto, after being nominated by Scott Richmond, director of the university's Centre for Culture and Technology. At Queer Directions, I presented the first version of the material that would become chapter 2. I am grateful to Liat Berdugo, who invited me to speak as part of the Living Room Light Exchange salon series in 2019, where I shared some of my earliest thoughts on queer game physics, the subject of chapter 3. I am also grateful to Ari Gass, Josef Nguyen, and Kara Stone, who were my co-panelists for a 2021 Society of Cinema and Media Studies conference panel titled "Queer Embodiment in Video Games: Erotic Encounters with Computational Technologies." As part of this panel, I presented a second work-in-progress attempt to articulate the queer potential of game physics. Thank you in addition to Laine Nooney, the managing editor of *ROMchip: A Journal of Game Histories*, who invited me to write my 2022 article "Playing with 'Real Women': A Sexual Prehistory of Realism in Video Games," which has served as the springboard for my discussion of breast physics and the trouble with "realistic" graphics found in chapter 3.

Thank you to the many game designers, developers, and artists who have generously supported this project in a variety of ways. My thanks to Adam Robinson-Yu, the creator of *A Short Hike* (2019), who okayed the reproduction of screenshots from a presentation about his worldbuilding process found in the introduction. Thanks also to Elizabeth LaPensée, who allowed me to publish a screenshot from a video she produced of her virtual reality game *Along the River of Spacetime* (2020), since it was not feasible for me to use an image from the game itself. The developers at Triband, the Swedish studio that made *What the Golf* (2019), have been especially lovely in expressing their enthusiasm for a queer analysis of their game. Tom Astle generously gave his blessing for my analysis of his developer diaries, which are core to my discussion of his game *Wobbledogs* (2021) in chapter 3. Ken Watanabe, the new media artist who created *San Andreas Deer Cam* (2016), kindly shared additional documentation from the deer-cam project that was not publicly available. All the way back in 2019, T. J. Hughes, the creator of *Nour: Play with Your Food* (2023), which I discuss in the conclusion, gave me the opportunity to play an early build of the game over lunch at the Game Developers Conference; this intimate early encounter with *Nour* solidified my ongoing fascination with (and affection for) the game.

Academic work is a human endeavor that can feel, at times, strangely distant from human connection. A few lines tucked away in the acknowledgments of a monograph cannot begin to express my gratitude and love for the people who make me feel, in my own strange way, human. Thank you to Eli, for all your moral support and the countless hours of child care you have undertaken on nights and weekends so that I can do . . . this. But thank you also for being my safe, warm place where I can let down my mask, ramble about obscure historical facts, and simply exist. Thank you to Jonah, whom I adore beyond words, for all of the ecstatic silliness and goofy intimacies that come with parenting a small child who is, like me, a strange creature in a strange world that is filled with constant perils but also ever-present possibilities for joy.

Lastly, I am grateful, in a bittersweet sort of way, to my father, who has played an important role in my lifelong (decidedly amateur) fascination with physics—a subject that recurs throughout this book. At the age of seven, I came home from the library with a college textbook about quantum mechanics; I had recently read *A Wrinkle in Time*, and the idea of quantum physics felt to me then, as it does to me now, like a kind of deep magic that lay just beneath the surface of the logical world. My otherwise stoic father, who himself had always wanted to be a physicist, was initially thrilled by my interest. Of course, as a second grader trying to parse the contents of a textbook designed for physics majors, I failed to make heads or tails of quantum mechanics. I returned the book to the library in defeat. My father was clearly disappointed in me, but he briefly held out hope. A few years later, when I was eight or nine, he bought me a workbook designed to accompany a different college textbook about physics—one of the very few gifts he had ever given me or has given me since. For that reason, it was a cherished object. But without the main textbook, and still only in the third or fourth grade, I couldn't figure out how to use the workbook. So, it sat on my shelf as a constant reminder that, despite my best efforts, I was not living up to be the person my father wanted me to be.

And, indeed, I did not grow up to be a physicist. Instead, I became a creative writing major, a journalist, a comparative literature graduate student, and then a humanities scholar. All of these years later, my father will still tell you, with the bitterness of a man freshly scorned, that once upon a time I pretended to be interested in physics but that I had lied. I hadn't lied, though. I've just always felt too ashamed to try again. And so the idea of physics has retained for me both this childlike feeling of magic and a childlike feeling of loss: a loss for the things that I could have learned, a loss for the version of myself that I could have been, a loss for the relationship that I could have had with my father, if only a million things had been different, if only this had been a different world.

I recognize that this feeling, like the functioning of the universe at both infinitely small and infinitely grand scales, seems illogical. Studying physics would not have fixed anything. I would still be a disappointment. I would still be queer. Yet, in truth, the world is rarely built on logic. Allowing myself to return to my interest in physics, as I have done in this book, has also allowed me to begin unpacking that sadness, to begin questioning that shame, to begin reconsidering the nature of that loss, and to begin seeing myself as a person who is allowed to take pleasure in new ways of understanding the world.

NOTES

INTRODUCTION

1. Butler, *What World Is This?*, 13, 14.
2. In using the word "otherwise," I am nodding toward Jack Halberstam's discussion of queerness in *Queer Art of Failure*, 2.
3. Keeling, *Queer Times, Black Futures*, 15.
4. For texts that introduce readers to Afrofuturism and map its multiple manifestations, see Womack, *Afrofuturism*; and Anderson and Jones, *Afrofuturism 2.0*.
5. J. Brown, *Black Utopias*, 2, 7.
6. De Veaux, Gumbs, and Imarisha, "Writing New Worlds," 84.
7. De Veaux, Gumbs, and Imarisha, "Writing New Worlds," 86.
8. See, for example, Dyer-Witheford and de Peuter, *Games of Empire*; Consalvo, "There Is No Magic Circle."
9. McRuer, *Crip Theory*, 2.
10. A recent example of a volume that explores these intersections is Patterson and Fickle, *Made in Asia/America*.
11. Gray, *Intersectional Tech*, 29.
12. Doyle-Myerscough et al., "Other Worlds Are Possible."
13. Mejeur, "Games as Critical Literature," 67.
14. Lothian, *Old Futures*, 138.
15. Some key examples of scholarship that explores queer worldmaking include Muñoz, "Ephemera as Evidence"; Muñoz, *Disidentifications*; Berlant and Warner, "Sex in Public"; Ahmed, *Queer Phenomenology*. For recent overviews of existing scholarship on queer worldmaking, see Zaino, "Queer Worldmaking"; Otis and Dunn, "Queer Worldmaking."
16. The theme of queerness beyond representation is one that I have explored in a number of my earlier works, most notably, Ruberg, *Video Games Have Always Been Queer*.
17. Fassone, *Every Video Game Is an Island*, 2.
18. Fassone, *Every Video Game Is an Island*, 2, 3.
19. Taylor, *Play between Worlds*.
20. A. Chang, *Playing Nature*, 11.
21. For a description of these original *Super Mario Bros.* worlds and a discussion of how they have been translated from digital to analog form in board games, see Altice, "Super Mario Bros."

22 Consalvo, "MOOs to MMOs," 326.
23 Pearce, *Communities of Play*; Boellstorff, *Coming of Age in Second Life*. The use of different international "shards" in long-standing games like *World of Warcraft* (Blizzard Entertainment, 2004–present) or geographically grouped servers in competitive games like *Rocket League* (Psyonix, 2015) could also be seen as dividing online games into multiple parallel worlds. For a description of how multiple servers operate in *World of Warcraft* and the different cultural norms that develop on various servers, see MacCallum-Stewart and Parsler, "Role-Play vs. Gameplay."
24 Kocurek and Payne, *Ultima and World-Building*, 6, 8, 13.
25 In addition, in many games that require navigating large or complicated terrain, players are often shown multiple layers of in-game maps and head-up displays: interfaces that constantly establish and reestablish the conditions of game spaces as navigable worlds. Thus, many video games contain worlds within worlds.
    For the prevalence of head-up displays (HUDs) in video games, see Caroux and Isbister, "Influence of Head-Up Displays' Characteristics"; for the use of maps in establishing players' understandings of navigable space in video games, see Wolf, "Theorizing Navigable Space in Video Games."
26 A. Phillips, *Gamer Trouble*, 13.
27 Consalvo, "Confronting Toxic Gamer Culture."
28 For a discussion of how player cultures differ even within LGBTQ gaming communities, see Shaw, "Trouble with Communities."
29 Bulut, "Fantasy of Do What You Love."
30 cárdenas, "Ones Who Walk Away." I was one of the co-organizers of this event. Due to COVID-19, the in-person version of this conference was canceled, and presentations shifted online. In response to this shift, cárdenas chose to change the topic of her keynote.
31 I am thinking here of ongoing debates within games culture about what constitutes a "real game," which came to the fore in 2014 and the years following with the rise of the online harassment campaign #GamerGate. In these debates, video games made by marginalized people and/or those that did not privilege conflict and skill were publicly reviled as being insufficiently "real." For more on the discriminatory attitudes underlying efforts to police so-called realness in video games, see Consalvo and Paul, *Real Games*.
32 For a discussion of walking simulators and their relationship to definitions of "real" games, see Kagen, *Wandering Games*, 24.
33 Boluk and Lemieux, *Metagaming*, 8.
34 Murray, *On Video Games*, 141–182.
35 LaPensée, "Restoration through Activation"; video presented and discussed in "Artist Talk."
36 Fullerton, "Surveying the Soul," 96, 100.
37 Discussions of the magic circle can be found across game studies texts. The concept originates in Huizinga, *Homo Ludens*. It was introduced to the contemporary study of video games through Salen and Zimmerman, *Rules of Play*.

38 Boni, "Introduction," 10.
39 Boni, "Introduction," 13.
40 For an overview of different ways that narrative worlds are built in media, see Wolf, *Routledge Companion to Imaginary Worlds*.
41 See, for example, Heussner et al., *Game Narrative Toolbox*.
42 See, for example, Paterson, Williams, and Cordner, *Once Upon a Pixel*.
43 For an example of new work in this area, see Tremblay, *Collaborative Worldbuilding*.
44 See, for example, Wolf, "Bioshock Infinite."
45 Wolf, "World Design," 67.
46 GDC, "World Design for Different Player Types"; GDC, "Designing the Settlements."
47 GDC, "Designing the Settlements."
48 GDC, "Designing the Settlements."
49 A. Phillips, "Negg(at)ing the Game Studies Subject."
50 GDC, "Crafting a Tiny Open World."
51 GDC, "Crafting a Tiny Open World."
52 GDC, "Crafting a Tiny Open World."
53 Consalvo, "From MOOs to MMO," 329.
54 Samutina, "Fan Fiction as World-Building."
55 Dolan, "Performance, Utopia, and the 'Utopian Performative,'" 476.
56 Somerville, "Queer," 198.
57 Reddy, "Queer," 172 (emphasis in the original).
58 Tongson, "Queer," 157.
59 Puar, *Terrorist Assemblages*, 2.
60 Haritaworn, Tauqir, and Erdem, "Gay Imperialism," 76.
61 See, for example, Ruberg, "Queerness and Video Games." For texts that overview the subfield of queer game studies, see Ruberg and Shaw, *Queer Game Studies*; Harper, Blythe-Adams, and Taylor, *Queerness in Play*.
62 Valentine, "Last of Us Part 2."
63 Ruberg, *Queer Games Avant-Garde*.
64 Ruberg, *Queer Games Avant-Garde*, 140.
65 Doyle-Myerscough, "New Indie Board Games."
66 See, for example, Evans, "Video Game Showed Me."
67 Ruelos, "Queer Gamer Assemblages," 49.
68 Ruberg, "Forty-Eight-Hour Utopia."
69 In referencing art gallery shows, I am thinking in particular of the show "SHE KEEPS ME DAMN ALIVE," which featured the work of Danielle Brathwaite-Shirley and was hosted at the arebyte Gallery in London from November 2021 to March 2022. Information about the show can be accessed at arebyte Gallery, "SHE KEEPS ME DAMN ALIVE."
70 Halberstam, "Queer Gaming"; E. Chang, "Queergaming"; Adrienne Shaw and Bo Ruberg, "Introduction"; Jennessa Hester, "Warm Glow of a Pixelated Campfire"; Jeffrey Sens, "Queer Worldmaking Games."

71 Ruberg, "No Fun"; Ruberg, "Permalife."
72 Muñoz, *Cruising Utopia*, 1.
73 Macklin, "Finding the Queerness in Games," 256–257.
74 Muñoz, *Disidentifications*, 195.
75 Stryker, foreword to *Transgender Studies Reader Remix*, xi.
76 Jenkins, "Transmedia," 15.
77 I am thinking here of Heather Love's description of queer scholarship as dealing "centrally with untidy issues like desire, sexual practice, affect, sensation, and the body." Love, "How the Other Half Thinks," 28.
78 Haraway, "Companion Species." Halberstam discussed the concept of unworlding in a 2022 lecture at the University of Glasgow titled "Unworlding: An Aesthetics of Collapse." In addition, a discussion of the contents of the lecture can be found in Birch, "Theological House That Jack (Un)Built."
79 Bey, *Black Trans Feminism*, 32.
80 I am positioning my own thinking here against work from within the "serious games" or "games for change" movements that uses "gamification" to instrumentalize video game design in the name of a normative, neoliberal vision of making the world a better place. A text that exemplifies this approach is McGonigal, *Reality Is Broken*.
81 Macklin, "Finding the Queerness in Games," 257.
82 Pederson, *Gaming Utopia*, 2.
83 Anable, "Platform Studies."
84 For more on the murky ontologies of indie games, see Ruffino, *Independent Videogames*.
85 For more on work from this period, see Jagoda, *Experimental Games*.
86 See, for example, Kawitzky, "Magic Circles."
87 Amin, "Against Queer Objects," 105.
88 In respecting this distinction, I am thinking about Cael Keegan's call to resist eliding trans studies into queer studies in "Against Queer Theory."
89 For examples of this work, see Pow, "Trans Historiography of Glitches and Errors"; Berge, "Table and the Tomb"; Thatch, "Cross-Game Look"; Schmalzer, "Transition Games"; Gass, "Glitch as a Trans Representational Mode"; Mejeur, "Playing Trans Stories."
90 Jerng, *Racial Worldmaking*, 2.
91 Kondo, *World-Making*, 4.
92 Benjamin, "Introduction," 14.
93 Muñoz, *Sense of Brown*, 118.
94 Barad, "Nature's Queer Performativity," 137.
95 Ahmed, *Queer Phenomenology*, 15.
96 Chapter 5 has been adapted from an earlier article with permission of the journal: Ruberg, "Straight Paths through Queer Walking Simulators."
97 Chapter 6 has also been adapted from an earlier article with permission of the journal: Ruberg, "After Agency."

CHAPTER 1. NINE THOUSAND LITTLE WORLDS

1. *What the Golf* was originally released by Triband Studios in September 2019 for iOS (Apple devices) and the subscription service Apple Arcade. It was released for PC (distributed through Steam) in October 2019. In May 2020, it was released for the Nintendo Switch.
2. This chapter was originally written in early 2023, when the "A Hole New World" collection was the most recent episode released by Triband. In November 2023, shortly before I returned to this chapter to revise it in December 2023, Triband released its now newest (as of this writing) episode, "Slime Time." This chapter is therefore based on the game's contents as they existed before the "Slime Time" release, with the exception that I have adjusted my estimate of the total number of level-worlds the game includes to reflect the inclusion of the "Slime Time" content.
3. T. Phillips, "*What the Golf*'s *A Whole New World* Update."
4. Nintendo Dads, "Nintendo Dads Interview with Rune K. Drewsen."
5. Nintendo Dads, "Nintendo Dads Interview with Rune K. Drewsen."
6. Lo, "Everything Is Wiped Away."
7. Some elements of the levels in *What the Golf* do repeat, in the sense that a handful of holes are sometimes set on the same putting green. However, no two levels of *What the Golf* are exactly the same. By contrast, the content options in *Queers in Love at the End of the World* are identical each time the clock resets and play begins again.
8. For more on this, including specific references, see the introduction.
9. Mary Flanagan addresses connections between surrealism, dadaism, and games at a number of points in *Critical Play*. For an additional discussion of the history of dadaism in the context of digital games, see Schrank, *Avant-Garde Videogames*, 55–63.
10. *What the Golf* includes levels that explicitly reference these games, clearly nodding to them by using strikingly similar imagery and mechanics.
11. I am playing here on the phrase "I know it when I see it," which was famously used in the 1964 US Supreme Court case *Jacobellis v. Ohio* as a placeholder definition for pornography, raising ongoing questions about the subjectiveness of legal interpretations of so-called obscene materials. Morrow, Fahmy, and Fradella, "Obscenity and Pornography."
12. The *Super Monkey Ball* games have been developed by a variety of studios over the course of the series. The original *Super Monkey Ball* games for the Nintendo GameCube were developed by Amusement Vision and published by Sega, for example. Slightly later titles for mobile platforms like the Nintendo DS were both developed and published by Sega. The most recent games in the series as of this writing—*Super Monkey Ball: Banana Blitz HD* (2019) and *Super Monkey Ball Banana Mania* (2021)—were both developed by Ryu Ga Gotoku Studio.
13. Kasting and Siefert, "Life and the Evolution of Earth's Atmosphere."

14 Serna, "Atmosphere," 122.
15 Serna, "Atmosphere," 106.
16 Serna, "Atmosphere," 105.
17 Brock, "When Keeping It Real Goes Wrong," 446, 444.
18 Fletcher, "Black Gamer's Refuge."
19 Serna, "Atmosphere," 122.
20 Couture, "Road to the IGF."
21 Kunzelman, *World Is Born from Zero*, 15.
22 Lorde, *Sister Outsider*, 48.
23 In the hub world, where players navigate between levels, the player moves by hitting the ball. For this reason, we could say that the ball is technically the player's main object-qua-avatar in the game. However, this avatar shifts so rapidly with each new level that the game leaves no stabile sense of identification with one object.
24 Fickle, *Race Card*, 113–137.
25 Trammell, *Repairing Play*, 9.
26 Trammell, *Repairing Play*, 5.
27 Trammell, *Repairing Play*, 6.
28 "Serious games" is a label commonly applied to video games that are seen as tackling important social topics, often with the assumption that they will educate players about issues faced by marginalized people. For an example of scholarship that uses this framework, see Sanford et al., "Serious Games."
29 Pozo, "Queer Games after Empathy."
30 Bem and Paasonen, "Play! A Special Issue," 809.
31 I explore the queer erotics of hole-based game mechanics in my article "Hungry Holes and Insatiable Balls."
32 This scene is a direct reference to the opening sequence of *Octodad: Dadliest Catch* (Young Horses, 2014), in which Octodad flails his way through a similar church to meet his human bride at the altar.
33 Berlant and Warner, "Sex in Public," 547.
34 Berlant and Warner, "Sex in Public," 558.
35 Yep, Olzman, and Conkle, "Seven Stories," 136.
36 Muñoz, *Sense of Brown*, 118.
37 Muñoz, *Cruising Utopia*, 1.
38 J. Brown, *Black Utopias*.
39 Patterson, *Open World Empire*, 3.
40 Ward, "Dyke Methods," 262.
41 Muñoz, "Ephemera as Evidence"; Berlant and Warner, "Sex in Public."
42 Nakayama and Morris, "Worldmaking and Everyday Interventions," v.
43 Zaino, "Queer Worldmaking," 580.
44 Muñoz, *Disidentifications*, 200.
45 Muñoz, "Ephemera as Evidence," 12 (emphasis in the original).
46 Muñoz, *Disidentifications*, 195, 200.

47 For work on performance, gender performativity, and related forms of labor in live streaming, see Zhang and Hjorth, "Live-Streaming"; Woodcock and Johnson, "Affective Labor."
48 Nakamura, *Cybertypes*; Papacharissi, *Affective Publics*, 95.
49 Fernández-Vara, "Play's the Thing," 1.
50 Fernández-Vara, "Play's the Thing," 6.
51 Lothian, *Old Futures*, 138.
52 Yep, "Violence of Heteronormativity," 35.
53 Berlant and Warner, "Sex in Public," 558.
54 Soderman, *Against Flow*, 19.
55 Muñoz, *Disidentifications*, 196.
56 LeMaster, "Notes on Trans Relationality," 89.
57 E. Chang, "Queergaming," 19.

CHAPTER 2. INVERTING THE LAWS OF THE UNIVERSE

1 For more information about Llaura McGee and her work, see Ruberg, *Queer Games Avant-Garde*, 73–80.
2 Barad, "Nature's Queer Performativity," 137.
3 Mirowski, "Making (Outer) Space to Play," 10.
4 As I discuss more later in this section, my knowledge of black holes comes from a range of recent books by astrophysicists, scientific historians, or science writers translating astrophysics for a general audience. The books I draw from most directly include Smethurst, *Brief History of Black Holes*; Gubser and Pretorius, *Little Book of Black Holes*; Blundell, *Black Holes*; Cox and Forshaw, *Black Holes*.
5 Blundell, *Black Holes*, 1.
6 Cox and Forshaw write that, inside the singularity of a black hole, "nature breaks down. . . . It's not obvious that gravity should be related to space and time. . . . Black holes take centre stage in exploring this deep relationship because they are gravity's most extreme observable creations" (*Black Holes*, 2–3).
7 Though it falls beyond the boundaries of this book's focus on video game worldbuilding, I see potential in expanding this reflection on the queerness of black holes, which could be explored through works like Leo Bersani's classic 1987 queer theory essay "Is the Rectum a Grave?" (in *Is the Rectum a Grave? and Other Essays*) or Georges Bataille's earlier 1931 "The Solar Anus" (in *Visions of Excess*).
8 Cox and Forshaw, *Black Holes*, 3, 11; Smethurst, *Brief History of Black Holes*, 7, 106.
9 In referring to anti–South Asian racism, I am referring to the confluence of two particular, notable incidents in the intellectual history of black holes. The first is the extremely dismissive response of the white (predominantly British) scientific community to Subrahmanyan Chandrasekhar's calculation of electronic pressure degeneracy limits, which he performed in 1930; Chandrasekhar, an Indian student then traveling to study in England, was awarded the Nobel Prize for this work, which functionally proved the existence of black holes, in 1983. See Cox and Forshaw, *Black Holes*, 13–14. The second is the naming of black holes themselves. The

name was reportedly coined when the white American physicist Robert H. Dicke, speaking at a symposium in Texas in 1961, compared "gravitationally completely collapsed stars" (what we would now call black holes) to the "black hole of Calcutta," a reference to an infamous prison cell in Fort William in Kolkata, India—a facility that was itself built to defend the interests of the occupying British East India Company. See Smethurst, *Brief History of Black Holes*, 71–72.

10 Wallace, *Invisibility Blues*, 218.
11 Hammonds, "Black (W)holes," 138. Smethurst explains this concept from an astrophysics perspective: "The term black hole leads people to believe that black holes are the absence of something. That they are negative space. Something that takes away. . . . A black hole is the furthest thing from a hole you can get. A black hole isn't the absence of something; it's the presence of *everything*; matter in its densest possible form." Smethurst, *Brief History of Black Holes*, 59 (emphasis in original).
12 S. Brown, *Dark Matters*; Glissant, *Poetics of Relation*; Bey, *Black Trans Feminism*.
13 Astrophysicists and other science writers seem endlessly fascinated with reiterating that no information can leave the event horizon of a black hole—which is to say, in part, that anything that travels beyond the event horizon (a kind of point of no return) will be irreversibly pulled in by the black hole's gravity, even light. Thus, whatever lies inside the black hole can never be seen from the outside. See, for example, Smethurst, *Brief History of Black Holes*, 118; Blundell, *Black Holes*, 28.
14 Cox and Forshaw, *Black Holes*.
15 Indeed, McGee herself grew up in County Donegal, also along Ireland's west coast. Ruberg, *Queer Games Avant-Garde*, 66.
16 Mejeur and Pellegrini, "Introduction," 127.
17 Flanagan and Nissenbaum, *Values at Play in Digital Games*.
18 Chess, *Ready Player Two*, 48.
19 We might also think here of a media trope like "bury your gays"—a critical term often applied by queer fans to media franchises that conspicuously kill off their LGBTQ characters—as a form of erasure, removing queer and trans characters from the world of the media object at hand. See, for example, Cover and Milne, "'Bury Your Gays' Trope."
20 I am using he/him pronouns for Shans because these are the pronouns that the game's other characters use for him. However, it is hinted at that Shans himself may also be trans (he looks up to Kasio and says he sees himself in her). Indeed, a character that strikingly resembles Shans appears at the end of Cassiopeia's narrative, where this character is depicted as nonbinary and described using they/them pronouns.
21 Gardner and Tanenbaum, "At the Edge."
22 Hanson, *Game Time*, 12, 2.
23 Wilcox, "Illusions of Space and Time," 116, 117.
24 Keeling, *Queer Times, Black Futures*; Freeman, *Time Binds*; Halberstam, *In a Queer Time and Place*.

25 A frequently cited example of this, also mentioned in chapter 1, is Anna Anthropy's Twine game *Queers in Love at the End of the World*; for an analysis of its queer temporality, see Lo, "Everything Is Wiped Away." An exception to this focus on smaller-scale indie games is Matt Knutson's queer reading of the time-based mechanics in the *Life Is Strange* series (Dontnod Entertainment, 2015–2022). See Knutson, "Backtrack, Pause, Rewind, Reset."
26 For more on the implications for worldbuilding of the time-based mechanics in *Mainichi*, see Ruberg, "Permalife"; for more on queer temporality in *Ritual of the Moon*, see Stone, "Time and Reparative Game Design."
27 Love, *Feeling Backwards*, 3, 7.
28 J. Brown, *Black Utopias*, 8, 15.
29 Keegan, "Against Queer Theory."
30 Devun and Tortorici, "Trans, Time, and History," 518, 521.
31 Malatino, *Queer Embodiment*, 110.
32 I say "men and women" here because these dominant transition narratives rarely account for the identities or experiences of nonbinary people.
33 Lau, "Trans-Temporality," 414.
34 Snorton, *Black on Both Sides*, 2.
35 Malatino, *Side Effects*, 21.
36 J. Chen, *Trans Exploits*, 6.
37 Malatino, *Side Effects*, 8.
38 Additionally, because transnormative narratives foreground progress and forward movement, they fail to account for experiences of trans time that are not about transition in the first place. Not all trans folks transition; not all transitions are visible or legible from the outside; not all transitions are permanent or immutable. Rather than understanding transness as a state of motion, a directional movement though time, we might do well instead to imagine it as a state of being: a commingled experience of one's identity and one's body as out of sync with normative gender expectations. This experience may shift over time, or it might not. We might change our bodies or our self-presentations in response to it, or we might not. We might follow the winding path to gender self-actualization, or we might give up on the very notion of reaching some future destination imagined as gender truth or gender euphoria. Many trans and nonbinary folks experience transness as a transition, surely, but some of us (like myself) more often experience it as stasis, a stuckness, the inability to move into one gendered world or another. Theorizations of trans temporality must remain open enough to account for our lived experiences of time, too. Despite the motion implied in the very term "trans," some of us are going nowhere at all.
39 Andrucki and Kaplan, "Trans Objects."
40 Greenfieldboyce, "Goodbye Fuzzy Donut." Cox and Forshaw explain this circle of light: "The bright disk surrounding the shadow [the inner area of the black hole] is formed mainly by rays of light emitted from gas and dust spiraling around and

into the black hole, their paths twisted and forged into a distinctive donut shape by the hole's gravity" (*Black Holes*, 6).

41 Cox and Forshaw, *Black Holes*, 11.
42 Regarding gravitational tidal forces, see Gubser and Pretorius, *Little Book of Black Holes*, 65; and Cox and Forshaw, *Black Holes*, 101.
43 Cox and Forshaw, *Black Holes*, 23.
44 Cox and Forshaw, *Black Holes*, 104.
45 I use "entity" rather than "person" here to acknowledge that, in reality, a human being would be destroyed by the gravitational force of a black hole long before they could reach its core. I am always baffled and entertained how many professional physicists describe black holes using diagrams and thought experiments that ask, "What kind of time dilation would a person experience around a black hole?" or "What would a person see from inside a black hole?" as if a person would not have already been long ago disintegrated into bits and recompressed into a point of infinite mass.
46 Lim, *Translating Time*, 2, 12.
47 Cox and Forshaw make a similar point in drawing parallels between physics, mathematics, and computer science. They write, "The mathematics of the twentieth century described a Universe populated by a limited number of different types of fundamental particles interacting with each other in an arena known as space-time according to a collection of rules that can be written down on the back of an envelope. If the Universe were designed, it seemed, the designer was a mathematician." Today, they posit, with the rise of the "language of information," we might instead say, "If the Universe is designed, it seems, the designer is a programmer" (*Black Holes*, 20). More fitting still, I would argue, would be to claim something like, If the Universe is designed, the designer is a game designer.

CHAPTER 3. QUEER BODIES IN MOTION

1 Bennett, *Vibrant Matter*, xvi.
2 Caracciolo, "Animal Mayhem Games."
3 For a description of gravity as attraction, see Cox and Forshaw, *Black Holes*, 4.
4 Hutchinson, "Making the Water Move."
5 Shinkle, "Of Particle Systems," 64.
6 Nicoll and Keogh, *Unity Game Engine*, 67.
7 Epic Games, "Fluid Simulation"; Epic Games, "Hair Physics Overview."
8 Monnens and Goldberg, "Space Odyssey," 124.
9 This claim that *Spacewar!* began as a physics simulation is drawn from statements made by the game's creators at a 2018 event at the Smithsonian's National Museum of American History. Information about the event, which featured a panel of speakers who had contributed to developing the original game, can be found in this press release: Havel, "*Spacewar!*"
10 Ruberg, "Playing with 'Real Women.'"
11 See, for example, Bourg and Bywalec, *Physics for Game Developers*, xii.

12 Wardrip-Fruin, "Gravity in Computer Space."
13 Wing, "Not without Matter or Substance."
14 Galloway, "Social Realism in Gaming."
15 For a discussion of "realness" in both its original meanings for queer cultures and in its present-day appropriation by straight discourse, see Heller, "RuPaul Realness."
16 Galloway, "Social Realism in Gaming."
17 Galloway, "Social Realism in Gaming."
18 Freedman, *Persistence of Code*, 124.
19 A. Phillips, "Dicks, Dicks, Dicks."
20 Pozo, "Queer Games after Empathy."
21 Khaw, "With a Popsicle."
22 Ruberg, *Queer Games Avant-Garde*, 96.
23 Love, "How the Other Half Thinks," 28.
24 Gass, "Machine Embodiment."
25 PC Gamer, "Weird Arm Physics of Jurassic Park."
26 Ruberg, "Playing with 'Real Women.'"
27 Rogers and Liebler, "Jubblies, Mammaries, and Boobs."
28 Cadorniga, "*Goat Simulator 3*."
29 Admittedly, these games sometimes offer players opportunities to shift the appearance of their characters—temporarily transforming the goat into a giraffe or an ostrich, for instance—but playing in goat mode is the games' real focus.
30 Ibrisagic, "How *Goat Simulator* Really Did Become Our Next IP."
31 A. Chang, *Playing Nature*, 188.
32 For a discussion of the term "floatiness," as well as evidence that designers and gamers themselves often disagree on its precise meaning, see this thread: r/gamedesign, "What the hell does 'floaty' mean?"
33 A "hit box" is the designated area around an in-game object that the game recognizes as describing its interactable, physical presence. For example, if a game presents a clump of grass for the player to slash with a sword, the grass will probably be enclosed within a hit box that is somewhat larger and less intricately contoured than the clump of grass itself. This allows the player to swipe their sword and "hit" the clump without needing to literally contact an individual blade of grass.
34 A notable example of this is quantum physics, which is based around probabilities rather than absolutes. See Cox and Forshaw, *Black Holes*, 191–192; Gubser and Pretorius, *Little Book of Black Holes*, 148–157.
35 Cox and Forshaw, *Black Holes*, 4.
36 Smethurst, *Brief History of Black Holes*, 61.
37 This comes from a Twitter thread that Ana Valens posted in 2019 but has since taken down.
38 A. Phillips, "Dicks, Dicks, Dicks."
39 Cox and Forshaw, *Black Holes*, 4.

40 Eve Sedgwick makes a similar rhetorical move in linking "gravity" and "gravitas" in a brief discussion of how queer of color theory "deepens and shifts" what she refers to as the "gravity . . . of the term 'queer'" (*Tendencies*, 9).
41 For a discussion of the place of asexuality under the larger umbrella of queerness, see, for example, Przybylo and Cooper, "Asexual Resonances."
42 See, for example, Chesney and Lawson, "Illusion of Love."
43 The game gives "Mingle" as the default name for this first dog, but the player can also choose to toggle through other name options or write in their own.
44 See, for example, the "community showcase" video series created by the YouTuber Cork, "Smallest AND Largest Dog!"
45 Aziz, "Over 65 Million Creations Made"; Queerness N'Games, "Beautiful Monsters."
46 For more on Freeman's games and *How Do You Do It?*, see Ruberg, *Queer Games Avant-Garde*, 171–179.
47 Fiedler, "Mixed-Race Child," 51.
48 A classic example of this is the 1992 novel *Children of Men* (P. D. James) and the 2006 film by the same name (*Children of Men*, dir. Alfonso Cuarón), which Lee Edelman addresses in his introduction to *No Future* (11–13), though these examples admittedly reflect straight cultural anxieties about queer reproduction rather than queer speculative thinking about reproductive futures.
49 M. Chen, *Animacies*.
50 Strings, *Fearing the Black Body*.
51 Though Josh Widera does not make an explicit connection to queerness, he does intriguingly connect non-Newtonian fluids to political resistance in his writing on the substance oobleck. In a description that has clear queer implications, he writes, "Non-Newtonian fluids are fluids that exhibit both liquid and solid attributes. Chemico-physical misfits [and] misbehaving substances" ("One Part Water," 160).
52 TIGForums, "Wobbledogs."
53 Tom Astle, comment on TIGForums, "Wobbledogs," February 22, 2016, https://forums.tigsource.com/index.php?topic=53994.0.
54 Tom Astle, comment on TIGForums, "Wobbledogs," June 1, 2016, https://forums.tigsource.com/index.php?topic=53994.140.
55 Tom Astle, comment on TIGForums, "Wobbledogs," June 12, 2016, https://forums.tigsource.com/index.php?topic=53994.140.
56 Tom Astle, comment on TIGForums, "Wobbledogs," June 29, 2016, https://forums.tigsource.com/index.php?topic=53994.160.
57 Regarding the charm of "goofy physics," see Tom Astle, comment on TIGForums, "Wobbledogs," September 22, 2016, https://forums.tigsource.com/index.php?topic=53994.300.
58 Tom Astle, comment on TIGForums, "Wobbledogs," September 17, 2018, https://forums.tigsource.com/index.php?topic=53994.640.
59 Astle, "Genetic Algorithm."

60 Tom Astle, comment on TIGForums, "Wobbledogs," August 1, 2016, https://forums.tigsource.com/index.php?topic=53994.220.
61 Tom Astle, comment on TIGForums, "Wobbledogs," August 17, 2016, https://forums.tigsource.com/index.php?topic=53994.240.
62 Tom Astle, comment on TIGForums, "Wobbledogs," October 5, 2016, https://forums.tigsource.com/index.php?topic=53994.300.
63 Tom Astle, comment on TIGForums, "Wobbledogs," October 29, 2018, https://forums.tigsource.com/index.php?topic=53994.640.

CHAPTER 4. BUILDING WORLDS THROUGH GRAPHICAL DEPTH

1 J. Brown, *Black Utopias*, 2, 7.
2 For more on the history of computer graphics, see Gaboury, *Image Objects*.
3 For more on the history of 3D cinema, see Zone, *3-D Revolution*.
4 Halberstam, "Queer Gaming," 197.
5 Halberstam, "Queer Gaming," 198.
6 Murray, "Horizons Already Here," 42.
7 Murray, "Horizons Already Here," 42, 47. In raising these questions, Murray is herself pointing back to valuable questions raised by artists like the filmmaker and intellectual Harun Farocki, whose creative work explored the meaning of game space.
8 For the concept of the spatial turn in game studies, see Günzel, "Lived Space of Computer Games," 168. For another recent example of collected work on video games, architecture, and culture, see Meinel, *Video Games and Spatiality*.
9 Günzel, "Lived Space of Computer Games," 170.
10 Whistance-Smith, *Expressive Spaces*, 4.
11 Wolf, "Theorizing Navigable Space in Video Games," 18.
12 Moralde, "Haptic Landscapes."
13 Nakamura, *Cybertypes*, 40.
14 Thompson, "Queer/ing Game Space."
15 Murray, *On Video Games*, 141–182.
16 Murray, *On Video Games*, 143.
17 Reinhard, "Mapping, Colonialism, and No Man's Sky."
18 Gray, "Gaming Out Online"; Kocurek, *Coin-Operated Americans*; DeAnda, "Interview with Drag Bingo Host"; Fletcher, "Esports and the Color Line."
19 See, for example, promotional text for virtual reality software development studios like Delusion (delusion.fr) or Sandbox VR (https://sandboxvr.com).
20 Nitsche, *Video Game Spaces*, 2.
21 See, for example, Keogh, "Across Worlds and Bodies"; Soderman, *Against Flow*, 11.
22 For a discussion of a parallel return to 3D in film, see Elsaesser, "'Return' of 3-D."
23 Campana, "Fold, Flip, Stick," 81.
24 Campana, "Fold, Flip, Stick," 82.
25 Campana, "Fold, Flip, Stick," 85.

26 The history of video games is full of telling examples of gamers getting angry when a beloved franchise changes the aesthetics of its games. Nintendo's release of *The Legend of Zelda: The Wind Waker* (2003), for instance, was met with highly gender-inflected snark in online gamer spaces for its colorful, stylized, supposedly childlike look. This, I strongly suspect, shaped Nintendo's decision to radically shift the aesthetic of the next game in the series, *The Legend of Zelda: Twilight Princess* (2006), which uses a much more "realistic," gritty style with a muted, masculinist color scheme.

27 Sugawa-Shimada, "Emerging '2.5-Dimensional' Culture," 124.

28 Interestingly, since the time I began writing this chapter (in early 2022, shortly after *OlliOlli World*'s release), *OlliOlli World* has eclipsed the earlier *OlliOlli* games as speedrunning favorites. Given the game's considerably quirkiness, not to mention its queerness, I was curious to see whether competitive players would pick up the game or stick with the earlier titles in the series. For a perspective on how *OlliOlli World* is similar to or different from earlier games in the series and a discussion of how it lands with gamers, see Webster, "*OlliOlli World*."

29 Simlish is the name of the gibberish language spoken by characters in the *Sims* video game series (Maxis, 2004–2023).

30 Roh, Huang, and Niu, *Techno-Orientalism*; Fickle, *Race Card*, 1–28.

31 The figures that I use for *OlliOlli World* in this chapter are screenshots taken from gameplay videos uploaded by YouTuber GabeHype rather than screenshots taken during gameplay. As I explain later in the chapter, many visual elements of the game pass by too quickly to be captured by a screenshot midgame. GabeHype, "OLLIOLLI WORLD."

32 Muscle Beach is a beach in Venice, California, with a long history as a center for gay men's bodybuilding culture. Johnson, *Buying Gay*, 27–28.

33 Tongson, *Relocations*, 202.

34 March, "Queer and Trans* Geographies of Liminality." The Halberstam text that March references is *In a Queer Time and Place*. The Gieseking text that she references is "Queer Geographer's Life."

35 March, "Queer and Trans* Geographies of Liminality," 464.

36 Lancaster, *Dragging Away*, 7.

37 Lancaster, *Dragging Away*, 3, 32, 8.

38 Johnston and Longhurst, *Space, Place, and Sex*, 2, 3.

CHAPTER 5. STRAIGHT PATHS THROUGH QUEER VIDEO GAMES

1 This chapter has been adapted from an earlier article that I published on queer movement and speedrunning in *Gone Home* ("Straight Paths through Queer Walking Simulators"). The present version has been updated and expanded; it has also been placed more squarely within the conceptual framework of worldbuilding. In addition, I have attempted to allow for more nuance in my interpretation of speedrunning practices since, in the intervening years, I have been more aware of queer and trans participants in speedrunning communities.

2   Ahmed, *Queer Phenomenology*, 15, 1.
3   Ahmed, "Orientations Matter," 235, 236.
4   Ahmed, *Queer Phenomenology*, 15, 21.
5   Schalk, "Coming to Claim Crip."
6   For examples of how *Gone Home* has been celebrated in the decade since its release, see Carpenter, "Why *Gone Home*"; Frank, "As *Gone Home* Turns Five."
7   I am basing my understanding of the time period in which *Gone Home* was most popular among speedrunners on the patterns I have seen in YouTube videos, Twitch live streams, and online speedrunning leaderboards. Together these imply that, though some speedrunners do still run *Gone Home*, the game's popularity in the speedrunning community peaked between roughly 2015 and 2019.
8   Ahmed, *Queer Phenomenology*, 92.
9   I have made the argument that speedrunning represents a queer form of play in my earlier monograph, *Video Games Have Always Been Queer*, 195–200. Additional work on this subject is addressed in the final section of this chapter.
10 Greer, "Queer Representation in Games"; Riley, "Why the Best Video Games."
11 Curiously, since I wrote the original version of this chapter as an article in 2018, GLAAD has removed its coverage of *Gone Home*, along with all of the blog posts in its "gaming" category from 2017 to 2019. Here I provide the original citation for the referenced piece, though the link is therefore no longer active. Townsend, "LGBT-Inclusive Video Game"; Quinlan, "*Gone Home* Is Still Queer"; Connolly, "Why This Indie Game Studio"; Piccoli, "Review."
12 kopas, "On *Gone Home*."
13 GameSpot Forums: System Wars, "Was *Gone Home* a Propaganda Game?"
14 Hart, "GLAAD Gives the Outstanding Video Game Award"; Kim, "*Tell Me Why.*"
15 Pavlounis, "Straightening Up the Archive," 583.
16 Veale, "*Gone Home.*"
17 Snyder, "Impossible Relationship."
18 Tullocha, Hoadband, and Young, "Riot Grrrl Gaming."
19 Fu et al., "Theme Park Storytelling."
20 Flanagan, "Navigating the Narrative in Space," 83.
21 GDC, "Environmental Narratives."
22 Morrissette, "I'd Like to Buy the World a Nuka-Cola."
23 Robertson, "Tacoma Isn't a Groundbreaking Story."
24 Ruberg, *Video Games Have Always Been Queer*, 200–203.
25 Anable, *Playing with Feelings*, 13.
26 Waszkiewicz and Bakun, "Towards the Aesthetic of Cozy Video Games."
27 Briscoe, "Joy of Walking."
28 Kagen, *Wandering Games*, 2.
29 W. Benjamin, *Charles Baudelaire*; Ivanchikova, "Sidewalks of Desire."
30 For example, Gaspard Pelurson proposes "positioning the gamer as a flaneur" in order to perform a queer reading of *The Path* (Tale of Tales, 2009) ("Flânerie in the Dark Woods," 919). More recently, Pelurson has argued for a recuperation of

the queer potential in linear narratives, arguing (also building from Ahmed) that lines themselves are not necessarily straight but may instead move queerly at a slant ("Cathartic Corridors").
31 Shah, "Race, Gender, and Sex Education"; Fields, "Children Having Children."
32 For more on chrononormativity and its place in video games, see Knutson, "Backtrack, Pause, Rewind, Reset."
33 Rahn, "Dark Ride of Snow White," 88.
34 Kagen, *Wandering Games*.
35 Boluk and Lemieux, *Metagaming*.
36 Hope, "Games Done Quick."
37 Hemmingsen, "Code Is Law."
38 Brewer, "Coming Out While Going Fast."
39 Schmalzer, "Transition Games," 6.
40 Bailey, "Celeste's Five-Year Journey."
41 Polygon, "Speed Rundown."
42 McElroy, "Speed Rundown."
43 Rutledge, "*Gone Home* Speedrunner."
44 This information is drawn from the current (as of December 2023) leaderboard for *Gone Home* on Speedrun.com, available at www.speedrun.com/gonehome.
45 Scully-Blaker, "Practiced Practice."
46 Scully-Blaker, "Practiced Practice."
47 Polygon, "Speed Rundown."
48 Ruberg, "Straight-Washing *Undertale*"; Ruberg, "Performances of Homophobia."
49 Ford, "Speedrunning."
50 Smith and Walters, "Desire Lines."
51 Schmalzer, "Transition Games," 1.
52 E. Chang, "Queer Glitches"; Halberstam, "Queer Gaming"; Pow, "Trans Historiography of Glitches and Errors."
53 Gass, "Glitch as a Trans Representational Mode," 5.
54 Pow, "Trans Historiography of Glitches and Errors," 203.
55 Pavlounis, "Straightening Up the Archive."

CHAPTER 6. UNPLAYABLE WORLDS

1 See, for example, MacDonald, "*Grand Theft Auto V* Review."
2 A. Chang, *Playing Nature*, 109.
3 For a discussion of the cultural debates that have surrounded the *Grand Theft Auto* series, as well as a feminist rereading of the series, see Ketterling, "You Do It for the Good Times."
4 See, for example, Plunkett, "Modded Deer Is Running Buck Wild."
5 A. Chang, "Rambunctious Games," 69, 75, 73.
6 BBC, "*Grand Theft Auto* Deer Causes Chaos."
7 Rundle, "Watching an AI Deer"; Smith, "Artificial Life."
8 Plante, "Watch an Invincible Deer"; Gerwin, "Immortal Deer."

9 These accounts existed primarily on Twitter but have since been deleted.
10 A. Chang, *Playing Nature*, 110.
11 *San Andreas Streaming Deer Cam.*
12 San Andreas Community Cams, *Official San Andreas Community Cam.*
13 Galloway, *Gaming*, 118.
14 Regarding *Big Buck Hunter*, see Kassel, "This Guy Spent Thousands."
15 DeAnda, "Thou Shall Never Use a Fire Stone on Eevee."
16 As of October 2023, *Grand Theft Auto V* was ranked the "the best-selling console/PC-only game of all time," with 185 million copies reportedly sold. Sirani, "10 Best-Selling Video Games of All Time."
17 *San Andreas Streaming Deer Cam.*
18 See, for example, Jenny Brusk et al. "DEAL"; Warpefelt and Verhagen, "Model of Non-Player Character Believability"; Simonov, Zagarskikh, and Fedorov, "Applying Behavior Characteristics."
19 Coanda and Aupers, "Post-Human Encounters."
20 Sheehan, "Posthuman Bodies," 245.
21 An example of work that centers plants is Tsing, *The Mushroom at the End of the World*; an example of work that centers metals is M. Chen, *Animacies*.
22 Badmington, "Posthumanism," 374.
23 Sheehan, "Posthuman Bodies," 245.
24 Asberg and Braidotti, "Feminist Posthumanities," 16.
25 Luciano and Chen, "Has the Queer Ever Been Human?," 194.
26 Jackson, "Outer Worlds," 215, 216.
27 Anable, "Platform Studies."
28 Joy, "Improbable Manners of Being," 222.
29 Joy, "Improbable Manners of Being," 222–223.
30 See, for example, Nurka, "Animal Techne."
31 Giffney and Hird, "Introduction," 4.
32 Muñoz, "Sense of Brownness," 209, 210.
33 MacCormack, "Queer Posthumanism," 111.
34 For more on the connections between Afrofuturism and posthumanism, see Lavender and Murphy, "Afrofuturism"; Rodine, "Janelle Monáe."
35 Sheehan, "Posthuman Bodies," 245.
36 Hayles, *How We Became Posthuman*; A. Chang, *Playing Nature*, 12.
37 Ruffino, "Nonhuman Games," 11.
38 Caracciolo, "Animal Mayhem Games."
39 Tyler, "New Tricks." See also Tyler, *Game*.
40 Ferreday, "Becoming Deer."
41 Caracciolo, "Animal Mayhem Games."
42 CBC, "Running with the *Grand Theft Auto* Deer."
43 Dictionary of Obscure Sorrows, "Kenopsia."
44 M. Chen, *Animacies*, 104.
45 Halberstam, *Wild Things*, 3.

46 Fizek, "Self-Playing Games."
47 Barr, "Game Ideas"; Garcia, "100 Oeubres d'art impossibles."

CONCLUSION

1 Mejeur, "Games as Critical Literature," 67.
2 Butler, *What World Is This?*, 13.
3 For a transcript of this speech, see "Ursula K Le Guin's Speech at National Book Awards."
4 Brewster, "Everything Review."
5 Lada, "*Noby Noby Boy*'s GIRL."
6 See Steam, "Nour: Play with Your Food."
7 See the official website for *Nour*: https://food.game (accessed January 13, 2024).
8 I am thinking of an example like Microsoft's ongoing "Gaming for Everyone" program, a corporate initiative that includes branches dedicated to LGBTQ gaming. See, for example, information about Microsoft's "Gaming for Everyone" programming at the 2020 Game Developers Conference, as listed in Ifeguni, "GDC 2020."
9 Tsing, *Mushroom at the End of the World*, 2.
10 Muñoz, *Disidentifications*, 200.

WORKS CITED

Ahmed, Sara. "Orientations Matter." In *New Materialisms: Ontology, Agency, and Politics*, edited by Diana Coole and Samantha Frost, 234–257. Durham, NC: Duke University Press, 2010.

———. *Queer Phenomenology*. Durham, NC: Duke University Press, 2006.

Altice, Nathan. "*Super Mario Bros.* vs. *Super Mario Bros.* vs. *Super Mario Bros.*" ROMchip: A Journal of Game Histories 2, no. 1 (2020). www.romchip.org.

Amin, Kadji. "Against Queer Objects." *Feminist Formations* 28, no. 2 (Summer 2016): 101–111.

Anable, Aubrey. "Platform Studies." *Feminist Media Histories* 4, no. 2 (Spring 2018): 135–140.

———. *Playing with Feelings: Video Games and Affect*. Minneapolis: University of Minnesota Press, 2018.

Anderson, Reynaldo, and Charles E. Jones, eds. *Afrofuturism 2.0: The Rise of Astro-Blackness*. Lanham, MD: Lexington Books, 2016.

Andrucki, Max J., and Dana J. Kaplan. "Trans Objects: Materializing Queer Time in US Transmasculine Homes." *Gender, Place & Culture* 25, no. 6 (2018): 781–798.

arebyte Gallery. "SHE KEEPS ME DAMN ALIVE." Accessed September 2, 2024. www.arebyte.com.

"Artist Talk: Along the River of Spacetime, by Elizabeth LaPensée." *Digital Culture & Education* 12, no. 2 (June 26, 2020). www.digitalcultureandeducation.com.

Asberg, Cecilia, and Rosi Braidotti. "Feminist Posthumanities: An Introduction." In *A Feminist Companion to the Posthumanities*, edited by Cecilia Asberg and Rosi Braidotti, 1–22. Cham, Switzerland: Springer, 2018.

Astle, Tom. "The Genetic Algorithm." Video posted by GlitchCityLA, June 20, 2017. www.youtube.com/watch?v=LQZv2J8K2z4.

———. "*Wobbledogs* Dogtech Deep Dive." YouTube, November 20, 2018. www.youtube.com/watch?v=66nymnESYhQ&t=8s.

Aziz, Hamza. "Over 65 Million Creations Made in Spore, No Word on How Many Are Penises." *Destructoid*, January 22, 2009. www.destructoid.com.

Badmington, Neil. "Posthumanism." In *The Routledge Companion to Literature and Science*, edited by Bruce Clarke and Manuela Rossini, 374–384. London: Routledge, 2012.

Bailey, Kat. "*Celeste*'s Five-Year Journey to Becoming One of the Most Important Trans Games Ever." IGN, June 26, 2023. www.ign.com.

Barad, Karen. "Nature's Queer Performativity." *Qui Parle* 19, no. 2 (Spring/Summer 2011): 121–158.
Barr, Pippin. "Game Ideas." Artist's website. Accessed September 2, 2024. www.pippinbarr.com.
Bataille, Georges. *Visions of Excess: Selected Writings, 1927–1939.* Minneapolis: University of Minnesota Press, 1985.
BBC. "*Grand Theft Auto* Deer Causes Chaos in the Game World." March 24, 2016. www.bbc.com.
Bem, Caroline, and Susanna Paasonen. "Play! A Special Issue." *Sexualities* 26, no. 8 (2023): 809–818.
Benjamin, Ruha. "Introduction: Discriminatory Design, Liberating Imagination." In *Captivating Technology: Race, Carceral Technoscience, and Liberatory Imagination in Everyday Life*, edited by Ruha Benjamin, 1–22. Princeton, NJ: Princeton University Press, 2019.
Benjamin, Walter. *Charles Baudelaire: A Lyric Poet in the Age of High Capitalism.* London: Verso, 1997.
Bennett, Jane. *Vibrant Matter: A Political Ecology of Things.* Durham, NC: Duke University Press, 2010.
Berge, P. S. "The Table and the Tomb: Positioning Trans Power and Play amid Fantasy Realism in *Dungeons & Dragons*." *Games and Culture*, October 11, 2023. https://doi.org/10.1177/15554120231204145.
Berlant, Lauren, and Michael Warner. "Sex in Public." *Critical Inquiry* 24, no. 2 (1998): 547–566.
Bersani, Leo. *Is the Rectum a Grave? and Other Essays.* Chicago: University of Chicago Press, 2010.
Bey, Marquis. *Black Trans Feminism.* Durham, NC: Duke University Press, 2022.
Birch, Jonathan C. P. "The Theological House That Jack (Un)Built: Halberstam on an Aesthetics of Collapse and Mushrooms among the Ruins." *Theology in Scotland* 29, no. 2 (2022): 60–73.
Blundell, Katherine. *Black Holes: A Very Short Introduction.* Oxford: Oxford University Press, 2015.
Boellstorff, Tom. *Coming of Age in Second Life: An Anthropologist Explores the Virtually Human.* Princeton, NJ: Princeton University Press, 2015.
Boluk, Stephanie, and Patrick Lemieux. *Metagaming: Playing, Competing, Spectating, Cheating, Trading, Making, and Breaking Videogames.* Minneapolis: University of Minnesota Press, 2017.
Boni, Marta. "Introduction: Worlds, Today." In *World Building: Transmedia, Fans, Industries*, edited by Marta Boni, 9–27. Amsterdam: Amsterdam University Press, 2017.
Bourg, David M., and Bryan Bywalec. *Physics for Game Developers.* Sebastopol, CA: O'Reilly, 2013.
Brewer, Johanna. "Coming Out While Going Fast: Queer Conviviality in Speedrunning Live Streams." *Proceedings of the Digital Games Research Association*, 2023, 1–16.

Brewster, Kat. "*Everything* Review: A Joyfully Expansive Dream of a Game." *The Guardian*, March 24, 2017. www.theguardian.com.

Briscoe, Amy. "The Joy of Walking." *Wired*, August 27, 2021. www.wired.com.

Brock, André. "'When Keeping It Real Goes Wrong': Resident Evil 5, Racial Representation, and Gamers." *Games and Culture* 6, no. 5 (2011): 429–452.

Brown, Jayna. *Black Utopias: Speculative Life and the Music of Other Worlds*. Durham, NC: Duke University Press, 2021.

Brown, Simone. *Dark Matters: On the Surveillance of Blackness*. Durham, NC: Duke University Press, 2015.

Brusk, Jenny, Torbjorn Lager, Anna Hjalmarsson, and Preben Wik. "DEAL: Dialogue Management in SCXML for Believable Game Characters." *Proceedings of the 2007 Conference on Future Play*, November 2007, 137–144.

Bulut, Ergin. "The Fantasy of Do What You Love and Ludic Authoritarianism in the Videogame Industry." *Television and New Media* 24, no. 8 (2023): 851–869.

Butler, Judith. *What World Is This? A Pandemic Phenomenology*. New York: Columbia University Press, 2022.

Cadorniga, Callie (Carlos). "'Goat Simulator 3' Was Announced Back in August—There Has Never Been a 'Goat Simulator 2.'" *Distractify*, November 15, 2022. www.distractify.com.

Campana, Andrew. "Fold, Flip, Stick: *Paper Mario*, 2.5-Dimensionality and the Media Mix." *Kinephanos* 5, no. 1 (2015): 77–111.

Caracciolo, Marco. "Animal Mayhem Games and Nonhuman-Oriented Thinking." *Game Studies* 21, no. 1 (May 2021). https://gamestudies.org.

cárdenas, micha. "Ones Who Walk Away." Planned Keynote for the Queerness and Games Conference, Montreal, Canada, October 2020.

Caroux, Loïc, and Katherine Isbister. "Influence of Head-Up Displays' Characteristics on User Experience in Video Games." *International Journal of Human-Computer Studies* 87 (2016): 65–79.

Carpenter, Nicole. "Why *Gone Home* Is the Most Important Game of the Decade." *Polygon*, November 13, 2019. www.polygon.com.

CBC. "Running with the *Grand Theft Auto* Deer." April 8, 2016. www.cbc.ca.

Chang, Alenda. *Playing Nature: Ecology in Video Games*. Minneapolis: University of Minnesota Press, 2019.

———. "Rambunctious Games: A Manifesto for Environmental Game Design." *Art Journal* 79, no. 2 (2020): 68–75.

Chang, Edmond. "Queergaming." In *Queer Game Studies*, edited by Bo Ruberg and Adrienne Shaw, 15–23. Minneapolis: University of Minnesota Press, 2017.

———. "Queer Glitches, or, the Recuperation of Vanellope Von Schweetz." Author's website, October 7, 2013. www.edmondchang.com.

Chen, Jian Neo. *Trans Exploits: Trans of Color Cultures and Technologies in Movement*. Durham, NC: Duke University Press, 2019.

Chen, Mel. *Animacies: Biopolitics, Racial Mattering, and Queer Affect*. Durham, NC: Duke University Press, 2012.

Chesney, Thomas, and Shaun Lawson. "The Illusion of Love: Does a Virtual Pet Provide the Same Companionship as a Real One?" *Interaction Studies* 8, no. 2 (January 2007): 337–342.

Chess, Shira. *Ready Player Two: Women Players and Designed Identity*. Minneapolis: University of Minnesota Press, 2017.

Coanda, Julia, and Step Aupers. "Post-Human Encounters: Humanizing the Technological Other in Videogames." *New Media & Society* 23, no. 5 (May 2021): 1236–1256.

Connolly, Matt. "Why This Indie Game Studio Chose a Feminist Drama over Guns and Zombies." *Mother Jones*, September 10, 2013. www.motherjones.com.

Consalvo, Mia. "Confronting Toxic Gamer Culture: A Challenge for Feminist Game Studies Scholars." *Ada: Journal of Gender, New Media, and Technology* 1, no. 1 (2012). No longer available at the *Ada* website but available at https://scholarsbank.uoregon.edu.

———. "MOOs to MMOs: The Internet and Virtual Worlds." In *The Handbook of Internet Studies*, edited by Mia Consalvo and Charles Ess, 326–347. Oxford, UK: Wiley-Blackwell, 2011.

———. "There Is No Magic Circle." *Games and Culture* 4, no. 4 (2009): 408–417.

Consalvo, Mia, and Christopher Paul. *Real Games: What's Legitimate and What's Not in Contemporary Videogames*. Cambridge, MA: MIT Press, 2019.

Cork. "The Smallest AND Largest Dog! Wobbledogs Community Showcase! EP 1." YouTube, July 22, 2022. www.youtube.com/watch?v=RRbRHOI0094.

Couture, Joel. "Road to the IGF: Triband's *What The Golf*." *Game Developer*, March 14, 2019. www.gamedeveloper.com.

Cover, Rob, and Cassandra Milne. "The 'Bury Your Gays' Trope in Contemporary Television: Generational Shifts in Production Responses to Audience Dissent." *Journal of Popular Culture* 56, nos. 5–6 (2023): 810–823.

Cox, Brian, and Jeff Forshaw. *Black Holes: The Key to Understanding the Universe*. London: William Collins, 2022.

DeAnda, Michael A. "An Interview with Drag Bingo Host, Sofonda Booz: Exploring Accessible Game Design and the Construction of Liminal Play Spaces of Gender and Sexuality." *WiderScreen* 1, no. 2 (2019). widerscreen.fi.

———. "'Thou Shall Never Use a Fire Stone on Eevee': *Twitch Plays Pokémon* and the Articulation of Game Brands as Cultural Texts." In *Real Life in Real Time: Live Streaming Culture*, edited by Johanna Brewer, Bo Ruberg, Amanda L. L. Cullen, and Christopher J. Persaud, 231–243. Cambridge, MA: MIT Press, 2023.

De Veaux, Alexis, Alexis Pauline Gumbs, and Walidah Imarisha. "'Writing New Worlds,' Allied Media Conference 2020 Plenary." *American Studies* 60, nos. 3–4 (2021): 83–94.

Devun, Leah, and Zeb Tortorici. "Trans, Time, and History." *TSQ: Transgender Studies Quarterly* 5, no. 4 (November 2018): 518–539.

Dictionary of Obscure Sorrows, The. "Kenopsia." Accessed September 2, 2024. www.dictionaryofobscuresorrows.com.

Dolan, Jill. "Performance, Utopia, and the 'Utopian Performative.'" *Theatre Journal* 53, no. 3 (October 2001): 455–479.

Doyle-Myerscough, Kaelan. "New Indie Board Games Build Worlds without Capitalism or Colonialism." *The Conversation*, March 3, 2021. https://theconversation.com.

Doyle-Myerscough, Kaelan, Patrick Jagoda, Sarah Edmands Martin, and Allison Yang Jing. "Other Worlds Are Possible." Presentations to the 2023 Digital Games Research Association Conference, Seville, Spain, June 20, 2023.

Dyer-Witheford, Nick, and Greig de Peuter. *Games of Empire: Global Capitalism and Video Games*. Minneapolis: University of Minnesota Press, 2009.

Edelman, Lee. *No Future: Queer Theory and the Death Drive*. Durham, NC: Duke University Press, 2004.

Elsaesser, Thomas. "The 'Return' of 3-D: On Some of the Logics and Genealogies of the Image in the Twenty-First Century." *Critical Inquiry* 39, no 2 (Winter 2013): 217–246.

Epic Games. "Fluid Simulation." Accessed December 30, 2023. https://docs.unrealengine.com.

———. "Hair Physics Overview." Accessed December 30, 2023. https://docs.unrealengine.com.

Evans, Margaret. "A Video Game Showed Me Who I Really Am." *Polygon*, April 12, 2019. www.polygon.com.

Fassone, Riccardo. *Every Video Game Is an Island: Endings and Extremities in Video Games*. London: Bloomsbury Academic, 2017.

Fernández-Vara, Clara. "Play's the Thing: A Framework to Study Videogames as Performance." *Proceedings of the 2009 DiGRA International Conference: Breaking New Ground: Innovation in Games, Play, Practice and Theory*, September 2009, 1–9.

Ferreday, Debra. "Becoming Deer: Nonhuman Drag and Online Utopias." *Feminist Theory* 12, no. 2 (2011): 219–225.

Fickle, Tara. *The Race Card: From Gaming Technologies to Model Minorities*. New York: New York University Press, 2019.

Fiedler, Brigitte. "The Mixed-Race Child Is Queer Father to the Man." In *Queer Kinship: Race, Sex, Belonging, Form*, edited by Tyler Broadway and Elizabeth Freeman, 48–70. Durham, NC: Duke University Press, 2022.

Fields, Jessica. "'Children Having Children': Race, Innocence, and Sexual Education." *Social Problems* 52, no. 4 (November 2005): 549–571.

Fizek, Sonia. "Self-Playing Games: Rethinking the State of Digital Play." Paper presented at the Philosophy of Computer Games Conference, Kraków, Poland, November 28–December 1, 2017.

Flanagan, Mary. *Critical Play: Radical Game Design*. Cambridge, MA: MIT Press, 2009.

———. "Navigating the Narrative in Space: Gender and Spatiality in Virtual Worlds." *Art Journal* 59, no. 3 (2000): 74–85.

Flanagan, Mary, and Helen Nissenbaum. *Values at Play in Digital Games*. Cambridge, MA: MIT Press, 2016.

Fletcher, Akil. "Black Gamer's Refuge: Finding Community within the Magic Circle of Whiteness." In *The Routledge Companion to Media Anthropology*, edited by

Elisabetta Costa, Patricia G. Lange, Nell Haynes, and Jolynna Sinanan, 368–378. New York: Routledge, 2022.

———. "Esports and the Color Line: Labor, Skill, and the Exclusion of Black Players," *Proceedings of the 53rd Hawaii International Conference on System Sciences*, 2020, 2670–2676.

Ford, Dom. "Speedrunning: Transgressive Play in Digital Space." *Proceedings of the 2018 Nordic Digital Games Research Association Conference*, November 2018.

Frank, Allegra. "As *Gone Home* Turns Five, We Look Back at Its Polarizing Legacy." *Polygon*, September 7, 2018. www.polygon.com.

Freedman, Eric. *The Persistence of Code in Game Engine Culture*. New York: Routledge, 2020.

Freeman, Elizabeth. *Time Binds: Queer Temporalities, Queer Histories*. Durham, NC: Duke University Press, 2010.

Fu, Xiaoxiao, Carissa Baker, Wen Zhang, and Ruoyang (Effie) Zhang. "Theme Park Storytelling: Deconstructing Immersion in Chinese Theme Parks." *Journal of Travel Research* 62, no. 4 (April 2023): 893–906.

Fullerton, Tracy. "Surveying the Soul: Creating the World of *Walden, a Game*." In *World-Builders on World-Building: An Exploration of Subcreation*, edited by Mark J. P. Wolf, 93–109. New York: Routledge, 2020.

GabeHype. "*OLLIOLLI WORLD* - FULL GAME + ENDING - Gameplay Walkthrough [4K PC ULTRA] - No Commentary." YouTube, January 4, 2023. www.youtube.com/watch?v=JDKBzoGnHsQ&t=1009s.

Gaboury, Jacob. *Image Objects: An Archaeology of Computer Graphics*. Cambridge, MA: MIT Press, 2021.

Galloway, Alexander R. *Gaming: Essays on Algorithmic Culture*. Minneapolis: University of Minnesota Press, 2006.

———. "Social Realism in Gaming." *Game Studies* 4, no. 1 (November 2004). www.gamestudies.org.

GameSpot Forums: System Wars. "Was *Gone Home* a Propaganda Game?" 2014. www.gamespot.com/forums/system-wars-314159282/was-gone-home-a-propaganda-game-29441524/.

Garcia, Dora. "100 Oeubres d'art impossibles." Rhizome. Accessed September 2, 2024. http://archive.rhizome.org.

Gardner, Daniel L., and Theresa J. Tanenbaum. "At the Edge: Periludic Elements in Game Studies." *Game Studies* 21, no. 4 (December 2021). https://gamestudies.org.

Gass, Ari. "Glitch as a Trans Representational Mode in Video Games." *Media-N* 20, no. 1 (Spring 2024): 5–27.

———. "Machine Embodiment and the Ethics of Touch." Paper presented at the Queerness and Games Conference, Montreal, Canada, September 29–30, 2018.

GDC. "Crafting a Tiny Open World: A Short Hike Postmortem." Presentation by Adam Robinson-Yu to the 2020 Game Developers Conference, virtual. YouTube, March 27, 2020. www.youtube.com/watch?v=ZW8gWgpptI8.

———. "Designing the Settlements in the World of 'Horizon Forbidden West.'" Presentation by Roland Ijzermans to the 2022 Game Developers Conference, San Francisco, California. YouTube, September 28, 2022. www.youtube.com/watch?v=LRQCmIHbq14.

———. "Environmental Narratives: Telling Stories in Spaces without Saying Anything Aloud." Presentation by Laura E. Hall to the 2019 Game Developers Conference, San Francisco, California. YouTube, July 9, 2021. www.youtube.com/watch?v=0XZTz30R30A.

———. "World Design for Different Player Types." Presentation by Raylene Deck to the 2021 Game Developers Conference, San Francisco, California. YouTube, March 29, 2021. www.youtube.com/watch?v=Mlf_pXwYajE.

Gerwin, Daniel. "The Immortal Deer an Artist Set Loose in *Grand Theft Auto.*" *Hyperallergic*, March 29, 2016. https://hyperallergic.com.

Gieseking, Jen Jack. "A Queer Geographer's Life as an Introduction to Queer Theory, Space, and Time." In *Queer Geographies*, edited by Lasse Lau, Mirene Arsanios, Felipe Zunga-Gonzalez, Mathias Kryger, and Omar Mismar, 14–21. Roskilde, Denmark: Museet for Samtidskunst, 2013.

Giffney, Noreen, and Myra J. Hird. "Introduction: Queering the Non/Human." In *Queering the Non/Human*, edited by Noreen Giffney and Myra J. Hird, 1–16. New York: Routledge, 2008.

Glissant, Édouard. *The Poetics of Relation*. Ann Arbor: University of Michigan Press, 1997.

Gray, Kishonna. "Gaming Out Online: Black Lesbian Identity Development and Community Building in Xbox Live." *Journal of Lesbian Studies* 22, no. 3 (2018): 282–296.

———. *Intersectional Tech: Black Users in Digital Gaming*. Baton Rouge: Louisiana State University Press, 2020.

Greenfieldboyce, Nell. "Goodbye Fuzzy Donut: The Famous First Black Hole Photo Gets Sharpened Up." NPR, April 13, 2023. www.npr.org.

Greer, Sam. "Queer Representation in Games Isn't Good Enough, but It Is Getting Better." *Games Radar*, May 15, 2018. www.gamesradar.com.

Gubser, Steven S., and Franz Pretorius. *The Little Book of Black Holes*. Princeton, NJ: Princeton University Press, 2017.

Günzel, Stephan. "The Lived Space of Computer Games." In *Architectonics of Game Spaces: The Spatial Logic of the Virtual and Its Meaning for the Real*, edited by Andri Gerber and Ulrich Götz, 167–181. Bielefeld, Germany: Transcript, 2019.

Halberstam, Jack. *In a Queer Time and Place: Transgender Bodies, Subcultural Lives*. New York: New York University Press, 2005.

———. *The Queer Art of Failure*. Durham, NC: Duke University Press, 2011.

———. "Queer Gaming: Gaming, Hacking, and Going Turbo." In *Queer Game Studies*, edited by Bo Ruberg and Adrienne Shaw, 187–199. Minneapolis: University of Minnesota Press, 2017.

———. "Unworlding: An Aesthetics of Collapse." Lecture, University of Glasgow, September 15, 2022. https://echo360.org.uk.

———. *Wild Things: The Disorder of Desire*. Durham, NC: Duke University Press, 2020.

Hammonds, Evelyn. "Black (W)holes and the Geometry of Black Female Sexuality." *Differences: A Journal of Feminist Cultural Studies* 6, nos. 2–3 (1994): 126–145.

Hanson, Christopher. *Game Time: Understanding Temporality in Video Games*. Bloomington: Indiana University Press, 2018.

Haraway, Donna J. "Companion Species, Mis-recognition, and Queer Worlding." In *Queering the Non/Human*, edited by Noreen Giffney and Myra J. Hird, xxiii–xxvi. New York: Routledge, 2008.

———. "A Cyborg Manifesto: Science, Technology, and Socialist-Feminism in the Late Twentieth Century." In *The Transgender Studies Reader*, edited by Susan Stryker and Stephen Whittle, 103–118. New York: Routledge, 2006.

Haritaworn, Jin, Tamsila Tauqir, and Esra Erdem. "Gay Imperialism: Gender and Sexuality Discourse in the 'War on Terror.'" In *Out of Place: Silences in Queerness/Raciality*, edited by Adi Kuntsman and Esperanza Miyake, 71–95. York, UK: Raw Nerve Books, 2009.

Harper, Todd, Meghan Blythe-Adams, and Nicholas Taylor, eds. *Queerness in Play*. Cham, Switzerland: Palgrave, 2018.

Hart, Aimee. "GLAAD Gives the Outstanding Video Game Award to *Tell Me Why* and *The Last of Us Part 2*." *Gayming*, April 8, 2021. https://gaymingmag.com.

Havel, Laura. "*Spacewar!* Creators Honored at Smithsonian 'Innovative Lives' Event." Lemelson Center for the Study of Invention and Innovation, November 8, 2018. https://invention.si.edu.

Hayles, N. Katherine. *How We Became Posthuman: Virtual Bodies in Cybernetics, Literature, and Informatics*. Chicago: University of Chicago Press, 1999.

Heller, Meredith. "RuPaul Realness: The Neoliberal Resignification of Ballroom Discourse." *Social Semiotics* 20, no. 1 (2020): 133–147.

Hemmingsen, Michael. "Code Is Law: Subversion and Collective Knowledge in the Ethos of Video Game Speedrunning." *Sports, Ethics and Philosophy* 15, no. 3 (2021): 435–460.

Hester, Jennessa. "The Warm Glow of a Pixelated Campfire: Queer Generosity and Community Building in the Worlds of Anna Anthropy." *QED: A Journal in GLBTQ Worldmaking* 8, no. 3 (2021): 189–195.

Heussner, Tobias, Toiya Kristen Finley, Jennifer Brandes Hepler, and Ann Lemay. *The Game Narrative Toolbox*. New York: Focal, 2015.

Hope, Robyn. "Games Done Quick, Organizational Presence, and Speedrunning Identity." In *Real Life in Real Time: Live Streaming Culture*, edited by Johanna Brewer, Bo Ruberg, Amanda L. L. Cullen, and Christopher J. Persaud, 289–302. Cambridge, MA: MIT Press, 2023.

Huizinga, Johan. *Homo Ludens: A Study of the Play Element in Culture*. New York: Routledge and Kegan Paul, 1949.

Hutchinson, Andrew. "Making the Water Move: Techno-Historic Limits in the Game Aesthetics of *Myst* and *Doom*." *Game Studies* 8, no. 1 (September 2008). www.gamestudies.org.

Ibrisagic, Armin. "How *Goat Simulator* Really Did Become Our Next IP." *Game Developer Blogs*, March 4, 2014. www.gamedeveloper.com.

Ifeguni, Jewel. "GDC 2020: Gaming for Everyone Community Events." Xbox Wire, February 5, 2020. https://news.xbox.com.

Ivanchikova, Alla. "Sidewalks of Desire: Paradoxes of the Postmodern Flaneur in Contemporary Queer Fiction." PhD diss., State University of New York, Buffalo, 2007.

Jackson, Zakiyyah Iman. "Outer Worlds: The Persistence of Race in Movement 'Beyond the Human.'" *GLQ: A Journal of Lesbian and Gay Studies* 21, nos. 2–3 (June 2015): 215–218.

Jagoda, Patrick. *Experimental Games: Critique, Play, and Design in the Age of Gamification*. Chicago: University of Chicago Press, 2020.

Jenkins, Henry. "Complete Freedom of Movement: Video Games as Gendered Play Spaces." In *From Barbie to Mortal Kombat: Gender and Computer Games*, edited by Justine Cassell and Henry Jenkins, 262–296. Cambridge, MA: MIT Press, 1998.

———. "Transmedia, Speculative World-Building and the Civic Imagination." In *Medien—Demokratie—Bildung: Normative Vermittlungsprozesse und Diversität in mediatisierten Gesellschaften*, edited by Gudrun Marci-Boehncke, Matthias Rath, Malte Delere, and Hanna Höfer, 13–24. Dortmund: Springer VS, 2022.

Jerng, Mark C. *Racial Worldmaking: The Power of Popular Fiction*. New York: Fordham University Press, 2018.

Johnson, David K. *Buying Gay: How Physique Entrepreneurs Sparked a Movement*. New York: Columbia University Press, 2019.

Johnston, Lynda, and Robyn Longhurst. *Space, Place, and Sex: Geographies of Sexuality*. Lanham, MD: Rowman and Littlefield, 2010.

Joy, Eileen. "Improbable Manners of Being." *GLQ: A Journal of Lesbian and Gay Studies* 21, nos. 2–3 (June 2015): 221–224.

Kagen, Melissa. *Wandering Games*. Cambridge, MA: MIT Press, 2022.

Kassel, Nat. "This Guy Spent Thousands on *Buck Hunter* . . . and Is Now Ranked #4 in the World." *Vice*, January 22, 2019. www.vice.com.

Kasting, James F., and Janet L. Siefert. "Life and the Evolution of Earth's Atmosphere." *Science* 296, no. 5570 (2002): 1066–1068.

Kawitzky, Felix Rose. "Magic Circles: Tabletop Role-Playing Games as Queer Utopian Method." *Performance Research* 25, no. 8 (2020): 129–136.

Keegan, Cáel M. "Against Queer Theory." *TSQ: Transgender Studies Quarterly* 7, no. 3 (2020): 349–355.

Keeling, Kara. *Queer Times, Black Futures*. New York: New York University Press, 2019.

Keogh, Brendan. "Across Worlds and Bodies: Criticism in the Age of Video Games." *Journal of Games Criticism* 1, no. 1 (2014): 1–26.

Ketterling, Jean. "'You Do It for the Good Times': Rival Feminist Readings of Torture and Kink in *Grand Theft Auto V*." *Feminist Media Studies* 23, no. 7 (2023): 3452–3467.

Khaw, Cassandra. "With a Popsicle and 'Immersive Cheek Physics,' Succulent Takes on Sex in Games." *Motherboard*, June 18, 2015. www.vice.com.

Kim, Michelle Hyun. "*Tell Me Why* Is the First Major Video Game to Feature a Transgender Main Character." *Them*, September 11, 2020. www.them.us.
Knutson, Matt. "Backtrack, Pause, Rewind, Reset: Queering Chrononormativity in Gaming." *Game Studies* 18, no. 3 (December 2018). http://gamestudies.org.
Kocurek, Carly A. *Coin-Operated Americans: Rebooting Boyhood at the Video Game Arcade*. Minneapolis: University of Minnesota Press, 2015.
Kocurek, Carly A., and Matthew Payne. *Ultima and World-Building in the Computer Role-Playing Game*. Amherst, MA: Amherst College Press, 2024.
Kondo, Dorinne. *World-Making: Race, Performance, and the Work of Creativity*. Durham, NC: Duke University Press, 2018.
kopas, merritt. "On *Gone Home*." In *Queer Game Studies*, edited by Bo Ruberg and Adrienne Shaw, 145–149. Minneapolis: University of Minnesota Press, 2017.
Kunzelman, Cameron. *The World Is Born from Zero: Understanding Speculation and Video Games*. Berlin: De Gruyter, 2022.
Lada, Jenni. "*Noby Noby Boy*'s GIRL Has Reached the Sun." *Siliconera*, December 14, 2015. www.siliconera.com.
Lancaster, Lex Morgan. *Dragging Away: Queer Abstraction in Contemporary Art*. Durham, NC: Duke University Press, 2022.
LaPensée, Elizabeth. "Restoration through Activation in *Along the River of Spacetime*." Vimeo, 2020. https://vimeo.com.
Lau, Jacob. "Trans-Temporality: Hermeneutic Affect and Queer/Trans of Color Critique." In *The Routledge Companion to Gender and Affect*, edited by Todd W. Reeser, 408–420. New York: Routledge, 2022.
Lavender, Isiah, and Graham J. Murphy. "Afrofuturism." In *The Routledge Companion to Cyberpunk Culture*, edited by Anna McFarlane, Lars Schmeink, and Graham Murphy, 353–361. New York: Routledge, 2019.
LeMaster, Benny. "Notes on Trans Relationality." *QED: A Journal in GLBTQ Worldmaking* 4, no. 2 (2017): 84–92.
Lim, Bliss Cua. *Translating Time: Cinema, the Fantastic, and Temporal Critique*. Durham, NC: Duke University Press, 2009.
Lo, Claudia. "Everything Is Wiped Away: Queer Temporality in *Queers in Love at the End of the World*." *Camera Obscura: Feminism, Culture, and Media Studies* 95 (32), no. 2 (2017): 184–192.
Lorde, Audre. *Sister Outsider: Essays and Speeches*. Berkeley, CA: Crossing, 1984.
Lothian, Alexis. *Old Futures: Speculative Fiction and Queer Possibility*. New York: New York University Press, 2018.
Love, Heather. *Feeling Backwards: Loss and the Politics of Queer History*. Cambridge, MA: Harvard University Press, 2007.
———. "'How the Other Half Thinks': An Introduction to the Volume." In *Imagining Queer Methods*, edited by Amin Ghaziani and Matt Brim, 28–42. New York: New York University Press, 2019.
Luciano, Dana, and Mel Chen. "Has the Queer Ever Been Human?" *GLQ: A Journal of Lesbian and Gay Studies* 21, nos. 2–3 (June 2015): 183–207.

MacCallum-Stewart, Esther, and Justin Parsler. "Role-Play vs. Gameplay: The Difficulties of Playing a Role in *World of Warcraft*." In *Digital Culture, Play, and Identity: A "World of Warcraft" Reader*, edited by Hilde G. Corneliussen and Jill Walker Rettberg, 225–246. Cambridge, MA: MIT Press, 2008.

MacCormack, Patricia. "Queer Posthumanism: Cyborgs, Animals, Monsters, Perverts." In *The Ashgate Research Companion to Queer Theory*, edited by Noreen Giffney and Michael O'Rourke, 111–126. London: Routledge, 2009.

MacDonald, Keza. "*Grand Theft Auto V* Review." *IGN*, September 16, 2013. www.ign.com.

Macklin, Colleen. "Finding the Queerness in Games." In *Queer Game Studies*, edited by Bo Ruberg and Adrienne Shaw, 249–275. Minneapolis: University of Minnesota Press, 2017.

Malatino, Hil. *Queer Embodiment: Monstrosity, Medical Violence, and Intersex Experience*. Lincoln: University of Nebraska Press, 2019.

———. *Side Effects: On Being Trans and Feeling Bad*. Minneapolis: University of Minnesota Press, 2022.

March, Loren. "Queer and Trans* Geographies of Liminality: A Literature Review." *Progress in Human Geography* 45, no. 3 (June 2021): 455–471.

McElroy, Griffin. "Speed Rundown: Learning the Ropes, Losing Our Minds with *Gone Home*." *Polygon*, July 9, 2015. www.polygon.com.

McGonigal, Jane. *Reality Is Broken: Why Games Make Us Better and How They Can Change the World*. New York: Penguin, 2011.

McRuer, Robert. *Crip Theory: Cultural Signs of Queerness and Disability*. New York: New York University Press, 2006.

Meinel, Dietmar, ed. *Video Games and Spatiality in American Studies*. Berlin: De Gruyter, 2022.

Mejeur, Cody. "Games as Critical Literature: Playing with Transhumanism, Embodied Cognition, and Narrative Difference in *SOMA*." In *Global Perspectives on Digital Literature: A Critical Introduction for the Twenty-First Century*, edited by Torsa Ghosal, 67–80. New York: Routledge, 2023.

———. "Playing Trans Stories, Generations, and Community." *SQS* 16, no. 2 (February 2022): 47–55.

Mejeur, Cody, and Chiara Pellegrini. "Introduction: Contextualizing Trans Narratologies." *Narrative* 32, no. 2 (May 2024): 125–137.

Mirowski, Alexander John Daniel. "Making (Outer) Space to Play: A Cosmic History of the American Video Game." PhD diss., Indiana University, 2021.

Monnens, Devin, and Martin Goldberg. "Space Odyssey: The Long Journey of *Spacewar!* from MIT to Computer Labs around the World." *Kinephanos*, June 2015, 124–147.

Moralde, Oscar. "Haptic Landscapes: *Dear Esther* and Embodied Video Game Space." *Media Fields Journal* 8 (2014): 1–15.

Morrissette, Jess. "I'd Like to Buy the World a Nuka-Cola: The Purposes and Meanings of Video Game Soda Machines." *Game Studies* 20, no. 1 (February 2020). https://gamestudies.org.

Morrow, Weston, Chantal Fahmy, and Henry F. Fradella. "Obscenity and Pornography." In *Sex, Sexuality, Law and (In)justice*, edited by Henry F. Fradella and Jennifer M. Sumner, 256–293. New York: Routledge, 2016.

Muñoz, José Esteban. *Cruising Utopia: The Then and There of Queer Futurity*. Durham, NC: Duke University Press, 2009.

———. *Disidentifications: Queers of Color and the Performance of Politics*. Minneapolis: University of Minnesota Press, 1999.

———. "Ephemera as Evidence: Introductory Notes to Queer Acts." *Women and Performance* 8, no. 2 (1998): 5–16.

———. *The Sense of Brown*. Durham, NC: Duke University Press, 2020.

———. "The Sense of Brownness." *GLQ: A Journal of Lesbian and Gay Studies* 21, nos. 2–3 (June 2015): 209–210.

Murray, Soraya. "Horizons Already Here: Video Games and Landscape." *Art Journal* 79, no. 2 (2020): 42–49.

———. *On Video Games: The Visual Politics of Race, Gender and Space*. London: I. B. Tauris, 2017.

Nakamura, Lisa. *Cybertypes: Race, Ethnicity, and Identity on the Internet*. New York: Routledge, 2002.

Nakayama, Thomas K., and Charles E. Morris III. "Worldmaking and Everyday Interventions." *QED: A Journal in GLBTQ Worldmaking* 2, no. 1 (Spring 2014): v–viii.

Nicoll, Benjamin, and Brendan Keogh. *The Unity Game Engine and the Circuits of Cultural Software*. Cham, Switzerland: Palgrave Macmillan, 2019.

Nintendo Dads. "Nintendo Dads Interview with Rune K. Drewsen of Triband—*What the Golf*?" YouTube, May 19, 2020. www.youtube.com/watch?v=6HwuqkA5_Cs.

Nitsche, Michael. *Video Game Spaces: Image, Play, and Structure in 3D Worlds*. Cambridge, MA: MIT Press, 2008.

Nurka, Camille. "Animal Techne: Transing Posthumanism." *Trans Studies Quarterly* 2, no. 2 (2015): 209–226.

Otis, Hailey N., and Thomas R. Dunn. "Queer Worldmaking." In *Oxford Research Encyclopedia of Communication*. Oxford: Oxford University Press, 2021. https://oxfordre.com.

Papacharissi, Zizi. *Affective Publics: Sentiment, Technology, and Politics*. Oxford: Oxford University Press, 2015.

Paterson, Eddie, Timothy Williams, and Will Cordner. *Once upon a Pixel: Storytelling and Worldbuilding in Video Games*. Boca Raton, FL: CRC, 2020.

Patterson, Christopher B. *Open World Empire: Race, Erotics, and the Global Rise of Video Games*. New York: New York University Press, 2020.

Patterson, Christopher B., and Tara Fickle, eds. *Made in Asia/America: Why Video Games Were Never (Really) about Us*. Durham, NC: Duke University Press, 2024.

Pavlounis, Dimitrios. "Straightening Up the Archive: Queer Historiography, Queer Play, and the Archival Politics of *Gone Home*." *Television & New Media* 17, no. 7 (November 2016): 579–594.

PC Gamer. "The Weird Arm Physics of *Jurassic Park: Trespasser*." YouTube, February 19, 2020. www.youtube.com/watch?v=BBD_yU-ze5s.

Pearce, Celia. *Communities of Play: Emergent Cultures of Multiplayer Games and Virtual Worlds*. Cambridge, MA: MIT Press, 2011.

Pederson, Claudia Costa. *Gaming Utopia: Ludic Worlds in Art, Design, and Media*. Bloomington: Indiana University Press, 2021.

Pelurson, Gaspard. "Cathartic Corridors: Queering Linearity in *Final Fantasy XIII*." *Continuum* 35, no 1 (2021): 43–57.

———. "Flânerie in the Dark Woods: Shattering Innocence and Queering Time in *The Path*." *Convergence* 25, nos. 5–6 (December 2019): 918–936.

Phillips, Amanda. "Dicks, Dicks, Dicks: Hardness and Flaccidity in (Virtual) Masculinity." *Flow*, November 27, 2017. www.flowjournal.org.

———. *Gamer Trouble: Feminist Confrontations in Digital Culture*. New York: New York University Press, 2020.

———. "Negg(at)ing the Game Studies Subject: An Affective History of the Field." *Feminist Media Histories* 6, no. 1 (2020): 12–36.

Phillips, Tom. "*What the Golf*'s *A Whole New World* Update Adds 1000 New Holes." *Eurogamer*, July 12, 2021. www.eurogamer.net.

Piccoli, Dana. "Review: 'Gone Home' Is the Beautiful, Queer-Centric Video Game of Your Dreams." *AfterEllen*, August 22, 2013. https://afterellen.com.

Plante, Chris. "Watch an Invincible Deer on the Loose in *Grand Theft Auto V*." *The Verge*, March 21, 2016. www.theverge.com.

Plunkett, Luke. "Modded Deer Is Running Buck Wild in *GTA V*." *Kotaku*, March 20, 2016. https://kotaku.com.

Polygon. "Speed Rundown: *Gone Home* 100% Speed Run." YouTube, July 9, 2015. www.youtube.com/watch?v=z0X43tebnwg&t=21s.

Pow, Whit. "A Trans Historiography of Glitches and Errors." *Feminist Media Studies* 7, no. 1 (2021): 197–230.

Pozo, Teddy. "Queer Games after Empathy: Feminism and Haptic Game Design Aesthetics from Consent to Cuteness to the Radically Soft." *Game Studies* 18, no. 3 (December 2018). https://gamestudies.org.

Przybylo, Ela, and Danielle Cooper. "Asexual Resonances: Tracing a Queerly Asexual Archive." *GLQ: A Journal of Lesbian and Gay Studies* 20, no. 3 (2014): 297–318.

Puar, Jasbir K. *Terrorist Assemblages: Homonationalism in Queer Times*. Durham, NC: Duke University Press, 2017.

Queerness N'Games. "'Beautiful Monsters'—Rebecca Stimson | QGCon 2017." Presentation of "Beautiful Monsters: Building Space for Queer Gaming in *Monster Factory*," by Rebecca Stimson, to the 2018 Queerness and Games Conference, Los Angeles, California. YouTube, April 21, 2017. www.youtube.com/watch?v=RsPrvUFF9e8&t=3s.

Quinlan, Emma. "*Gone Home* Is Still Queer, Finally Here for PS4 and Xbox." *Autostraddle*, April 6, 2016. www.autostraddle.com.

Rahn, Suzanne. "The Dark Ride of Snow White: Narrative Strategies at Disneyland." In *Disneyland and Culture: Essays on the Parks and Their Influence*, edited by Kathy Merlock Jackson and Mark I. West, 87–105. Jefferson, NC: McFarland, 2010.

Reddy, Chandan. "Queer." In *Keywords for Gender and Sexuality Studies*, edited by the Keywords Feminist Editorial Collective, 172–177. New York: New York University Press, 2021.

Reinhard, Andrew. "Mapping, Colonialism, and No Man's Sky." *Archaeogaming*, October 7, 2018. https://archaeogaming.com.

r/gamedesign. "What the hell does 'floaty' mean?" Reddit. Accessed December 30, 2023. www.reddit.com/r/gamedesign/comments/6qv09c/what_the_hell_does_floaty_mean/.

Riley, Tonya. "Why the Best Video Games Are the Ones That Make Men Cry." *Bustle*, July 24, 2018. www.bustle.com.

Robertson, Adi. "*Tacoma* Isn't a Groundbreaking Story, but It's a Great Moment for Video Game Storytelling." *The Verge*, April 4, 2017. www.theverge.com.

Rodine, Zoe. "Janelle Monáe, Dirty Computers, and Embodied Posthumanism." *MELUS: Multi-Ethnic Literature of the United States* 41, no. 1 (Spring 2022): 154–174.

Rogers, Ryan, and Carol Liebler. "Jubblies, Mammaries, and Boobs: Discourses of Breast Physics in Video Games." *Journal of Gaming & Virtual Worlds* 9, no. 3 (2017): 257–278.

Roh, David S., Betsy Huang, and Greta A. Niu, eds. *Techno-Orientalism: Imagining Asia in Speculative Fiction, History, and Media*. New Brunswick, NJ: Rutgers University Press, 2015.

Ruberg, Bo. "After Agency: The Queer Posthumanism of Video Games That Cannot Be Played." *Convergence* 28, no. 2 (2022): 413–430.

———. "Forty-Eight-Hour Utopia: On Hope and the Future of Queerness in Games." In *Queer Game Studies*, edited by Bo Ruberg and Adrienne Shaw, 267–274. Minneapolis: University of Minnesota Press, 2017.

———. "Hungry Holes and Insatiable Balls: Video Games, Queer Mechanics, and the Limits of Design." *Journal of Cinema and Media Studies* 61, no. 3 (2022): 107–128.

———. "No Fun: The Queer Potential of Video Games that Annoy, Anger, Disappoint, Sadden, and Hurt." *QED: A Journal in GLBTQ Worldmaking* 2, no. 2 (2015): 108–124.

———. "Performances of Homophobia in Player Videos of Robert Yang's 'Gay Sex Games.'" Presentation to the 2019 Society of Cinema and Media Studies Conference, Seattle, Washington, March 13–17.

———. "Permalife: Video Games and the Queerness of Living." *Journal of Gaming and Virtual Worlds* 9, no. 2 (2017): 159–173.

———. "Playing with 'Real Women': A Sexual Prehistory of Realism in Video Games." *ROMchip: A Journal of Game Histories* 4, no. 1 (July 2022). https://romchip.org.

———. *The Queer Games Avant-Garde: How LGBTQ Game-Makers Are Reimagining the Medium of Video Games*. Durham, NC: Duke University Press, 2020.

———. "Queerness and Video Games: Queer Game Studies and New Perspectives through Play." *GLQ: A Journal of Lesbian and Gay Studies* 24, no. 4 (2018): 543–555.

———. "Straight Paths through Queer Walking Simulators: Wandering on Rails and Speedrunning in *Gone Home*." *Games and Culture* 15, no 6 (2020): 632–652.

———. "Straight-Washing *Undertale*: Video Games and the Limits of LGBTQ Representation." *Transformative Works and Cultures* 28 (September 2018). https://doi.org/10.3983/twc.2018.1516.

———. *Video Games Have Always Been Queer*. New York: New York University Press, 2019.

Ruberg, Bo, and Adrienne Shaw, eds. *Queer Game Studies*. Minneapolis: University of Minnesota Press, 2017.

Ruelos, Spencer Taylor Berdiago. "Queer Gamer Assemblages and the Affective Elements of Digital Games." *Press Start* 4, no. 2 (2018): 35–50.

Ruffino, Paolo, ed. *Independent Videogames: Cultures, Networks, Techniques and Politics*. New York: Routledge, 2021.

———. "Nonhuman Games: Playing in the Post-Anthropocene." In *Death, Culture and Leisure: Playing Dead*, edited by Matt Coward-Gibbs, 11–25. Leeds, UK: Emerald, 2020.

Rundle, Michael. "Watching an AI Deer Wander *GTA V* Is Strangely Hypnotic." *Wired*, March 21, 2016. www.wired.co.uk.

Rutledge, Spencer. "*Gone Home* Speedrunner Sets New Record." *Hardcore Gamer*, January 4, 2018. https://hardcoregamer.com.

Salen, Katie, and Eric Zimmerman. *Rules of Play: Game Design Fundamentals*. Cambridge, MA: MIT Press, 2003.

Samutina, Natalia. "Fan Fiction as World-Building: Transformative Reception in Crossover Writing." *Continuum* 30, no. 4 (2016): 433–450.

San Andreas Community Cams. *The Official San Andreas Community Cam*. Accessed January 4, 2023. http://sanandreascommunitycams.com.

San Andreas Streaming Deer Cam. Accessed January 4, 2023. http://sanandreasanimalcams.com.

Sanford, Kathy, Lisa J. Starr, Liz Merkel, and Sarah Bonsor Kurki. "Serious Games: Video Games for Good?" *E-Learning and Digital Media* 12, no. 1 (2015): 90–106.

Schalk, Sami. "Coming to Claim Crip: Disidentification with/in Disability Studies." *Disability Studies Quarterly* 33, no. 2 (2013). https://dsq-sds.org.

Schmalzer, Madison. "Transition Games: Speedrunning Gender." PhD diss., North Carolina State University, 2022.

Schrank, Brian. *Avant-Garde Videogames: Playing with Technoculture*. Cambridge, MA: MIT Press, 2014.

Scully-Blaker, Rainforest. "A Practiced Practice: Speedrunning through Space with de Certeau and Virilio." *Game Studies* 14, no. 1 (August 2014). https://gamestudies.org.

Sedgwick, Eve Kosofsky. *Tendencies*. Durham, NC: Duke University Press, 1993.

Sens, Jeffrey. "Queer Worldmaking Games: A Portland Indie Experiment." *QED: A Journal in GLBTQ Worldmaking* 2, no. 2 (2015): 98–107.

Serna, Laura Isabel. "Atmosphere: Mexican Extras and Race Making in Silent Hollywood." *Journal of Cinema and Media Studies* 63, no. 1 (2023): 100–123.

Shah, Courtney Q. "Race, Gender, and Sex Education in Twentieth-Century America." *Oxford Research Encyclopedia of American History*. Oxford: Oxford University Press, August 22, 2017. https://oxfordre.com.

Shaw, Adrienne. "The Trouble with Communities." In *Queer Game Studies*, edited by Bo Ruberg and Adrienne Shaw, 153–162. Minneapolis: University of Minnesota Press, 2017.

Shaw, Adrienne, and Bo Ruberg. "Introduction: Imagining Queer Game Studies." In *Queer Game Studies*, edited by Bo Ruberg and Adrienne Shaw, ix–xxxiii. Minneapolis: University of Minnesota Press, 2017.

Sheehan, Paul. "Posthuman Bodies." In *The Cambridge Companion to the Body in Literature*, edited by David Hillman and Ulrika Maude, 245–260. Cambridge: Cambridge University Press.

Shinkle, Eugénie. "Of Particle Systems and Picturesque Ontologies: Landscape, Nature, and Realism in Video Games." *Art Journal* 79, no. 2 (2000): 59–67.

Simonov, Andrey, Aleksandr Zagarskikh, and Victor Fedorov. "Applying Behavior Characteristics to Decision-Making Process to Create Believable Game AI." *Procedia Computer Science* 156 (2019): 404–413.

Sirani, Jordan. "The 10 Best-Selling Video Games of All Time." *IGN*, October 16, 2023. www.ign.com.

Smethurst, Becky. *A Brief History of Black Holes*. Dublin: Macmillan, 2022.

Smith, Adam. "Artificial Life: *Grand Theft Auto V*'s Live Deer Webcam." *Rock Paper Shotgun*, March 21, 2016. www.rockpapershotgun.com.

Smith, Naomi, and Peter Walters. "Desire Lines and Defensive Architecture in Modern Urban Environments." *Urban Studies* 55, no. 13 (2018): 2980–2995.

Snorton, C. Riley. *Black on Both Sides: A Racial History of Trans Identity*. Minneapolis: University of Minnesota Press, 2017.

Snyder, Shane. "The Impossible Relationship: Deconstructing the Private Space in *Gone Home*." *Journal of Gaming & Virtual Worlds* 10, no. 1 (March 2018): 7–20.

Soderman, Braxton. *Against Flow: Video Games and the Flowing Subject*. Cambridge, MA: MIT Press, 2021.

Somerville, Siobhan B. "Queer." In *Keywords for American Cultural Studies*, edited by Bruce Burgett and Glenn Hendler, 198–207. New York: New York University Press, 2020.

Steam. "*Nour*: Play with Your Food." Accessed January 13, 2024. https://store.steampowered.com.

Stone, Kara. "Time and Reparative Game Design: Queerness, Disability, and Affect." *Game Studies* 18, no. 3 (December 2018). www.gamestudies.org.

Strings, Sabrina. *Fearing the Black Body: The Racial Origins of Fat Phobia*. New York: New York University Press, 2019.

Stryker, Susan. Foreword to *The Transgender Studies Reader Remix*, edited by Susan Stryker and Dylan McCarthy Blackston, x–xi. New York: Routledge, 2022.

———. "My Words to Victor Frankenstein above the Village of Chamounix." In *The Transgender Studies Reader Remix*, edited by Susan Stryker and Dylan McCarthy Blackston, 67–79. New York: Routledge, 2022.

Sugawa-Shimada, Akiko. "Emerging '2.5-Dimensional' Culture: Character-Oriented Cultural Practices and 'Community of Preferences' as a New Fandom in Japan and Beyond." *Mechademia* 12, no. 2 (Spring 2020): 124–139.

Taylor, T. L. *Play between Worlds: Exploring Online Game Culture*. Cambridge, MA: MIT Press, 2009.

Thatch, Hibby. "A Cross-Game Look at Transgender Representation in Video Games." *Press Start* 7, no. 1 (2021): 19–44.

Thompson, Nathan. "Queer/ing Game Space: Sexual Play in *World of Warcraft*." *Media Fields Journal* 8 (2014): 1–12.

TIGForums. "Wobbledogs." First post February 22, 2016. https://forums.tigsource.com/index.php?topic=53994.720.

Tongson, Karen. "Queer." In *Keywords for Media Studies*, edited by Laurie Ouellette and Jonathan Gray, 157–160. New York: New York University Press, 2017.

———. *Relocations: Queer Suburban Imaginaries*. New York: New York University Press, 2011.

Townsend, Megan. "The LGBT-Inclusive Video Game 'Gone Home' Is Coming to Nintendo's Wii U." *GLAAD Blog*, 2014. www.glaad.org.

Trammell, Aaron. *Repairing Play: A Black Phenomenology*. Cambridge, MA: MIT Press, 2023.

Tremblay, Kaitlin. *Collaborative Worldbuilding for Video Games*. New York: Routledge, 2023.

Tsing, Anna Lowenhaupt. *The Mushroom at the End of the World: On the Possibility of Life in Capitalist Ruins*. Durham, NC: Duke University Press, 2015.

Tullocha, Rowan, Catherine Hoadband, and Helen Young. "Riot Grrrl Gaming: Gender, Sexuality, Race, and the Politics of Choice in *Gone Home*." *Journal of Media and Cultural Studies* 33, no. 3 (2019): 337–350.

Tyler, Tom. *Game: Animals, Video Games, and Humanity*. Minneapolis: University of Minnesota Press, 2022.

———. "New Tricks." In *Becoming Human: Between Animals and Technology*, edited by Ron Broglio and Frederick Young, 62–79. London: Routledge, 2014.

"Ursula K Le Guin's Speech at National Book Awards: 'Books Aren't Just Commodities.'" *The Guardian*, November 20, 2014. www.theguardian.com.

Valentine, Rebekah. "*The Last of Us Part 2*, *Tell Me Why* Tie for Outstanding Video Game at GLAAD Media Awards." *IGN*, April 2, 2021. www.ign.com.

Veale, Kevin. "*Gone Home*, and the Power of Affective Nostalgia." *International Journal of Heritage Studies* 23, no. 7 (2017): 654–666.

Wallace, Michelle. *Invisibility Blues: From Pop to Theory*. New York: Verso, 1990.

Ward, Jane. "Dyke Methods: A Meditation on Queer Studies and the Gay Men Who Hate It." In *Imagining Queer Methods*, edited by Amin Ghaziani and Matt Brim, 259–276. New York: New York University Press, 2019.

Wardrip-Fruin, Noah. "Gravity in Computer Space." *ROMchip: A Journal of Game Histories* 1, no. 2 (December 2019). www.romchip.org.

Warpefelt, Henrik, and Hargo Verhagen. "A Model of Non-Player Character Believability." *Journal of Gaming & Virtual Worlds* 9, no. 1 (March 2017): 39–53.

Waszkiewicz, Agata, and Martyna Bakun. "Towards the Aesthetic of Cozy Video Games." *Journal of Gaming & Virtual Worlds* 12, no. 3 (October 2020): 225–240.

Webster, Andrew. "*OlliOlli World* Captures the Essence of Skateboarding, and Then Makes It Weird." *The Verge*, February 2, 2022. www.theverge.com.

Whistance-Smith, Gregory. *Expressive Spaces: Embodying Meaning in Video Game Environments*. Berlin: De Gruyter, 2022.

Widera, Josh. "One Part Water, Two Parts Starch: Performing Oobleck as Political Resistance." *Performance Philosophy* 5, no. 1 (2019): 158–171.

Wilcox, Steve. "Illusions of Space and Time: An Ethical Approach to Temporality in Games." *Journal of Gaming & Virtual Worlds* 10, no. 2 (June 2018): 115–133.

Wing, Carlin. "'Not without Matter or Substance': On the Occasion of a Bouncing Ball." *ROMchip: A Journal of Game Histories* 4, no. 2 (December 2022). www.romchip.org.

Wolf, Mark J. P. "Bioshock Infinite: World-Building." In *How to Play Video Games*, edited by Matthew Payne and Nina Huntemann, 75–81. New York: New York University Press, 2019.

———, ed. *The Routledge Companion to Imaginary Worlds*. New York: Routledge, 2018.

———. "Theorizing Navigable Space in Video Games." In *DIGAREC Keynote-Lectures 2009/10*, edited by Stephan Günzel, Michael Liebe, and Dieter Mersch, 18–49. Potsdam: University of Potsdam Press, 2011.

———. "World Design." In *The Routledge Companion to Imaginary Worlds*, edited by Mark J. P. Wolf, 67–73. New York: Routledge, 2018.

Womack, Ytasha L. *Afrofuturism: The World of Black Sci-Fi and Fantasy Culture*. Chicago: Lawrence Hill Books, 2013.

Woodcock, Jamie, and Mark R. Johnson. "The Affective Labor and Performance of Live Streaming on Twitch.tv." *Television and New Media* 20, no. 8 (2018): 813–823.

Yep, Gust A. "The Violence of Heteronormativity in Communication Studies: Notes on Injury, Healing, and Queer World-Making." *Journal of Homosexuality* 2, no. 4 (2003): 11–59.

Yep, Gust A., Miranda Olzman, and Allen Conkle. "Seven Stories from the 'It Gets Better' Project: Progress Narratives, Politics of Affect, and the Question of Queer World-Making." In *Producing Theory in a Digital World*, edited by Rebecca Ann Lind, 123–141. New York: Peter Lang, 2012.

Zaino, Karen. "Queer Worldmaking." In *Encyclopedia of Queer Studies in Education*, edited by Kamden K. Strunk and Stephanie Anne Shelton, 578–582. Leiden: Brill, 2021.

Zhang, Ge, and Larissa Hjorth. "Live-Streaming, Games and Politics of Gender Performance: The Case of *Nüzhubo* in China." *Convergence: The International Journal of Research into New Media* 25, nos. 5–6 (2019): 807–825.

Zone, Ray. *3-D Revolution: The History of Modern Stereoscopic Cinema*. Lexington: University Press of Kentucky, 2012.

INDEX

Bold page numbers refer to figures

2.5D games, 30, 141–69, 197, 230

AAA games, 6, 19, 60, 85, 109, 173, 200, 214, 219
abstraction, 5, 22, 32, 38, 46, 51, 168, 204
absurdism, 5, 25, 74, 99, 105, 159, 168–69, 221–22; in *Everything*, 224; in *Nour: Play with Your Food*, 228; in *San Andreas Deer Cam*, 195; in *What the Golf*, 28, 35, 40, 46, 56, 58; in *Wobbledogs*, 140
Adventure Time, 155
aesthetics, 9, 14, 43; of *Legend of Zelda*, 258n26; of *OlliOlli World*, 155; of *Shumi Come Home*, 231; of *What the Golf*, 40; of *Wobbledogs*, 129
Africa, 54
African American studies, 18, 26
Afrofuturism, 2, 26, 204, 245n4, 261n34
AfterEllen, 173
Ahmed, Sara, 4, 30, 124, 170–72, 177, 179, 185, 232, 259n30
algorithms, 21, 31, 108, 138, 196–97, 208, 215–17
ALIEN CASENO (Grace Bruxner, 2016), 234–36
Along the River of Spacetime (Elizabeth LaPensée, 2020), 9–**10**
alternate dimensions, 29, 67, 141–42, 221, 229
Amin, Kadji, 26
Amusement Vision, 249n12

Anable, Aubrey, 176, 203
analog games, 20, 25, 245n21. *See also* tabletop games
Andrews, Jimmy: *Realistic Kissing Simulator* (2014), 112–14
Andrucki, Max, 88
animal gameplay, 200
animal mayhem games, 107, 208
Anishinaabe people, 10
Annapurna Interactive, 93
Anthropy, Anna: *Queers in Love at the End of the World* (2013), 39, 249n7, 253n25
anti-Blackness, 46, 132, 141
Apple Arcade, 249n1
arcades, 146, 200
Arcangel, Cory: *Super Mario Clouds* (2002), 200, 219
architecture, 144, 182, 189, 191–92, 197, 233; impossible, 143
Art Journal, 144
Asberg, Cecilia, 202
Asia, 54, 74, 156. *See also* individual countries
Asian media studies, 150
Asian women characters, 114–15
Assassin's Creed (various developers, 2007–2023), 84
Astle, Tom: *Wobbledogs* (2021), 29, 107–8, 125–40, 227–29
astrophysics, 106, 122; in *If Found . . .*, 28–29, 69–105, 225, 251n4
atmosphere, 9, 27, 43–46, 197, 210

284 | INDEX

augmented reality, 108, 147
Autostraddle, 173
avatars, 48, 51, 59, 152, 156, 166, 250n23
Awash, Peggy: *She Puppet* (2001), 200, 219

backward temporality: in *If Found . . .*,
    28–29, 69, 80–86, 91, 99–100, 225
Baldur's Gate 3 (Larian Studios, 2023), 9
Barad, Karen, 29
bar arcade games, 200
Barr, Pippin, 219
Bem, Caroline, 56
Benjamin, Ruha, 28
Benjamin, Walter, 176
Bennett, Jane, 29, 106
Berge, P. S., 26
Berlant, Lauren, 4, 59, 63, 66
Bey, Marquis, 22
Big Buck Hunter (Play Mechanix, Inc.,
    2000–2018), 200
black hole M87, 93–**94**
black holes, 28, 69–75, 79–80, 91–103, 106,
    225, 251n4, 251n9, 251nn6–7, 252n11,
    252n13, 253n40, 254n45
Black liberation, 2
Black speculative worldbuilding, 2, 85, 141
The Black Trans Archive (Danielle
    Brathwaite-Shirley, 2021), 18–19
Boellstorff, Tom, 6
Boluk, Stephanie, 9, 186
Boni, Marta, 11
bounce, 106, 108, 110, 114–15, 120–21, 131–32
"boy culture," 145
Braid (Jonathan Blow, 2008), 84
Braidotti, Rosi, 202
Brathwaite-Shirley, Danielle, 247n69
breast physics, 114–16, 131–32
Brewer, Johanna, 187
Brewster, Kat, 224
Brice, Mattie, 19; *EAT* (2013), 219;
    Mainichi (2012), 85, 253n26
Brock, André, 46
Brown, Jayna, 2, 29, 60, 85, 141–42

Brown, Simone, 74
Butler, Judith, 1, 221

California: Huntington Beach, 164; Los
    Angeles, 138, 194, 197–98, 207, 210, 214,
    234; Muscle Beach, 162, 258n32; San
    Francisco, 13–**14**, 32
Campana, Andrew, 150
capitalism, 20, 23, 202, 222, 236; playful, 66
Caracciolo, Marco, 107, 206, 208
cárdenas, micha, 8, 246n30
Celeste (Maddy Makes Games, 2018), 187
Chandrasekhar, Subrahmanyan, 251n9
Chang, Alenda, 6, 119, 195
Chang, Edmond, 21, 67, 192, 199–200
Chen, Jian Neo, 28, 87–88
Chen, Mel Y., 29, 132, 203, 205, 213, 217
Chess, Shira, 79
cisgender people, 56, 74, 86–87, 174, 183,
    219, 230
cisnormative temporality, 87
Coffee Stain: *Goat Simulator* (2014), 29,
    107, 116–25, 131, 136, 140, 200, 227–28;
    Goat Simulator 3 (2022), 116
colonialism/imperialism, 5, 9, 19–20, 27,
    30, 53, 60, 87, 104, 110, 145–46
color-blind ideology, 46
Colossal Cave Adventure (William
    Crowther, 1976), 176
Conkle, Allen, 59
Consalvo, Mia, 6
consoles. *See individual consoles*
COVID-19 pandemic, 1, 176, 221, 246n30
Cox, Brian, 123, 251n6, 253n40, 254n47
cozy games, 176
creature-creator games, 130
critical race theory, 26, 131, 203
cultural studies, 144, 149

dadaism, 40, 249n9
dark rides, 175, 184
Dead or Alive: Xtreme Beach Volleyball
    (Team Ninja, 2003), 115

DeAnda, Michael, 146
Dear Esther (The Chinese Room, 2012), 7, 145
Deeeer Simulator (Gibier Games, 2000), 200
depth, graphical, 25, 30, 141–69, 230. *See also* dimensionality
desire lines, 191–92
De Veaux, Alexis, 2
developer logs (devlogs), 29, 108, 133–39
Devun, Leah, 86
Dicke, Robert H., 251n9
Digital Games Research Association, 3
dimensionality, 4, 231; 1D, 142, 149; 2.5D, 30, 141–69, 197, 230; 2D, 10, 29, 69, 108, 132, 142–44, 147–57, 159, 165–67; 3D, 30, 108, 118, 135, 142–44, 147–53, 166–68, 198, 230; 4D, 147, 149; alternate dimensions, 29, 60, 141–42, 221, 229. *See also* depth, graphical
disability studies, 3, 171
discrimination, 3, 7, 53, 86, 116, 124, 164, 177, 217, 246n31
Dolan, Jill, 17
Donut County (Ben Esposito, 2018), 40
Doyle-Myerscough, Kaelan, 3, 20
drag bingo, 146
Dragon Age: Inquisition (Bioware, 2014), 13
Dream Daddy (Game Grump, 2017), 55
Dreemfeel: *If Found . . .* (2022), 28–29, 69–105, 225–26
Drewson, Rune K., 38, 56, 68

EAT (Mattie Brice, 2013), 219
Edelman, Lee, 256n48
Elden Ring (FromSoftware Inc., 2022), 9
empathy, 55, 173–74
The Endless Forest (Tale of Tales, 2005), 200
Epic Games, 109
erasing mechanics, 71–72, 79–82, 85, 90–91, 96, 100
Erdem, Esra, 19
Escher, M. C., 143

esports, 64, 146
Event Horizon Telescope, 93–**94**
Everything (David O'Reilly, 2017), 224–25

fan studies, 17, 22
Fassone, Riccardo, 5
fatphobia, 132
femininity, 79, 176
feminism, 173–74, 183, 202–4; Black, 22, 74; intersectional, 18; trans, 22
feminist studies, 29, 61
feminist technoscience, 26
Fernández-Vara, Clara, 65
Ferreday, Debra, 206
Fickle, Tara, 53–54, 156
Fiedler, Brigitte, 131
first-person shooter games, 9, 147
Fizek, Sonia, 219
Flanagan, Mary, 77, 175, 249n9
flâneur, 176–77, 259n30
Fletcher, Akil, 46, 146
floatiness, 107, 116–25, 131, 255n32
floppiness, 36, 48, 51, 112–13, 116, 119, 127, 136
Forshaw, Jeff, 123, 251n6, 253n40, 254n47
Freeman, Elizabeth, 84
Freeman, Eric, 112
Freeman, Nina: *How Do You Do It?* (2014), 130
Fullerton, Tracy, 10

GabeHype, **157**, 258n31
Galloway, Alexander, 111, 200
Game Developer (magazine), 47
Game Developers Conference, 13, 175
Game Developers of Color Expo, 20
Game Grump: *Dream Daddy* (2017), 55
game levels, 4–7, 14, 144; in *Goat Simulator*, 118–20; in *Gone Home*, 177; in *LittleBigPlanet*, 152; in *Nour: Play with Your Food*, 228–**29**; in *OlliOlli World*, 154–64; in *Paper Mario*, 153; in *What the Golf*, 35–60, 224–25, 249n2, 249n7, 249n10, 250n23

INDEX

game mechanics, 5, 77, 106, 197, 250n31, 253nn25–26; in *If Found . . .*, 28–29, 69–105, 225; in *Noby Noby Boy*, 226; in *OlliOlli World*, 157, 161; in *What the Golf*, 39, 47, 49, 249n10; in *Wobbledogs*, 127, 130, 134, 229; and worldbuilding, 14, 49, 66

game physics, 29, 106–40, 142, 171, 228–29

gamer culture, 112, 187, 200; toxic, 7, 173

GamerGate, 173, 246n31

gamers, 60, 115, 151, 155, 191, 255n32, 258n26, 258n28, 259n30; Black lesbian, 146; hardcore, 112; mainstream, 9

Games Done Quick, 186

games for change, 248n80

game studies, 2, 5, 11, 46, 49, 60, 145; on dimensionality, 149; exclusions in, 13; on *Gone Home*, 173; on interactivity, 197; on magic circle, 11, 246n37; on play, 53, 68; on posthumanism, 203; queer, 19, 21, 84–85, 112, 236; and queer worldmaking, 66; on realistic representation, 111; on speedrunning, 187; on temporality, 84; trans, 26, 172; on worldbuilding, 21

gamification, 248n80

Garbos, Tim, 47–48

Garcia, Dora, 219

Gass, Ari, 26, 113, 192

gay assimilation, 19. *See also* homonationalism

GaymerX, 20

gender, 107, 124, 187, 203–5, 219; in astrophysics, 74; and game physics, 108–16; gender dysphoria, 32; gender norms, 4, 20; gender transition, 87–89, 96, 98, 226, 253n32, 253n38; in *Gone Home*, 173–74; and gravity, 123; and identity tourism, 64; in *If Found . . .*, 70, 75, 86–99; in *OlliOlli World*, 156, 168; and queerness, 18; in *San Andreas Deer Cam*, 196, 198; in serious games, 55; in video game culture, 3, 146, 258n26; and walking simulators, 176; and *What the Golf*, 56, 61–62; and worldbuilding, 4, 20, 27. *See also* femininity; feminism; masculinity; misogyny; sexism; transing; transnormativity; transphobia; trans temporalities

gender studies, 18

Genital Jousting (Free Lives, 2016), 112–13

Genshin Impact (miHoYo, 2020), 7

Getting Over It with Bennett Foddy (Bennett Foddy, 2017), 112

Gieseking, Jen Jack, 30, 166

Giffney, Noreen, 204

"girl games," 145

GLAAD, 19, 173–74, 185, 259n11

Glissant, Édouard, 74

Glitch City, 138

glitches, 113–14, 186, 189, 192, 199, 214

Global South, 104

goat-likes, 117

Goat Simulator (Coffee Stain, 2014), 29, 107, 116–25, 131, 136, 140, 200, 227–28

Goat Simulator 3 (Coffee Stain, 2022), 116

God of War Ragnarök (Sony Interactive Entertainment, 2022), 9

golf games, 38, 58, 68, 224

Gone Home (The Fullbright Company, 2013), 30, 55, 170–93, 232–33, 258n1, 259n11, 259nn6–7

Grand Theft Auto series (Rockstar Games, 1997–2021), 118, 260n3; *Grand Theft Auto San Andreas* (2004), 200; *Grant Theft Auto V* (2013), 31, 194–95, 198–200, 206, 212, 217–19, 234, 261n16

gravity, 222, 251n6, 251n9, 252n13, 253n40, 254n45, 256n40; in *Goat Simulator*, 29, 106–10, 116–25, 228; in *If Found . . .*, 73–74, 93–96, 100; in *Wobbledogs*, 136, 139–40

Gray, Kishonna, 3, 146

Great Britain, 19, 251n9

The Ground Itself (Everest Pipkin, 2019), 20
Gumbs, Alexis Pauline, 2

Halberstam, Jack, 21–22, 84, 143, 166, 192, 213, 245n2
Hall, Laura E., 175
Hammonds, Evelyn, 74
Hanson, Christopher, 84–85
Haraway, Donna, 22, 204
Hardcore Gamer, 188
Haritaworn, Jin, 19
Hayles, N. Katherine, 205
head-up displays (HUDs), 246n25
Hemmingsen, Michael, 186
Hester, Jennessa, 21
heteronormativity, 18, 63, 74, 170, 196, 214, 236; cis-, 79, 105, 130
heterosexuality, 57–59, 115, 124, 131, 183
Hird, Myra J., 204
hit boxes, 122, 255n33
Hoadband, Catherine, 174
homonationalism, 19. See also gay assimilation
homophobia, 1, 61, 173, 191, 215–16. See also GamerGate; MAGA supporters
Horizon: Forbidden West (Guerilla Games, 2022), 13–**14**
House of the Dead series (Sega, 1996–2018), 183
How Do You Do It? (Nina Freeman, 2014), 130
Hughes, T. J.: *Nour: Play with Your Food* (Terrifying Jellyfish, 2023), 228–**29**, 243

I Am Bread (Bossa Studios, 2015), 112
I Am Fish (Bossa Studies, 2021), 233
Ibrisagic, Armin, 117
identity tourism, 64, 145
ideology, 4, 9–10, 18, 46, 64, 191, 223
If Found . . . (Dreemfeel, 2022), 28–29, 69–105, 225–26
Ijzermans, Roland, 13

Imarisha, Walidah, 2
immersion, 7, 29, 56, 112, 143, 149
impossible architecture, 143
IndieCade, 20
indie games, 14, 19, 23, 25, 138, 154–55, 253n25
Indigenous studies, 10
interaction design, 9, 25
interactive visual novels, 8, 28, 69
interfaces, 9, 24–25, 28, 53, 246n25
Itch.io, 9

Jackson, Zakiyyah Iman, 31, 203
Jacobellis v. Ohio (1964), 249n11
Jagoda, Patrick, 3
Japan, 152, **154–156**
Jenkins, Henry, 22, 145
Jerng, Mark, 27
jiggle physics, 115, 131
Jing, Allison Yang, 3
Johnston, Lynda, 169
joy, 22, 25, 68, 87, 167, 176, 190, 217
Joy, Eileen, 203–4

Kagen, Melissa, 176, 184
Kaplan, Dana, 88
Katamari Damacy series (Bandei Namco Studios, 2004–2018), 40
Keegan, Cael, 248n88
Keeling, Kara, 1, 84
Kentucky Route Zero (Cardboard Computer, 2013), 176
Keogh, Brendan, 109
Knutson, Matt, 253n25
Kocurek, Carly, 6, 146
Kondo, Dorinne, 27
kopas, merritt, 173
Kunzelman, Cameron, 49

Lancaster, Lex Morgan, 168
LaPensée, Elizabeth: *Along the River of Spacetime* (2020), 9–**10**
Lau, Jacob, 87

Lefebvre, Henri, 144
The Legend of Zelda series (Nintendo, 1986–2023), 187; *The Legend of Zelda: Breath of the Wild* (Nintendo, 2017), 6–7; *The Legend of Zelda: The Wind Waker* (2003), 258n26; *The Legend of Zelda: Twilight Princess* (2006), 258n26
Le Guin, Ursula K., 222
LeMaster, Benny, 67
Lemieux, Patrick, 9, 186
level design, 4, 47, 119, 177
Life Is Strange (Dontnod Entertainment, 2015), 84, 253n25
Lim, Bliss Cua, 104
Line Wobbler (Robin Baumgarten, 2015), 149
LittleBigPlanet (Media Molecule, 2008), 152–53
LittleBigPlanet 2 (Media Molecule, 2011), 152
live streaming, 31, 64, 154, 186, 188, 191, 198, 200, 206, 251n47, 259n7
Lo, Claudia, 39
Longhurst, Robyn, 169
looping/repeating mechanics, 39, 81, 85, 133, 149, 207, 215
Lorde, Audre, 50
Lothian, Alexis, 3, 65
Love, Heather, 85, 113, 248n77
Luciano, Dana, 203, 205, 217
ludo-Orientalism, 156

Macklin, Colleen, 21, 23
MAGA supporters, 216
magic circle, 11, 246n37; of whiteness, 46
Malatino, Hil, 28, 87–88
March, Loren, 166
Martin, Sarah Edmands, 3
masculinity, 9, 88, 112, 124, 183, 187, 205, 258n26
massively multiplayer online roleplaying games (MMORPGs), 6, 200
Mathias, Lora, 112

McElroy, Griffin, 187–91
McRuer, Robert, 3
mechanics of speculation, 49
media studies, 3, 11, 150
Mejeur, Cody, 3, 26, 76
meneely, 188
messiness, 81, 103, 122–23, 201; and queerness, 22–23, 60, 113, 172, 182, 192–93; and transness, 87, 89
Metal Gear Solid V: The Phantom Pain (Kojima, 2015), 146
methodology of book, 23–28
Metroid (various developers, 1986–2003), 187
Michigan: Lansing, 10
Microscope Explorer (Ben Robbins, 2011), 20
Microsoft: Gaming for Everybody, 262n8
Middle East, 54
Mirowski, Alexander, 72
misogyny, 60, 195. *See also* GamerGate; MAGA supporters; sexism
Monster Factory video series, 130
Monument Valley (UsTwo Games, 2014), 143
Moralde, Oscar, 145
Morriss, Charles E., III, 63
Morrissette, Jess, 175
Mother Jones, 173
multiuser dungeons (MUDs), 6
Muñoz, José Esteban, 4, 21, 24, 28, 40, 60–61, 63–67, 204, 217–18, 237
Murray, Soraya, 9, 144, 146, 257n7
Myst (Cyan, 1993), 7–**8**

Nakamura, Lisa, 64, 145
Nakayama, Thomas K., 63
narrative, 84–85, 149, 187, 189, 218, 221, 230, 259n30; in *Dear Esther*, 145; in *Gone Home*, 173–83, 232; in *Horizon: Forbidden West*, 13; in *If Found . . .* , 28, 69, 71–72, 75–76, 79–82, 88–91, 97–101, 225–26; in *OlliOlli World*, 159–64; and

race, 27, 88; in *A Short Hike*, 14–16; and storytelling, 12–13; *versus* structural elements, 9; transition narratives, 75, 87–89, 226, 253n32; and transnormativity, 87–89, 225, 253n38; in *What the Golf*, 39–41, 47, 55; in *Wobbledogs*, 139, 228; and worldbuilding, 3, 5, 11, 19, 24–25, 49, 63. *See also* storytelling
new materialism, 26, 70
Nicoll, Benjamin, 109
Nintendo: 3DS, 149; *The Legend of Zelda* series (Nintendo, 1986–2023), 6–7, 187, 258n26; Nintendo DS, 249n12; Nintendo GameCube, 249n12; *Nintendogs* (Nintendo, 2005), 126; Nintendo Switch, 116, 125, 249n1; *Super Mario* series (Nintendo, 1983–2024), 6, 38, 147–**48**, 150–53, 166, 187, 245n21; *Yoshi's Woolly World* (2015), 152
Nissenbaum, Helen, 77
Noby Noby Boy (Namco Bandei Games, 2009), 226–**27**
No Man's Sky (Hello Games, 2016), 146
non-Euclidian geometry, 143, 166
nonnarrative games, 39
non-player characters (NPCs), 13, 139; in *Grand Theft Auto* series, 194, 200; in *OlliOlli World*, 156, 159–61, 163; in *San Andreas Deer Cam*, 198–99, 201, 206–8, 212–16; in *What the Golf*, 44–47, 56
Nour: Play with Your Food (Terrifying Jellyfish, 2023), 228–**29**, 243

Octodad (Young Horses, 2014), 112
Octodad: Dadliest Catch (Young Horses, 2014), 40, 250n32
OlliOlli series (Rolly7, 2014–2022): *OlliOlli* (2014), **154**–156; *OlliOlli 2* (2015), 154–55; *OlliOlli World* (2022), 30, 141–69, 197, 230, 258n28, 258n31
Olzman, Miranda, 59
on rails, 30, 171, 181–86
open-world games, 6–7, 118

operational logics, 75, 110, 221
O'Reilly, David: *Everything* (2017), 224–25
Orientalism, 54; ludo-, 156; techno-, 156
orientation, 118, 156; disorientation, 81, 103, 143, 181, 189, 231; in *Gone Home*, 183, 185, 190–91, 193, 232; and queer space, 30, 170–71, 177–78; sexual, **90**, 124, 170; and transnormativity, 87
overbuilding, 30, 170–93, 232–33

Paasonen, Susanna, 56
Papacharissi, Zizi, 64
The Path (Tale of Tales, 2009), 259n30
Patterson, Christopher, 60
Pavlounis, Dimitrios, 174, 193
Payne, Matt, 6
Pearce, Celia, 6
Pederson, Claudia Costa, 23
Pellegrini, Chiara, 76
Pelurson, Gaspard, 259n30
performance studies, 2, 17, 26, 63, 65, 141
pet simulator games, 107, 126–27, 139
Phillips, Amanda, 7, 13, 112, 123, 132
physics games, 107, 112–13, 117–18, 123, 200, 228
physics software, 29, 109, 115. *See also* breast physics
PhysX, 135–36
player-characters, 30, 112, 144, 146, 161, 194, 198, 206, 208, 211; in *Gone Home*, 183, 190; in *OlliOlli World*, 155–65; in *Realistic Kissing Simulator*, 113; in *What the Gold*, 46
playtesting, 17, 137
Polygon, 187, 190
posthumanism, 26; queer, 31, 194–220
Pow, Whit, 26, 192
Pozo, Teddy, 55, 112
Prince of Persia (various developers, 1989–2022), 84
Puar, Jasbir, 19
Puppeteer (Japan Studios, 2013), 152

QED: A Journal in GLBTQ Worldmaking, 63
quantum physics, 70, 255n34
queer, definition, 18
queer conviviality, 187
queer dimensionality, 141–69
queer games avant-garde, 19
queer game studies, 19, 21, 84–85, 112, 236
Queer Game Studies, 21
queer geographies, 30, 63, 166
queering, 4, 24, 58, 99–105, 145, 172, 225
queer mess, 13, 22–23, 60, 113, 172, 182, 192–93
Queerness and Games Conference, 20
queer physics, 107, 113, 123, 125, 140
queer posthumanism, 31, 194–220
queer publics, 59
queer romance options, 20, 55
Queers in Love at the End of the World (Anna Anthropy, 2013), 39, 249n7, 253n25
queer studies, 4, 21–22, 24, 68, 87, 176, 203, 214, 217; relation to trans studies, 26, 86, 248n88
queer theory, 4, 21, 39, 59, 62–63, 251n7
queer wandering, 183
queer worldbuilding, definition, 4
queer worldmaking, 4, 21–22, 26, 28, 30–31, 35–68, 167, 172, 191, 223
The Quiet Year (Avery Alder, 2013), 20

race-making, 27
racialization, 3, 19, 132, 203–4, 207, 236; and human/nonhuman divide, 31; and identity tourism, 64; in *OlliOlli World*, 156; and queer worldmaking, 63; racialized homophobia, 61; in silent films, 43; and visibility, 74; in *What the Golf*, 43–46; and worldbuilding, 27
racism, 1, 8, 27, 60; anti-Black, 46, 132, 141; anti–South Asian, 74, 251n9. *See also* GamerGate; MAGA supporters; white supremacy

ragdoll physics, 112–13, 118
Rahn, Suzanne, 184
rail shooters, 183–84
realism, 24, 46, 113–15, 120, 222, 229; in film, 43, 46; of game physics, 109–16; in *Grand Theft Auto* series, 195; in *If Found . . .*, 226; in *Legend of Zelda: Twilight Princess*, 258n26; in sports simulator games, 35
Realistic Kissing Simulator (Jimmy Andrews and Loren Schmidt, 2014), 112–14
Reddy, Chandan, 18
Reinhard, Andrew, 146
right-wing extremism, 1
riot grrrl, 174
Ritual of the Moon (Kara Stone, 2019), 85
Robinson-Yu, Adam: *A Short Hike* (2019), 14–17
Rocket League (Psyonix, 2015), 246n23
Ruelos, Spencer, 20
Ruffino, Paolo, 205
Ryu Ga Gotoku Studio, 249n12

San Andreas Deer Cam (Brent Watanabe, 2013), 31, 118, 194–220, 234–36, 243
Schalk, Sami, 171
Schmalzer, Madison, 26, 187, 192
Schmidt, Loren: *Realistic Kissing Simulator* (2014), 112–14
science and technology studies, 26
science fiction, 1, 3, 5, 11, 31, 49, 65, 72, 92, 221–22
Scully-Blaker, Rainforest, 189
Sedgwick, Eve Kosofsky, 256n40
Sega, 249n12
Sens, Jeffrey, 21
serious games, 55, 248n80, 250n28
Serna, Laura Isabel, 43, 46
sexism, 116. *See also* GamerGate; MAGA supporters; misogyny
Sexualities, 56
Shaw, Adrienne, 21

"SHE KEEPS ME DAMN ALIVE" (2021–2022), 247n69
Shinkle, Eugénie, 108
A Short Hike (Adam Robinson-Yu, 2019), 14–17
Shumi Come Home (SomeHumbleOnion, 2023), 230–32
side-scrolling platformers, 29, 147–50, 154, 157
Sims series (Maxis, 2004–2023), 258n29
Skate & Date (Geneva Hayward, 2020), 20
Smethurst, Becky, 122
Snorton, C. Riley, 87
Snyder, Shane, 174
Soderman, Braxton, 66
software studies, 112
Somerville, Siobhan, 18
Sonic the Hedgehog games (Sega, 1991–2023), 154
space games, 72
Spacewar! (Steve Russel, 1962), 109, 254n9
spatial turn, 144
Spec Ops: The Line (2K Games, 2012), 146
Speedrun.com, 186, 260n44
speedrunning, 259n9; fundraisers, 64; through *Gone Home*, 30, 172–93, 232, 258n1, 259n7, 260n44; through *OlliOlli* series, 154, 258n28
Spore (Maxis, 2008), 130
sports simulator games, 35
Steam, 133, 249n1
Steven Universe, 155
Stone, Kara: *Ritual of the Moon* (2019), 85
storytelling, 24, 140; in *Gone Home*, 174–85; in *If Found . . .* , 75–76; in *What the Golf*, 39; and worldbuilding, 3–4, 11–17, 21, 66. *See also* narrative
Street Fighter II (Capcom, 1991), 114–**15**
Strings, Sabrina, 132
Stryker, Susan, 22, 204
Sugawa-Shimada, Akiko, 152
Super Mario series (Nintendo, 1983–2024), 187, 245n21; *Paper Mario* (2000), 150–53, 166; *Super Mario 64* (1996), 147–**48**; *Super Mario Bros.* (1985), 6, 38, 147; *Super Mario Bros. 2* (1988), 147–**48**; *Super Mario Galaxy* (2007), 147; *Super Mario Kart* (1992), 150
Super Monkey Ball series (various developers, 2000–2021), 42, 249n12
surrealism, 40, 249n9

tabletop games, 25; role-playing games, 20
Tacoma (The Fullbright Company, 2017), 175–76
Tauqir, Tamsila, 19
Taylor, T. L., 5–6
techno-futurism, **154**–156
techno-Orientalism, 156
Tell Me Why (Dontnod Entertainment, 2020), 173–74
Thatch, Hibby, 26
The Last of Us Part II (Naughty Dog, 2020), 19
Thompson, Nathan, 145
TIGForums, 133
TIGSource, 133–**34**
Tongson, Karen, 18
Tortorici, Zeb, 86
toxic gamer culture, 7–8, 23
Trammell, Aaron, 54
Transgender Studies Quarterly, 86
transing, 22, 172
trans mechanics, 70–71, 91
transmedia studies, 11
transnormativity, 28, 87; transnormative temporality, 87–90, 225, 253n38
transphobia, 1, 61, 76. *See also* GamerGate; MAGA supporters
trans studies, 22, 28, 87, 105, 203–4; relation to queer studies, 26, 86, 248n88
trans temporalities, 28, 75, 86–92, 253n38
Trespasser (DreamWorks Interactive, 1998), 113
Triband: What the Golf (2019), 28, 35–68, 77, 122, 172, 224–25, 249n7, 249n10

Tsing, Anna Lowenhaupt, 232
Tullocha, Rowan, 174
Twine, 39, 253n25
Twitch, 130, 186, 198–99, 206, 259n7
Twitch Plays Pokémon (2014), 200
Tyler, Tom, 206

Ultima, 6
unbuilding, 4, 139, 221, 233–35, 237
Undertale (Toby Fox, 2015), 187, 191
Unity, 15, 109, 135
unplayability, 194–220
Unravel (Coldwood Interactive, 2016), 152
Unreal 5, 109
Untitled Goose Game (House House, 2019), 123
unworlding, 22, 248n78
US Supreme Court, 249n11

Valens, Ana, 123, 255n37
Veale, Kevin, 174
virtual reality, 9, 147, 149, 205, 257n19
visual novels, 8, 28, 69

Walden, a Game (USC Game Innovation Lab, 2017), 10
walking simulators, 8, 176–77, 184, 187–88
Wallace, Michele, 74
wandering games, 184
Ward, Jane, 61
Wardrip-Druin, Noah, 110
Warner, Michael, 4, 59, 63, 66
Watanabe, Brent: *San Andreas Deer Cam* (2013), 31, 118, 194–220, 234–36, 243

What Remains of Edith Finch (Giant Sparrow, 2017), 184–85
What the Golf (Triband, 2019), 28, 35–68, 77, 122, 172, 224–25, 249n7, 249n10
Whistance-Smith, Gregory, 144
white supremacy, 2, 27, 164, 216. *See also* GamerGate; MAGA supporters
wholesome games, 176
Widera, Josh, 256n51
Wilcox, Steve, 84–85
Wing, Carlin, 110
The Witness (Jonathan Blow, 2016), 7
Wobbledogs (Tom Astle, 2021), 29, 107–8, 125–40, 227–29
Wolf, Mark J. P., 12, 144–45
world design, 12
worlding (Haraway), 22
worldmaking, 205; queer, 4, 21–22, 26, 28, 30–31, 35–68, 167, 172, 191, 223; racial, 27
World of Goo (2D Boy, 2008), 112
World of Warcraft (Blizzard, 2004–present), 145, 246n23
worldviews, 10, 51, 77, 85, 115, 146, 228

Xbox Live, 146
XOXO Festival, 138

Yang, Robert: *Succulent* (2015), 112
Yep, Gust A., 59
Yoshi's Woolly World (Nintendo, 2015), 152
Young, Helen, 174
YouTube, 113, 117, 130, 154, 188, 258n31, 259n7

Zaino, Karen, 63

ABOUT THE AUTHOR

BO RUBERG is Professor in the Department of Film and Media Studies at the University of California, Irvine. They are the author of three previous monographs, including *Video Games Have Always Been Queer*, the coeditor of two edited volumes, and the co-editor in chief of the *Journal of Cinema and Media Studies*. They received the Stonewall Book Award for LGBTQ Non-Fiction from the American Library Association in 2021 and the Anne Friedberg Innovative Scholarship Award from the Society of Cinema and Media Studies in 2023.